D0665416

How to Get What We Pay For

How to Get What We Pay For

A Handbook For Healthcare Revolutionaries:
Doctors, Nurses, Healthcare Leaders, Inventors, Investors,
Employers, Insurers, Governments, Consumers, YOU

Joe Flower

The Change Project, Inc.
2015

HOW TO GET WHAT WE PAY FOR: A HANDBOOK FOR HEALTHCARE
REVOLUTIONARIES — DOCTORS, NURSES, HEALTHCARE LEADERS,
INVENTORS, INVESTORS, EMPLOYERS, INSURERS, GOVERNMENTS,
CONSUMERS, YOU.
Copyright © 2015 by Joe Flower. All rights reserved. Print edition printed in the United
States of America.

No part of this book may be used or reproduced in any manner whatsoever without
written permission except in the case of brief quotations embodied in critical articles
and reviews.

For information address The Change Project, Inc., 3020 Bridgeway #282, Sausalito CA
94965.

ISBN, digital edition: 978-0-9839953-40

Editorial Note
Brief portions of this book have been previously published as columns or blog posts or
in the author's previous book, *Healthcare Beyond Reform: Doing It Right For Half The Cost*
(2012).

ISBN: 0983995338
ISBN 13: 9780983995333
Library of Congress Control Number: 2015915502
The Change Project, Incorporated, Sausalito, CA
AKM 9-18

for Jennifer Flower

Great partner, insightful critic, best friend, beloved wife

Table of Contents

Acknowledgements

There are many without whom this book could never have been written. But I wish especially to thank:

Kathryn Johnson, who got me started on healthcare many thousands of years ago, inspired me with her constant belief that we could do this so much better, and nurtured my learning over decades through my work writing for the Healthcare Forum Journal.

The crew at the American Hospital Association's Health Forum (the successor organization to The Healthcare Forum), including especially my editor Rick Hill at the Hospitals and Health Networks Daily for allowing me into their spaces to poke and prod the hospital world to greater excellence over the last 15 years.

John Irvine, head honcho of TheHealthcareBlog.com, for his continuing encouragement and support, and providing me an online home to work out many of these ideas.

My friends and fellow board members at the Center for Health Design, and especially our CEO Debra Levin, for their continuing support.

My hundreds of clients over the years, from national governments and Fortune 50 corporations to free clinics and rural hospitals, who have always been as much of an education for me as I have been for them.

The writers of the Writers Conference on The Well, the world's oldest and smartest social medium, for their continuing support over the past 25 years.

Finally, but most important of all: Jenni, Jennifer Flower Ph.D., president of The Change Project, Inc. not only for her loving support and partnership, her forbearance and patience, and her intelligent and helpful criticism and editing, but especially for her vast and unremitting labor in furthering this entire project. Thank you with all my heart.

How to Get What We Pay For

A Handbook For Healthcare Revolutionaries:
Doctors, Nurses, Healthcare Leaders, Inventors, Investors,
Employers, Insurers, Governments, Consumers, YOU

Basic Instructions

- Bring your heart to this.
- Bring all of your skills.
- Open your mind.

Bring your heart and your passion; bring your love and your anger, your guts and your generosity and your ferocity and your courage. You're going to need all of them. This is too hard a job to do with just your head.

Bring all of your skills. You're a clinician, a manager, an entrepreneur, a numbers guy, a coder, a builder of coalitions and connections, a caretaker for your aging parents or your children, or just a person with a body. You know more about your part of healthcare, your perspective, than I do, in some ways more than anyone else. Bring it. We need what you know, your experience, your tool kit.

Open your mind. The way we have been thinking got us here, but it won't get us out of here. This means more than "be flexible." This is an instruction to drop your story altogether. It's the only way we together can build a new story.

Healthcare The Day After Tomorrow

Carlton runs his EKG, and talks to his cardiologist about it — on his cell phone, while sitting on a bench at the park.

Alicia's mother is recovering from surgery in her own bedroom. Alicia and the hospital can continuously track how her mother is doing via the cell-phone-sized ICU-style monitor strapped to her mother's wrist.

Dexter calls his own personal doctor, whom he has on retainer, for an appointment that afternoon. Dexter is on Medicaid.

Eva needs a new hip, and her co-pay will be pretty big. But her employer's HR department offers her a deal: They will fly her to California; put her up in a hotel; have the hip redone at a top-flight facility; pay her part of the tab, pay for her drugs, her rehab, everything; and throw in a $5,000 bonus — all because the California facility will do it better and at one-quarter the price of the local facility.

Gareth picks up his cane and hobbles to answer the door. He is obese, his joints are inflamed, his lungs seem to be going, his diabetes is out of control, and he still hasn't signed up for insurance. The woman at the door introduces herself: she's his own personal nurse case manager, sent over by the hospital after his third appearance at the emergency department in the last month.

Healthcare tomorrow will look little like healthcare today. The hospital as we know it will deconstruct into something far more varied, personal, and smaller. Prices for many parts of healthcare may drop by 50 percent, 75 percent, or more. Much medical care will happen where you are, not where the doctor is. Many healthcare organizations that miss the twists and turns of adaptation will fail, their ruins absorbed by others.

What We Are Doing Here

1) We are seizing the revolutionary
   moment in healthcare.
2) We are drastically improving
   your healthcare situation.

You know healthcare needs changing.
You know you need to change what you're doing, whether it's to get more reliable, better healthcare for your people or your family, or seeing a new way forward for your career or your organization.

We are revolutionizing healthcare, top to bottom. We aim to rebuild it, reshape it, re-engineer it. We will shift the energy connections, the information flows, the revenue streams, the organizational structures. We will rebuild healthcare. *We already are rebuilding healthcare.*

What that means is that The Next Healthcare will be both vastly cheaper and vastly better, for everybody, for you. We will help the people, help the doctors, help the nurses, help the caregivers, help the families, help ourselves. Our aim for everyone: a good birth, a long life full of healthy strength, far less suffering, and in its time an easy death.

Ambitious? Sure. You have something better to do with your time, your love, your energy? If you do, please do it with all your heart. I don't.

The problem that is healthcare in the United States is much too complex for any simple paint-by-numbers approach. Here's what I will do in this book:

- Lay out the **causes of the problem** in the underlying economics.
- Identify the **Levers of Change** that can move us toward solutions.
- Give **examples of ideas** that are already working in parts of healthcare.
- Give you **resources** to explore solutions in the part of healthcare that you can affect.
- Give you **action steps** using each of the Levers of Change
- Help **connect you with others** in the same struggle, with the ideas, organizations, and individuals fighting to make a difference.

Of course, the resources and circumstances continue to evolve, there will be shifts in the landscape. For help in thinking your way through the tangle for your organization, talk to me. Start that conversation at ImagineWhatIf.com/want-help.

The point is: there are now answers, and more are coming. We can do this. We can rebuild healthcare to do much more, much better, for much less. So this a handbook of challenges; of questions; of possibilities; of directions forward; of answers, plans, and steps to take. We are not talking about how to compete better at the old ways. We are talking about creating new concepts and business models and modes of competition that we could not have considered before. This is an invitation to think of them now — to think, to do, to create.

How To Work This Book

This book has two big sections. In the first, I explain a few things, mostly some different ways to look at the basics of the problem. In the second, I lay out a variety of solutions and the resources you need to implement them.

Section 1: The Ideas

We can't get to real change without a solid grounding in the problem. How did we get here? What are the threads and currents and connections of the tangled mess that we are in? Only when we understand that can we see how pulling this thread or that one, remaking a connection or shifting a power flow, will cause the system to fairly rapidly reconfigure itself. Step through this with me in Section 1: The Ideas.

Before we get going on the solutions, I also have a special focus, "The Art of Thinking Differently." In order to come up with new solutions, we have to challenge some of our basic assumptions in the old way of doing things. That's not just a matter of "getting loose" or "being creative." It's an art, an activity. It takes specific methods and it takes practice. We will go over them in this short passage. You may be tempted to skip it. You may think you are pretty good at it already. Let me encourage you not to skip it, but to give the techniques a try. They can be very rewarding.

Section 2: The Levers of Change

There are seven identifiable levers of change in healthcare right now. Each one of them could, by itself, cause significant change. Together they have enormous power, feeding each other. They are:

- Shopping
- Transparency
- Results
- Prevention
- Targeting
- Trust
- Tech

For each "Lever" I first lay out the problem, then identify the emerging solutions specific to each of six groups:

- **Purchasers** (employers, pension plans, and other large private purchasers of healthcare)
- **Consumers** (the end users of and eventual payers for the whole system)
- **Health plans** (the middlemen in the private financing of the system)
- **Entrepreneurs, inventors, and investors** (people and organizations creating new products to make healthcare work better)
- **Providers** (the hospitals, physician groups, and health systems who actually provide us the medical care we need)
- **Government** (federal, state, and local legislators and policymakers who define the ground rules under which the whole system works)

Throughout each "Lever," I offer resources to help you implement the solutions for your role in healthcare. At the end of each "Lever," I provide checklists for each of the six groups: Here's what you need to do to make healthcare better and cheaper, as well as what's in it for you, your family, or your organization. Then, as I just said, you can find further resources on ImagineWhatIf.com/resources. You can also start a conversation with me at ImagineWhatIf.com/want-help to see if I can help you work through the issues for your organization or business.

Appendices

At the end of the book, there are four special sections: one on regulations, one on malpractice — and then there's the Acronymicon, a guide to the perplexed (what book on healthcare would be complete without a glossary of abbreviations?).

It's the first appendix, though, that I believe you will find most helpful. Appendix 1: Resources expands on those that I provide throughout the book for each of the six groups.

Section 1: The Ideas

Why This Book, Why Now?

HEALTHCARE IS BROKEN. U.S. healthcare costs us twice as much as in any other developed country, and it still doesn't take care of everybody, it still bankrupts people, it still does not do the best for the least of any healthcare system in the world. This is still true even after the passage and implementation of the Patient Protection and Affordable Care Act ("Obamacare" or ACA) and it is true in ways that the ACA cannot or will not reach.

We can change that because we are already changing it. This is the moment. The healthcare world is in chaos. Everyone is trying to figure out the new rules. Now is when we can change the rules.

Who is the "we" who can do this? Everyone who has anything to do with healthcare. It's more than something we can leave to Congress and the president and the bureaucrats in Washington, or the politicians in your state capital. All the rest of us — the clinicians who labor in healthcare; the boards, executives, and administrators who run it; the employers, unions, and pension funds who pay for much of it; the health plans that devise different ways to pay for it; the entrepreneurs, inventors, and investors who come up with new products to make it work better; and each of us as consumers and choosers of healthcare, as patients, as caregivers for our parents, spouses, or children, and as citizens and voters — finally, and for a brief time before the new shape hardens, we have the ability and the tools to effect massive change that goes far beyond what the ACA can do, or was designed to do.

Didn't We Just Have Healthcare Reform?

The Affordable Care Act brought access to many more people and laid a foundation for real change. But it did not and will not fundamentally fix healthcare.

The uninsured hit a peak of 56 million Americans (20.3 percent) in the fall of 2013, just before the ACA signups began. By the end of the sign-up rush on March 31, 2014, that number had fallen to 46 million (14.9 percent)1 and by spring of 2015 to 11.9 percent, with the greatest drops among African-Americans and lower-income people.2 So far, so good; the law was at least partially successful in doing what it set out to do, which was mainly to get more people insured.

However, tens of millions of people in the United States are still uninsured. People on the Bronze and Silver plans will act in many ways like uninsured people because their co-pays and co-insurance are so high. (Co-pays are set dollar amounts the patient has to pay for each encounter; co-insurance is a percentage of the total bill that the patient has to pay.) So people on these plans can still go medically bankrupt — and medical bills are still the most common cause of bankruptcy.

Most importantly, the ACA did not break the back of the cost structure. It's not forcing costs down.

This is the main way that healthcare is still broken: it costs too much. Any way you measure it, healthcare in the United States not only costs twice as much as healthcare in other medically advanced countries, we get far less for our dollar. One-third to one-half of all the money in healthcare is just plain wasted. We get overtreated in every way that can be industrialized and made profitable for the industry, and undertreated in every way that requires difficult human handling — and many types of problems and types of people are simply ignored and left to fend for themselves.

---

1 Gallup poll, "In U.S., Uninsured Rate Lowest Since 2008," April 7, 2014. Available at: http://www.gallup.com/poll/168248/uninsured-rate-lowest-2008.aspx
2 Gallup poll, "In U.S., Uninsured Rate Dips to 11.9% in First Quarter," April 13, 2015. Available at: http://www.gallup.com/poll/182348/uninsured-rate-dips-first-quarter.aspx
Health and Human Services report, "Health Insurance Coverage and the Affordable Care Act," March 2015. Available at: http://aspe.hhs.gov/health/reports/2015/uninsured_change/ib_uninsured_change.pdf

Healthcare has other deep problems, such as wasteful defensive medicine (when doctors over-treat out of fear of being sued), vast numbers of "medical misadventures" (serious mistakes), and "never events" (mistakes so serious they should literally never happen, even though they happen a lot). Yet, as I will explain, many of these deep problems grow from the same root and will be fixed by the same solutions.

Healthcare can be fixed.

The tools to fix it are now available. For the first time, this is now possible. I'll explain why. Who can fix it? We cannot look to government for the heavy lifting. Government can provide some of the tools and in many cases can get out of the way. The heavy work falls to employers and other purchasers and payers; to health plans; to healthcare providers such as hospitals, healthcare systems, and medical groups; and to us, the users of healthcare. We can do this. I'll show you how and who is doing it.

This is about what works. The goal: better healthcare for as many people as possible for vastly lower cost than we pay today — half or less per person, or as a percentage of the economy.

Wait! Wait!
Isn't Government the Root of All Evil?
Um, no.

Wait! Wait! Isn't the So-Called
"Free Market" the Root of All Evil?
Um, no.

Okay, I've got some 'splaining to do. Just sit tight for a few and see what you think.

The Right Choice Is Pragmatic
If you don't care what works, I'm not talking to you. Seriously.

When tasked by one particularly vociferous libertarian friend to defend providing access to healthcare for all citizens, I started to explain the practical effect of having a healthy work force and well-cared-for elderly people and children. He interrupted me with a loud exclamation: "Don't talk to me about what works!" That ended that conversation for me.

All of morality means recognizing that our choices, our actions, even our rhetoric has consequences. That's part one. Part two is caring about that. Having a moral backbone means dedicating yourself to actions and choices and speech that help others and do not hurt them. It means, absolutely, paying attention to what works to achieve those goals. It means being pragmatic.

So if you would not put saving people's lives and ending unnecessary suffering at the lowest cost possible at the top of the list because "socialism" or because "free market" or because "single payer" or whatever … don't bother reading this. Put the book down and back away slowly. This book deals with how the system actually works; what works best when done by the government; what needs to be done (and can be done) by private payers or citizens, healthcare providers, or employers. If you believe that nothing the government does works, or that government is inherently evil, or that market competition destroys everything and government should simply dictate everything, go argue about it on the Internet. Here, we are out to save lives and end suffering. Capiche?

If, like many people, you are eager for radical change in U.S. healthcare, I ask you to bear with me for a while and seriously consider what I am saying. The framework that I present here may be a little different from what you expect, a little more complex, informed by my 35 years of studying how the system we have actually works, interviewing leaders across healthcare, and consulting for organizations large and small. As I believe you'll see, looking at the problem this way is more practical, and more radical, more change-inducing than simply overturning the system, because the process for change is completely doable, based on knowledge and new methods … and it's being done. As a futurist, I study trends. This is a huge one and it's been developing globally and nationally for a long time, from deep causes. What we are talking about here is a true transformation, both economically and clinically, to the Next Healthcare.

The Right Choice Is Universal

Many political arguments about healthcare seem to be premised on a principle of fundamental selfishness: "I have to take care of myself and my family first. Anything I do (or am forced to do) to help others will hurt me. The pie is only so big, and I must have my piece."

But the pie is not "only so big." And there is not just one pie. We can make the supply of pie bigger by not throwing away half or a third of it. We can find a way to make better pie for less, and we can all have plenty of pie. Maybe most important: If we think there is only so much pie to go around, it doesn't matter how good the pie is or how much it costs, we all still want our piece. If there are lots of pies, and we can choose, and we can have tasting contests, we'll not only all have pie, we'll have really amazing pie.

Who Deserves Healthcare?

Everybody. I mean seriously, how many people do you know who get recreational hysterectomies, who fight cancer as a hobby, who bear children as a weekend project? Healthcare is not a luxury.

When Jefferson and his committee of Founders stretched their minds forward to imagine what this new nation would be about, and struggled to put it in a few words that would be understood around the world and down through the centuries, they settled on three concepts: "life, liberty, and the pursuit of happiness."

To Jefferson and Company these were not aspirations, hoped-for end points, or stretch goals. They were "unalienable rights." Do you believe you have a right to life, liberty, and the pursuit of happiness? Without access to doctors, medicine, and caregivers, all three of those can disappear at any moment.

Understanding Risk

People say they should not be forced to pay for other people's pregnancies, because they are not going to get pregnant, or addiction services because they are not addicted, or rare genetic diseases because they don't have that gene. Yet we pay for home insurance even though we have a sound roof and a sprinkler system and don't expect our house to burn down. Why? Lightning, fire storms, earthquakes, or a neighbor who likes to hoard gasoline and fireworks. We insure against the chance that something terrible might happen to us, as part of a system that helps the unlucky fellow whose house actually is destroyed.

Your true risk of disease and disability changes radically over your lifetime, sometimes slowly and obviously, as you age; sometimes suddenly and even invisibly, as you become exposed to some new pathogen or as a gene that you have expresses itself. And most of that risk is hidden from you.

Some of your risk comes from those around you — your family, your sexual partners, your co-workers, the people next to you on the subway, the busboy who sets your table in the restaurant. Whether they have been vaccinated, whom they have touched, how often they wash their hands, and how the health system handles pathogens from Ebola to the flu to AIDS — all these deeply affect your risk of disease.

You are terrible at correctly estimating your own medical risk. So am I. We all are. Maybe you are not overweight, and maybe you think you know how obese people get that way. But you don't, not really. Medical scientists are still debating it. You may feel that you take good care of yourself — you exercise, you don't smoke, you don't drink to excess — and you're probably right, you may have reduced some risks. But you have not and cannot rid yourself of all risks. I guarantee you that at some point you will need medical help for something that you didn't see coming. When that happens, you will be grateful that you have insurance that covers that unforeseen problem — and grateful that the system is paid for by many people, almost none of whom have that same problem.

Your financial profile also changes, sometimes radically. Economic studies show that most poverty is cyclical: Most Americans have been poor at some point in their lives, and most stand a fair chance of becoming poor again. The most common reasons people become poor are medical: They get sick and can't work, they spend their savings down, they lose their insurance. Or because of the ACA they have access to insurance but they can't afford the co-pays, the deductible, the co-insurance. So they stay poor and they likely stay sick or die. Unless you are one of the 0.01 percent of Americans who are ridiculously rich, this could be you.

This is the core principle of insurance: Spread the risk across as large a pool as possible, then take care of the pool to reduce the risk to all.

Why Cost Matters

When healthcare costs too much, it becomes a luxury good, freely accessible only to those who can afford it.

But healthcare is not a luxury good. It is about as basic a human need as it can be. It's about life and death and how much you suffer. It's about whether you are limited and debilitated by disease, or can be all that you hope to be. It's about whether you are a burden to others, or have the energy and ability to help others who need help.

We want such a basic human necessity to be available, good, and cheap. Instead it has been scarce, hard to access, poorer quality than it could be, and far more expensive than it has to be.

Compare this with food, the most basic human necessity. In 1870, 70 to 80 percent of the U.S. population was employed in agriculture. As of 2008, less than two percent of the population was directly employed in agriculture. We do have problems with our food supply. But food as a commodity is cheap and plentiful in America.

Healthcare that costs more than it needs to is not just an annoyance, it's a big factor in income inequality in the U.S. The financial, physical, and emotional burden of disease are major drivers of poverty. At the same time, the high cost of healthcare means that many people don't access it when they need it, and this in turn deprives large swathes of the population of their true economic potential as entrepreneurs, workers, and consumers. People who are burdened by disease and mental illness don't start businesses; don't show up for work; and don't spend as much money on cars, smartphones, and cool apartments. Unnecessary sickness is a burden to the whole economy.

Wait! Wait! Wouldn't "the Free Market" Fix Everything, if We Got Rid of Regulation?

No.

Markets and regulation are not fundamentally opposed to each other. Over-regulation, or the wrong regulations, can obviously stifle markets, and this is in fact a big problem in healthcare today (see the Appendix for more thoughts on this). But the answer is not to get rid of regulation. Smart regulation enables markets, even creates markets.

We can see this easily if we trace markets back to their birth in medieval market towns and the independent cities such as those in the Hanseatic League. What we find is that regulation defined the very birth of markets: Build a wall around the town to defend the goods that are gathered there. Hire some watchmen to watch over them at night, and some kind of guardsmen to deal with troublemakers, drunks, and thieves, so that the merchants feel safe enough to come and trade. Establish a toll for merchants who want to use the market, to support the regulation and security. Establish what is going to be traded, where, on which day, so that the buyers can find a good supply, and the sellers can find lots of buyers. Establish some regulation of weights, measures, and currency so that customers and merchants can feel comfortable that they are not being cheated. Get control, as far as possible, of the roads and sea lanes leading to your city, so that merchants worry less about pirates and brigands.

All of this is in support of the market economy, not in opposition to it. For a market to become efficient, it must be regulated and constrained. Unconstrained and uncompetitive markets rapidly become distorted, making them far less effective; prices and quality vary widely for the same products, supply is unreliable. Sound familiar?

So the question is not so much whether we can get rid of regulation, or even how much regulation is okay, but what kinds of regulations produce the effects we need.

Every market is shaped by the regulations that set up its goal posts and yard lines and rules. The healthcare market has been shaped not to bring us all the best care and the greatest health at the lowest cost, but mostly to make the companies and organizations that make up healthcare as comfortable and profitable as possible. If we change the goal posts and the yardage markers and the out-of-bounds lines, the market will reshape itself to provide us better healthcare for far less.

Wait! Wait!
Won't "Single Payer" Fix Everything?

No.

I was recently at a party with a number of friends I had not seen in a few years. Someone asked, in front of the group, what I was doing these days. I mentioned the title of my book and said that I am campaigning for ways to make healthcare better, cheaper, and more available. The group roared back at me, as if in chorus, "Yay! Single payer!"

Progressives widely share the assumption that "single payer" would fix healthcare. After all, if the government were the sole payer it could dictate prices and force the costs down, the way the government does in other countries. But we don't have to speculate what a single payer system would look like in the United States, how it would work, or what its effects would be, because we already have it — for people over 65.

Medicare is somewhat less expensive and more efficient than private healthcare, but only somewhat. It is not half as expensive as private healthcare. Why? Because Medicare can be gamed. We will see in greater detail how this works, but the short version is: In Medicare "single payer" largely means "single buyer." The people who decide what is covered, and set the price they will pay for it (the Centers for Medicare & Medicaid Services [CMS] and their advisory panels), are not making the decision on their own behalf. They are not shoppers in the usual sense. It is a classic case of "regulatory capture," in which the agencies that are supposedly forcing an industry into compliance are actually taken over, advised, and directed by representatives of the industry itself.

Doctors' rates for Medicare, for instance, are set according to a complicated relative value scale, which is adjusted and tweaked every year by a committee of the American Medical Association (the AMA RUC, the Relative Value Scale Update Committee).[3] Though it in many ways affects more Americans than any other committee, it is not a govern-

---

3 American Association of Family Practitioners, "Relative Value Scale Update Committee (RUC)." Available at: http://www.aafp.org/practice-management/payment/ruc.html

ment body. It is private, it meets in secret, its deliberations are open to no public scrutiny. It has 26 members appointed by various medical associations, the majority of them from specialist associations. No more than six represent primary care doctors. CMS, by law, has only limited ability to tweak the recommendations of the RUC before turning them into actual Medicare rates. These Medicare rates, in turn, become the baseline for what commercial insurers pay, thus setting the baseline for doctors for the entire industry. Commercial payers tend to more or less accept the relative values established by the RUC, and adjust and negotiate their reimbursements from there. Is it any surprise that rates have continuously risen, well beyond the rates paid in other medically advanced countries, well beyond the relative value of doctors to the economy as a whole; and for specialists, well beyond their value relative to the value of primary care doctors and nurse practitioners?

In the RUC as in other ways across healthcare, the doctors and hospitals who provide healthcare do compete — and compete fiercely. A dermatologist who served on the RUC described it in a trade journal: "Everybody sits around a table and tries to strip money away from another specialty." He compared it to "26 sharks in a tank with nothing to eat but each other."[4] But unlike other industries in which producers compete in the marketplace to see who can bring us the best products at the lowest price, healthcare producers compete across the table just to see who can get more for themselves.

The effects over decades of this regulatory capture have been devastating. Today there are an estimated 750 lobbyists in Washington, D.C., whose sole job is to represent doctors and make sure that their ability to make a nice profit is not restricted or reduced. The higher priced the specialty, the more lobbyists it has shoring up its price.[5]

Reason number two that a single payer system is not the answer to our prayers: In the fight to drastically lower costs and make better

---

4 Rosenthal E, "Patients' Costs Skyrocket; Specialists' Incomes Soar," *The New York Times*, January 18, 2014. Available at: http://www.nytimes.com/2014/01/19/health/patients-costs-skyrocket-specialists-incomes-soar.html

5 Rosenthal E, "Colonoscopies Explain Why U.S. Leads the World in Health Expenditures," *The New York Times*, June 1, 2013. Available at: http://www.nytimes.com/2013/06/02/health/colonoscopies-explain-why-us-leads-the-world-in-health-expenditures.html

healthcare more affordable and available to all, we consumers need all the allies we can get. In the current system, we have a powerful group of allies, the employers and other big purchasers of healthcare, a group that is just waking up to its power to change healthcare. Employers are deeply invested in finding ways to lower their healthcare costs at the same time they can help their employees and keep a healthy workforce with less absenteeism, less debility, and less turnover. And they can act more independently, trying more varied ways of solving the problem, than a Medicare-like government payer ever could.

If we managed to get a single-payer funding system, we would have cut employers out of the loop and lost their powerful leverage. We would have converted the entire funding of healthcare into a single political problem in Washington. Considering the difficult political environment in Washington, does that seem to be the best place to look for a maximally wonderful outcome?

A Medicare-for-all system might help in some ways, but it would not fix healthcare all by itself, and would not drive down costs to half of their current level, which is where they should and could be, by most criteria, as I explain later. Medicare-for-all would not even make all healthcare available to everyone — because the costs would still be far too high. And when the costs are too high, there will always be a powerful political urge to ration and cut and trim, which will necessarily leave some people out in the cold. Most importantly, a single payer system would remove one whole layer of possible competition from the healthcare market place: All those other payers like health plans and especially employers, who are only now beginning to understand their power to provoke real competition over cost and quality and drive real costs down.

Critically, the government cannot act as a true customer. Because it has to serve everyone, the entire nation and the entire industry, it cannot do the one coercive thing that defines a true customer: It cannot pick up its marbles and go play with someone else. The industry can game the system, as we have seen it do over the last several decades. It cannot game a true customer, a customer that has options to choose from, information on which to base that choice, and the means to execute on the choice.

No Blame

Years ago a club I was a member of threw a party. We rented a yacht club. Everybody brought food and drink. Some of the guys in the club liked to play music and had formed a band. They set up upstairs, where there was a dance floor.

The next time the club had a party, the band asked whether folks would like them to play again. To their surprise a lot of people said no. Why? Because they had played so loudly that for many people it was physically painful to be on the dance floor. People couldn't have conversations even downstairs in the dinner area. Some fled to the docks outside to be able to hear each other talk, and failed even there.

I asked the lead guitarist why they were so loud. It was simple: Their sound guy had not been able to make it, with his soundboard and mixing equipment and speakers. Each member of the band was setting a level for his own instrument and microphone on his own amplifier — and all were competing with the drummer, who did tend to play rather loudly.

"So you are each trying to be the loudest one of the room?"

"Not at all. We were each just trying to hear ourselves."

Each member of the band had control only over his own sound. No one controlled the sound of the whole band. Each was trying to position his sound appropriately in relation to the others, and each was competing with the loud drummer right behind him. As each one turned up his own amp, the others had to turn up theirs in order to hear them-selves — and the louder the band got, the harder the drummer hit the skins. The band never decided to be really loud, but the band was really loud — so loud that they ruined the party for everyone else.

Healthcare in the United States is like that band. No one is trying to make it the most expensive system in the world. The people running each part of the system — each hospital, medical practice, pharmaceutical company, surgical center, device manufacturer, health insurer, or any other node of the system — are doing their best to optimize their part, to make themselves and their organization as comfortable as possible, and to make sure that they are paid appropriately relative to other parts of the system. And as we shall see when we explore this in more detail, there is no sound man, no central authority setting the rates for everybody. Nor are there real feedback loops that would allow the market to push back, to tell the band definitively, "You're playing too loud. Turn it down."

Understanding that there is no one to blame is crucial to fixing the problem. If you think you can blame someone, you come up with solutions about how to control them. As we shall see, that has not worked in the past and is unlikely to work in the future. The invitation here is to play a bigger game. The author Harriet Rubin said a marvelous thing. She said, "Freedom is a bigger game than power. Power is about what you can control. Freedom is about what you can unleash." If we can unleash countervailing forces in healthcare, we can get this done.

What's Necessary

What are those forces? Think about this: For a system to drive toward better and cheaper, it must in one way or another include variety. It must also include buyers, at risk for their own money and health, making real shopping decisions. Like any real economic system that has a chance of self-regulating toward realistic prices, it must:

- Allow the real buyers to make choices
- Provide them with different options to choose from
- Reward them when they make a better choice
- Provide them with real information about price and quality, so that they can make an informed choice

Let's unpack these a little bit. Think about your smartphone. Pretty amazing object, isn't it? You choose it, you pay for it, and you benefit from it. You have all kinds of information about which one is better, from ads to reviews to online discussions to looking at what your friends have. There are a bunch of different ones, at different price points, and different phone systems to hook them up with. They are widely available within price ranges that most people can afford.

For a system to drive toward better and cheaper, the system must allow the real buyers (that is, the people who choose the product, pay for it, and benefit from it) to make choices. A system that decided what kind of smartphone everybody should have would not produce cheap, amazing smartphones.

At the same time, for the system to allow making choices, it must provide choices. If you had the theoretical ability to buy any smartphone you want, but only one manufacturer provided them, your choice would not matter much. For a health system to work, there must be multiple providers competing to provide you any particular bit of healthcare you need — and the scoreboard of that competition must tell us who is doing the best job at the lowest price. Information, availability, and the ability to choose, right?

This is how we get reasonably priced smartphones and tablets that can do everything but tuck us in at night. Why can't we have a healthcare system that improves as rapidly as that, and drives its costs down to a level we can all afford?

The answer is actually rather simple: Our system of paying for healthcare as it has existed up until now has largely not had any of these qualities. It is often hard to know who chooses for you to have a particular procedure, test, or medicine — you, your doctor, your insurance company? Most of that choosing is not done by a real buyer paying with his or her own money. And almost all of that choosing is done by someone who has no idea what the choice will actually cost, who will pay for it, or whether the thing is worth it or necessary at all.

Now all of that is changing, and we can change it further, deeper, more radically.

Seems impossible, no?

No. It's not impossible, just hard. Work through some of these changes with me, and you'll see what I mean. Then something that might seem even more impossible will happen: You'll become an advocate and a leader for whatever can be done from where you are, with the tools you can assemble, in the parts of the system that you can affect, to make healthcare much better and vastly cheaper and more available.

Reality

As Byron Katie put it, "If you argue with reality, you'll lose. But only 100 percent of the time."

This book is deeply pragmatic. It is about what we can do now, with the system as it exists, and how we realistically can push that system further. Where are the hinge points, the points of leverage, the forces we can unleash?

I say this as someone who actually likes the industry. I am awed by what it has been able to accomplish; by its great medical advances and seemingly miraculous new techniques; and by the hundreds of thousands of dedicated, compassionate clinicians and administrators who run it. I have written about the industry, studied it, and advocated for ways to make it better for 35 years. But I also see its enormous flaws, what systemically drives it to make itself steadily worse, how we can change that system, and why this is the moment that we can do it. Using the right levers and wedge points, we can shift the whole system in a new direction and help it help itself. As I explain later, the tipping point toward a new coherence is a lot closer than you think.

Let's get to work.

Special Focus: The Art Of Thinking Differently

HEALTHCARE IS A very complex problem. This whole book is about different ways of thinking about that very complex problem. Our ideas about it are rooted in the system that we have, our experiences with it, the political scream fests we have had about it, how it has helped or hurt us. We are not going to think our way through this using the same assumptions and definitions that got us into it.

But just like a fish trying to identify water, it is hard to even notice our own assumptions, the frames we naturally put around things.

Humans are story-making machines. That's how we make sense out of the universe. The most profound personal transformations always involve dropping your story, abandoning your sense of what it means to be you, and allowing a new one to unfold. Every time I work with a client, letting loose of the old story and shaping a new one is a major part of the process.

So if we suspect that we want to make a new story about some complex situation and really see it differently, there are essentially two things we can do: We can find other stories, from places in healthcare where people have tried something differently, maybe in other countries or in other parts of our system, or in other industries. Or we can puncture holes in our own story. We will consider other stories throughout this book. But first let's talk about how you can go about systematically and fruitfully and creatively puncturing your own story — even if you do not naturally think of yourself as a creative, "big thinker" type of person.

How do you do that? Go to the edge of your organization, your experience, your assumptions. My wife, Jennifer Flower, PhD, is a psychologist. She would put it this way: Go to the live edge of your experience, the edge of your knowledge and your certainty. That is where you are most alive and where you grow.

Here's one way to find that edge: When you hear about some new way of doing things, and you hear that inner voice saying, "But we're not the kind of organization that does ..." or "I'm not the kind of person who ..." Try this experiment. Say the sentence out loud, but this time add the words: "Yet." Or "so far." Then remind yourself, "There are others out there like me."

So walk out to that edge. Feel that wall. Then ask yourself what is on the other side. There are lots of methods for doing this in the fields of personal transformation and psychology, but here we will go over one particular method that is direct, simple in concept, and quite powerful. You can do it with a group using a facilitator, a conference room, and a bunch of flip charts. Or you can do it all by yourself, staring out the window with a notebook in your hands.

The method is The Work, originated by Byron Katie.[6] I highly recommend that you find out more about The Work at TheWork.com,[7] or in her books. You could think of it as a variant of cognitive behavioral therapy, for home use. You don't have to use The Work or a tool like it in order to get the value you'll need from this book. But the core of the exercise is very simple, so I recommend you try it. It can be liberating, and even fun.

First, write down some things that you know to be true about the situation. Let's imagine a personal situation first. Maybe you write down, "Julie doesn't trust me. I need Julie to trust me more."

---

6 http://www.thework.com.

7 Links that appear in the text will take you to resources that I have found useful in teaching and training at large organizations and board retreats. I recommend only products and services that I have found valuable and honorable. The web addresses of some resources (as opposed to reference footnotes) have been shortened to bit.ly addresses for the convenience of readers of printed editions.

Write down several such things about the situation with Julie, then come back and pick one to work with. Let's say you decide that trust is the core issue here, so you start with that one. Ask yourself if it is really true. Then imagine how that belief makes you feel, and finally imagine how your world would be different without that belief.

Then comes the big piece: Turn it around. Imagine at least three logically valid opposites of the statement. In the case of Julie, some opposites might be, "Actually, Julie does trust me. She is just fearful."

Or: "I don't need Julie's trust. I need to trust myself more."

Or: "I need to be more trustworthy."

Or: "Actually, Julie's the one who is untrustworthy. It has been a mistake to trust Julie so much."

You don't have to believe any of these; you're just trying them on. Take up each one in turn, and imagine that there is some way in which that is true. Think of several real examples that show a way that the statement is true. Maybe you can't think of any. Usually you can think of several.

Then ask yourself if you can think of any more such turn-arounds. Do the same with them. With each of these, explore what would change if you actually believed that.

In the experience of many people who have tried it, often one of these "counter-factuals" suddenly comes alive, suddenly comes to seem true, or at least more true than the original statement. There can be an "Aha!" moment when suddenly the landscape snaps into a new shape. Or you can see how the "counter-factual" could be true if just this or that little aspect were different. Suddenly you can see the path to a different story.

Do you see what we are doing here? We are purposely cracking open the story that we have about ourselves, chipping away at it, opening its heart so that a different story might arise.

What's fascinating is that we can do this with organizations and careers.

Write down some things you know to be true about your organization. Make them specific things, not generalities. And make them about your organization, not about what somebody should do in Washington or in some other organization.

So for example you might write down something that is just obviously true, like, "We can't make any money treating poor people with no insurance."

Or, "We need to spend billons on a massive proprietary IT system that will mean a huge hit on our bottom line."

Or, "We need to be reimbursed more for our procedures."

After you examine each one, you can try to turn it around: "We don't need higher reimbursements, because…"

Or, "If we get our cost structure down, we'll have a market advantage. We'll be the one organization not demanding higher reimbursements."

Or, "Actually, we don't need reimbursements at all. We'll be better off when we move to some completely different ways of getting paid."

Similarly, if you have a career in healthcare, reading a book about how to radically change healthcare will leave you wondering about your own career choices, and that inner voice that says, "I'm not the kind of person who could …" will get a lot of exercise. You can challenge that voice by stepping its statements through The Work. You just may find the way in which you are exactly the person to take on the challenges of the healthcare revolutionary.

What it Comes Down To

The work of revolutionizing healthcare is a powerful mental and creative and heart challenge to everyone involved. We've got to get in training for it, we have to work at it, we have to persist to end the unnecessary deaths, the useless suffering, the endless waste, the personal bankruptcies, and life disasters left in the wake of this mindlessly cruel machine that is the mainstream healthcare industry today.

I travel the country and the world to speak at conferences, do board retreats, consult with corporations and systems and governments. At the buffets and receptions, over drinks at the hotel bar, on the beach at picnic dinners, in the hallways at board retreats, people pull me aside and put it to me straight: "Okay, I know it has to be done, but can we do it? How can we do it?" They tell me stories of their private desperation to find some way to do the right thing from the bellies of organizations seemingly bent on doing the wrong things. These people often have great ideas, many have piloted programs, sponsored initiatives, at times with excellent, demonstrable results. But still they feel like they're paddling against a tide. They may have found a small pack of like-minded partners. They may be luckier and belong to large groups that are already doing the work of transforming healthcare, that are getting the reductions in cost and much better outcomes that so many are hunting for. Few know about them. What they're learning and thinking is not getting shared the way we need it to be.

This book is for them. This book is for you. It's a book, and it's an index, it's a way into a world where you'll be able to find the help and connections and camaraderie you need in a fight for something you still dare to believe in.

The Economics: Why And How Healthcare In The United States Costs Too Much

---

THE HIGH COSTS of healthcare are a complicated knot. To have any hope of untying it, we have to understand the knot — how it was tied, what the threads are, and what is keeping it in place. In recent years, the outrageous inflation rate of national health expenditures has slowed. The per-capita inflation rate (how much it rises per person, on average) dropped to 1.8 percent from 2007 to 2010, and since then has barely reached 1.3 percent. We'll talk about why a little further along, but the key point here is: This is a drop in the rate of inflation, not a drop in the cost. Healthcare costs are still rising, just not as fast.

And it still costs too much. Not by a little bit. Not by a lot. By an insane amount. Each item and service we buy has a much higher price than necessary, far more than its cost, far more than it costs in other countries, and often far more than it costs in this country in the very same markets.

To understand how we got here, we can start with this chart.[8] It shows national health expenditures as a percentage of the gross domestic product of all the countries in the Organization for Economic Cooperation and Development (OECD) over the last half century. That is, it shows all the money spent on health, whether public or private, in all the more developed countries in the world, as a percentage of their whole economy.

---

8 Information from the Organization for Economic Cooperation and Development (OECD).

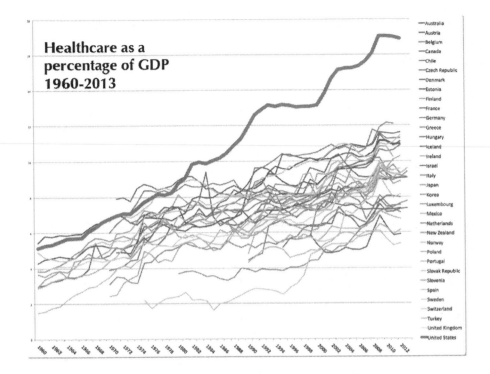

Healthcare as a percentage of GDP 1960-2013

You don't have to read the fine print to guess which line represents the United States. The right side of the graph is no surprise at all: We all know that healthcare takes about twice as much of a chunk out of the U.S. economy as it does out of anybody else's. It's the left side of the graph that is more interesting: Healthcare in the United States did not always cost wildly more than anyone else's. It was always one of the most expensive, but it was there in the pack with the rest.

Notice that the big spike did not happen when Medicare was adopted in 1964. But something big happened almost 20 years later. Between 1982 and 1983 suddenly the line jumps sharply upward. It levels for a while, then rises again between 1987 and 1993, then plateaus, then bumps up sharply again in the early 2000s.

The chart ends in 2013. By that point, U.S. healthcare accounts for about 18 percent of the economy. Imagine, for a moment, an alternative history, in which the U.S. line continued to follow the pattern on the left side of the chart. Healthcare today would cost about as much in the United States as in the other most expensive countries, about 11 percent of GDP. In other words, instead of $2.8 trillion per year, it would cost more like $1.6 trillion, a $1.2 trillion difference every single year. It doesn't matter who is counting; $1.2 trillion per year is a lot of money.

So what happened in 1983? What changed? Only one thing changed: the way we pay for Medicare. That year, the federal government adopted "diagnosis related groups" (DRGs), designated amounts that it would pay for particular baskets of hospital care. A heart attack would get this much, a bacterial pneumonia would get this much.

Note that this was just the hospital costs. The surgeon, the assistant surgeon, the anesthesiologist, the radiologist, the attending physician — all had their own fee schedules and were not part of the hospital fee. Even the basket of hospital costs did not cover everything involved in, say, a cancer operation. A CT scan, a bandage, a suture, a unit of blood — all could be billed separately. So the DRG did not give anyone the ability to guess how much the total cost of anything would be.

"Cost Control" Becomes a Manual for Making More Money

The DRG scheme was touted as a way for the government to get the upper hand on healthcare costs. That was the theory. But what happened in real life can be seen on the graph: Costs shot up. Here's why: In their attempt to control system costs, policy-makers had only controlled unit costs.

The actual pattern was not noticed by the policy-making world. The jump in healthcare costs seemed temporary, an artifact of adjusting to the new system, accounting for some costs that had been ignored previously. The idea still seemed so sensible and useful for the industry that it spread. Every time a new sector in the healthcare economy adopted the DRG manual for making money in healthcare, costs shot up again.

Private health insurance companies followed suit, negotiating their own "prospective payment" fee schedules with healthcare providers, declaring ahead of time what would be paid for each test, procedure, or visit. These were based on the Medicare DRG prices, but usually somewhat higher. Again, the insurance companies assured themselves and their customers that they were getting a handle on costs, because the prices they negotiated were steep discounts off of hospitals' list prices, which were much higher. These list prices (called "chargemaster" prices) became ever more divorced from any reality. Now, they were merely the starting point for negotiations between the hospitals and the payers. And who was the only one left paying chargemaster prices? Hapless patients without any coverage or information. There was no one to negotiate for them. So the people with the least ability to pay came to be charged the most.

The code-based payment practice spread from inpatient hospital charges to outpatient charges, to doctors' offices and clinics. Eventually almost all of U.S. healthcare came to be paid through one variant or another of this fee-for-service, insurance-supported, code-driven payment system. Let's call this the Default Model.

Yet over time the costs still rose, plateauing only when cost control in healthcare became a hot political topic, such as in the early 1990s (and today, since we began talking incessantly about healthcare reform in 2007).

It seems that, far from capping healthcare costs, the manual of DRGs (along with the prospective payment fee schedules of the private payers) became a manual for how to make more money in healthcare:

- Do more of the things that you can make more money at.
- Do more complex things that can justify a higher reimbursement.
- Do new things that get a new higher-paying code. Capture every single extra, from MRI scans to aspirins, on a charge sheet.
- Do lots of extras.

A method of cost control became a ladder of success for the whole industry.

New "Stuff" Means More Money

We have seen many new techniques, devices, and drugs introduced over the last 40 years. Until recently we have seen almost none that was simpler and cheaper than what it replaced. This has been a stark contrast to most other industries, which over the same decades kept producing new computers, handheld devices, kitchen appliances, guitars, cars, every manner of thing that either packed in greater value for the same price or brought the price down to ever-lower ranges.

Once the government set up this system, how did it decide on which new items to pay for, and how much? It set up various commissions and panels to advise them. These commissions naturally were filled with people from the industry, and naturally became the focus of intense interest from the industry. Whether your product, your program, your organization would thrive or wither depended on the prices (the "reimbursements") set by Medicare or negotiated with the private plans. So of course you lobbied and negotiated for the highest reimbursement you could get.

At the same time, suppliers and pharmaceutical companies and device manufacturers built higher inflation rates into their planning assumptions. For decades, even into the 2000s, the rule of thumb for makers of knee implants and CT scanners and stents was simple: Add seven percent to last year's price, even on the identical model. Plus, as often as possible, add new whistles and bells so that you can claim it is a different and better model that can be reimbursed at a higher price.

Looking at the graph, we can see clear evidence of this regulatory capture: Over time, the commissions steadily convinced the government to raise prices and pay for more (and more complex) medical stuff. List prices continued to escalate, so the discounts negotiated by health plans became more and more meaningless. (Negotiate a 50 percent discount on a $500 hammer, and you're still paying $250 for a hammer.) The costs continued to rise faster than general inflation, and faster than in any other country.

No Buyer

Think about this: In this setup, there is no real buyer.

What makes a real buyer? A real buyer is making a decision to buy, not buy, or look for an alternative. She is making the buy with her own money (or in some other way that puts her directly at risk for making a good choice). She has alternatives to choose among, she knows what those alternatives are, and she knows what they will cost. She has risk, alternatives, and information.

The traditional healthcare transaction has none of these features. You go to the doctor and say, "I have this problem." The doctor says, "You need these tests to find out what's going on." Maybe later he says, "You need this operation."

Nowhere is there a discussion of alternatives, or costs.

A personal example: In the 1990s, many insurance and health systems had begun using deductibles and co-pays, putting patients at some risk for healthcare costs. But few had absorbed what this meant: that you have to bring the client into the buying decision. Most patients hadn't absorbed that thought, either — including me. At just this moment in the history of healthcare I found a small bump on my hand. I thought it was some kind of wart, the kind the doctor could cut out or freeze off in a few minutes. I was (and am) a Kaiser patient. Until recently, Kaiser had not had co-pays or deductibles. You paid your monthly premium, and that took care of everything.

The doctor said it was not a wart but a ganglion cyst, and the surgery was a bit more complicated. He said I could have it cut out, or wait and see if it went away. I said, well, let's cut it out, and made an appointment for the hand surgery. On the day of the surgery, while my hand was being prepped, the desk clerk asked for a credit card for the co-pay. I gave her the card, imagining it would be a $50 co-pay, like everything I had experienced so far at Kaiser. She came back with a receipt for $2,500. It was the first time anyone mentioned the cost of the decision I had made.

Nor had anyone mentioned how likely it was that the surgery would succeed, and how likely it was that the cyst would go away on its own. It turns out that ganglion cysts have been traditionally called "Bible cysts," because the most popular treatment for one was to whack it with the biggest book around. According to one study,[9] after surgery 58 percent of the cysts stay gone, 42 percent come back. After not doing surgery, 61 percent go away, 39 percent don't. That is, doing no surgery has a slightly higher success rate than the surgery. Other studies find no difference in outcome between any of the methods of treating ganglion cysts and just leaving them alone.

I wasted $2,500. Had I known both the costs and the likely outcomes, I would have made a different decision.

This situation is not at all rare in healthcare. It is in fact quite common. If you imagine more real buyers at all levels of the system

---

9 Dias JJ, Dhukaram V, Kumar P, "The natural history of untreated dorsal wrist ganglia and patient reported outcome 6 years after intervention." J Hand Surg Eur Vol. 2007, Oct;32(5), pp. 502—8.

(patient, patient's family, employer or other big purchaser, payer), and you imagine them asking the basic buying question, "Is this worth the money?" you can begin to imagine a profoundly different healthcare system.

No Real Buyers, No Real Prices

What a hospital charges (the chargemaster list prices we mentioned before) is quite different from what a hospital is paid.

The actual amounts paid for the very same item can vary widely between regions and between institutions. You can stare straight into these differences on an interactive map provided by *The New York Times* based on data from the Centers for Medicare & Medicaid Services, at: http://bit.ly/HospitalsCharge.

Actual prices paid can vary even within the same institution depending on who's paying — or even within the same institution with the same payer, depending on how hard either the patient or the payer bargained.

The key point here: All prices in healthcare are squishy. They are phantoms. The real prices paid, especially to large institutions by private payers, are often made up on the spot in the middle of constant ongoing negotiations.

Think about that. Or maybe try not to think about it too much, because if you are one of the millions of uninsured Americans whose family life was turned upside down, or who were forced into bankruptcy while trying to do the right thing and pay overwhelming medical bills, that way lies madness. Those massive numbers on your medical bills were just made up out of thin air.

So if we are trying to imagine a future in which we spend a lot less on healthcare, the first thing we need to drop is the idea that what we currently pay in healthcare is based on any solid reality.

Aren't These Differences Regional?

You would think that the biggest differences are between, say, Massachusetts hospitals and Louisiana hospitals. To some extent, on average, that is true. But there are far larger differences between different hospitals and clinics and medical practices in the same market. For example:

Ankle MRI Prices- Washington, DC Area

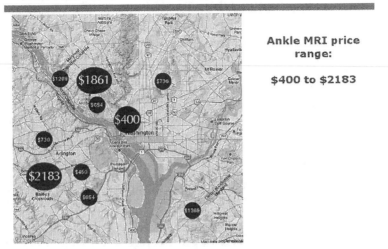

Ankle MRI price range:

$400 to $2183

This anonymized map of prices for an ankle MRI in the Washington, D.C. area is from Castlight Health,[10] an organization that is in the business of casting light on healthcare prices. All of the places mentioned are good-quality providers. These are not chargemaster prices, but the actual prices paid by private insurers. The spread of prices is enormous. Of the 10 mentioned, six run between $400 and $730, two are double that range, at $1,269, one is triple that range at $1,861, and the highest one is nearly four times the bottom group at $2,183.

So the question is: Who is paying $2,183? Probably not anyone who is conscious, has a choice about it, knows that there are alternatives, is paying any part of it out of their own pocket, and has a DC Metro card in their pocket.

Such large local variations in actual prices paid are a sign of an inefficient market. If anything happens to make it more efficient (such as an influx of real buyers with real information paying at least partly with their own money) we will see those prices collapse.

10 http://www.castlighthealth.com

But Surely Quality Costs More?

You'd think. It's true that academic teaching hospitals have higher charges, because they have the teaching overhead, and they typically take more complex cases. For-profit hospitals have higher charges because, well, they're in the business to make a profit. But in the aggregate, it's a scatter plot: The relationship between cost and quality is random.

For instance, think about the fact that prices for individual items are not really what's interesting. The interesting question is, "How much does the whole thing cost?" That is harder to measure in the Default Model of traditional fee-for-service healthcare. A few years back the Dartmouth Institute for Health Policy and Clinical Practice asked a very interesting question:[11] What is the cheapest place to die in the United States? That is, sure, there are bridges you can fling yourself off of. But most of us in our final struggles spend a great deal of time and resources in particular healthcare institutions. So they asked, what are the most and least expensive healthcare institutions in which to spend the last two years of life? This is actually a very good measure of total cost, since people trying to stave off death use a wide variety of resources — surgeries, CT scans, pharmaceuticals, lab tests, practically everything that a health system has to offer. The most expensive? Cedars-Sinai in L.A., "Hospital to the Stars." Not surprising. The second most expensive was similar: UCLA Medical Center right next to Beverly Hills. The third: NYU Langone in Manhattan. The surprise was on the other end. The least expensive institution in which to spend the last two years of life: Mayo Clinic in Rochester, Minnesota. Second least expensive: the Cleveland Clinic. These two cost half as much as Cedars-Sinai, and are among the most respected systems in the country.[12]

How can the best healthcare in the world cost half as much as the best healthcare in the world?

The overall cost of healthcare in a given medical system has little to do with quality and much to do with how they are organized and who gets paid to do what.

---

11 Pear R, "Researchers Find Huge Variations in End-of-Life Treatment," *The New York Times*, April 7, 2008.

12 *Ibid.*

What Costs So Much?

Everything.

In the last seven years of incessant debate about healthcare reform, there were lots of fingers pointed: It was the fault of those greedy doctors, hospitals, pharmaceutical companies, device manufacturers, health insurers — take your pick. And every finger-pointer could back up the accusation with facts. And they were all correct: Every part and aspect of healthcare costs far too much.

Take a look at this:

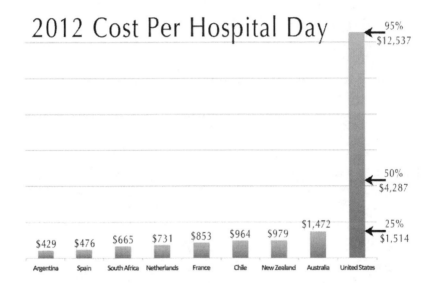

This chart[13] is from the International Federation of Health Plans. Again, it represents actual prices paid by health plans in various countries with modern healthcare, not phantom chargemaster prices. Their report has 20 similar graphs covering all aspects of healthcare, from drugs to devices to services to procedures, comparing the United States with a variety of different countries. All show a similar profile, with the United States towering over all others.

A few things to notice here: All the other countries are typically represented by one number, usually representing a price set by the government in one way or another. The United States always shows three wildly different

13 International Federation of Health Plans 2012 Comparative Price Report. Available at: http://www.ifhp.com/market-intelligence

prices. Here, for instance, $12,537 represents the 95th percentile, that is, five percent of room charges in U.S. hospitals are higher than that. $4,287 is the average price. $1,514 is the 25th percentile, that is, 25 percent of room charges in U.S. hospitals are lower than that, yet somehow those hospitals manage to eke out a living. On many of these charts, this 25th percentile, as here, is about on a par with the more expensive other countries. As we have seen, that 25th percentile often exists side by side in the same market with institutions that are much more expensive for the very same item.

The forecast here: When a more efficient market develops (through more actual buyers armed with information looking out for their own interest) these huge price spreads will collapse. They will collapse probably not to a range around the average price, but to a narrower range closer to the 25th percentile.

On the other hand, it doesn't matter how much something costs if you could just do without it. How much of today's healthcare is just plain waste?

Waste

Most studies conclude that we waste about a third of every healthcare dollar. That's about $900 billion every year. How big is this?

- It is 50 percent greater than the entire US military budget.
- The federal part alone through Medicare and other medical spending is greater than the entire federal budget deficit.

This is not about doing things inefficiently. This is about doing things that don't need to be done, unnecessary, unhelpful things, such as these:

- Anesthesiologists routinely attend colonoscopies, where they are not needed. Colonoscopies do not require general anesthesia, only a mild sedative or a low dose of propofol. The use of an anesthesiologist typically adds $2,000 or more to the bill. Ending this practice would save an estimated $1.1 billion per year.[14]

---

14 Rosenthal E, "Colonoscopies Explain Why U.S. Leads the World in Health Expenditures," *The New York Times*, June 1, 2013. Available at: http://www.nytimes.com/2013/06/02/health/colonoscopies-explain-why-us-leads-the-world-in-health-expenditures.html; Liu H, Waxman DA, Main R, and Mattke S, "Utilization of Anesthesia Services During Out-

- Most of the $10 billion in colonoscopies themselves done in the United States every year are unnecessary. Screening for colon cancer is very important, but there are several less-invasive tests that could substitute for most colonoscopies at a tiny fraction of the price.[15]

- The extra cost of computerized mammograms (a computer program searches the scan to mark out possible tumors before the radiologist looks at it) is climbing to $500 million per year. How much is that per extra tumor found or extra life saved? Can't be computed, because several studies have calculated that the number of extra tumors found = zero.[16]

- Mammography of any kind is useless for mass screening, according to the results of the Canadian National Breast Screening Study, which followed nearly 90,000 women over 25 years,[17] published in the *British Medical Journal* in 2014. Of the 44,925 women who received breast exams and mammograms, 3,250 had diagnoses of breast cancer and 500 died from breast cancer. Of the 44,910 women who received breast exams but no screening mammograms, 3,133 had diagnoses of breast cancer and 505 women died of breast cancer — nearly identical numbers. For mass screening purposes, adding a mammogram to a proper manual breast exam offers no benefit.

---

patient Endoscopies and Colonoscopies and Associated Spending in 2003–2009," *Journal of the American Medical Association*, Vol. 307, No. 11, March 21, 2012, pp. 1178–1184. Available at: http://jama.jamanetwork.com/article.aspx?articleid=1105089;

Liu H, Waxman DA, Main R, and Mattke S, "Eliminating Discretionary Use of Anesthesia Providers During Gastroenterology Procedures Could Generate $1.1 Billion in Savings per Year," RAND Corporation Research Highlight, March 2012. Available at: http://www.rand.org/pubs/research_briefs/RB9648.html

15 Rosenthal, *ibid.*

16 Fenton J *et al.*, "Influence of Computer-Aided Detection on Performance of Screening Mammography," *New England Journal of Medicine*, Vol. 356, 2007, pp. 1399–409. Available at: http://www.nejm.org/doi/full/10.1056/NEJMoa066099#t=articleTop

17 Miller *et al.*, "Twenty five year follow-up for breast cancer incidence and mortality of the Canadian National Breast Screening Study: randomised screening trial," *British Medical Journal*, February 11, 2014, BMJ 2014;348:g366. Available at: http://www.bmj.com/content/348/bmj.g366

- Knee surgery for arthritis[18] or a torn meniscus have been found to be no more helpful for most patients than physical therapy and painkillers.[19] Same with complex back fusion surgery for simple back pain: It is simply not medically indicated.[20] Yet these continue to be among the most common surgeries in the country. Kyphoplasty and vertebroplasty, two less-invasive back interventions, cost Medicare nearly $1 billion a year, despite the fact that no strong, controlled study has shown their usefulness.[21]

- Implanted defibrillators can be very valuable for people with life-threatening cardiac arrhythmias. But a 2011 study discovered

---

18 Mosely *et al.*, "A Controlled Trial of Arthroscopic Surgery for Osteoarthritis of the Knee," *New England Journal of Medicine*, July 11, 2002. Available at: http://www.nejm.org/doi/full/10.1056/NEJMoa013259;

Kirkley *et al.*, "A Randomized Trial of Arthroscopic Surgery for Osteoarthritis of the Knee," *New England Journal of Medicine*, September 11, 2008. Available at: http://www.nejm.org/doi/full/10.1056/NEJMoa0708333

19 Sihvonen *et al.*, "Arthroscopic Partial Meniscectomy versus Sham Surgery for a Degenerative Meniscal Tear," *New England Journal of Medicine*, December 26, 2013. Available at: http://www.nejm.org/doi/full/10.1056/NEJMoa1305189

20 Wheeler AH *et al.*, "Low Back Pain and Sciatica," Medscape reference, May 16, 2011. Available at: http://emedicine.medscape.com/article/1144130-overview#a1;

Weber H, "Lumbar Disc Herniation. A Controlled, Prospective Study with Ten Years of Observation," *Spine* (Phila Pa 1976), Vol. 8, No. 2, March 1983, pp. 131–40.

Atlas SJ, Keller RB, Robson D, Deyo RA, and Singer DE, "Surgical and Nonsurgical Management of Lumbar Spinal Stenosis: Four-Year Outcomes from the Maine Lumbar Spine Study," *Spine* (Phila Pa 1976), Vol. 25, No. 5, March 1, 2000, pp. 556–62.

Atlas SJ, Keller RB, Chang Y, Deyo RA, and Singer DE, "Surgical and Nonsurgical Management of Sciatica Secondary to a Lumbar Disc Herniation: Five-Year Outcomes from the Maine Lumbar Spine Study," *Spine* (Phila Pa 1976), Vol 26, No. 10, May 15, 2001, pp. 1179–87.

Deyo R *et al.*, "Trends, Major Medical Complications, and Charges Associated with Surgery for Lumbar Spinal Stenosis in Older Adults," *Journal of the American Medical Association* Vol. 303, No. 13, 2010, pp. 1259–65.

Cahill KS *et al.*, "Prevalence, Complications, and Hospital Charges Associated with Use of Bone-Morphogenetic Proteins in Spinal Fusion Procedures," *Journal of the American Medical Association*, Vol. 302, No. 1, 2009, pp. 58–66.

Levin DA *et al.*, "Comparative Charge Analysis of One- and Two-Level Lumbar Total Disc Arthroplasty vs Circumferential Lumbar Fusion," *Spine* (Phila PA 1976), Vol. 32, No. 25, 2007, pp. 2905–9.

21 Goodman B, "New Studies Raise Doubts about the Benefits of Vertebroplasty," *Arthritis Today*, August 5, 2009.

Buchbinder R *et al.*, "A Randomized Trial of Vertebroplasty for Painful Osteoporotic Vertebral Fractures," *New England Journal of Medicine*, Vol. 361, No. 6, 2009, pp. 557–68.

Kallmes DF *et al.*, "A Randomized Trial of Vertebroplasty for Osteoporotic Spinal Fractures," *New England Journal of Medicine*, Vol. 361, No. 6, 2009, pp. 569–79.

that 22 percent of them end up in people who, by guidelines of electrocardiology, should not be getting them — and may even be harmed by the operation. That's another cost of nearly $1 billion per year.[22]

- An estimated $1 billion in unnecessary, unhelpful coronary artery stents are put in patients every year, patients whose low-level, stable heart disease does not call for them.[23]

- About one in three U.S. births are by C-section,[24] far above the five percent to 10 percent rate considered necessary by World Health Organization studies. Studies show that healthy women with good pre-natal care should see about a four percent C-section rate. C-section is major surgery, with all the risks that implies. Cesarean section approximately doubles the cost of a normal birth to around $7,000 — another $2.8 to $3.5 billion added to the system cost every year. Tellingly, hospitals and doctors with a financial incentive to perform C-sections perform more of them — and they perform fewer when the patient herself is a doctor.[25]

- Of the some 100 million CT scans done in the United States every year at a cost of $100 billion, some 35 percent are estimated to be unnecessary — at the cost of $35 billion down the drain.[26]

---

22 "Non–Evidence-Based ICD Implantations in the United States," *Journal of the American Medical Association*, January 5, 2011, Vol. 306, No. 1, pp 43—49. Available at: http://jama.jamanetwork.com/article.aspx?articleid=644551

23 Boden WE *et al.*, "Optimal Medical Therapy with or without PCI for Stable Coronary Disease," *New England Journal of Medicine*, Vol. 356, 2007, pp. 1503–16., Available at: http://www.nejm.org/doi/full/10.1056/NEJMoa070829

Redberg R, "Squandering Medicare's Money," *The New York Times*, May 25, 2011. Available at: http://www.nytimes.com/2011/05/26/opinion/26redberg.html

24 Multiple studies cited in "Why Does the National U.S. Cesarean Section Rate Keep Going Up?" *Childbirth Connection*. Available at: http://www.childbirthconnection. org/article. asp?ck=10456

25 Rehavi M and Johnson E, "Physicians Treating Physicians: Information and Incentives in Childbirth," July 2013. NBER Working Paper No. w19242. Available at SSRN: http://ssrn.com/abstract=2295856;

Vedantam S, "Money May Be Motivating Doctors To Do More C-Sections" National Public Radio, August 30, 2013. Available at: http://www.npr.org/blogs/health/2013/08/30/216479305/money-may-be-motivating-doctors-to-do-more-c-sections

26 LaPook J, "Too Many Unnecessary MRIs and CT Scans?" CBS News, September 25, 2009.

As Senator Everett Dirksen famously commented half a century ago, "A billion here, a billion there, pretty soon you're talking real money!"

These are just a few of the more common examples. Healthcare is riddled with unproven, not helpful, unnecessary therapies and tests that are often quite expensive.

Beyond new practices, even many existing therapies and tests are useless or worse. A 2013 study published in the *Mayo Clinic Proceedings* sorted through thousands of studies of both new and existing practices in medicine published from 2000 to 2010.[27] Perhaps the most surprising finding was that the studies only validated 38 percent of existing practices; 22 percent of the studies could not find any benefit for the existing practice over lesser practices; 40 percent of the studies in fact found the established practices to be inferior to the lesser practices that they replaced. Two examples of those not found to be superior are the routine use of hormone therapy in postmenopausal women and the mixture of high-dose chemotherapy and stem cell transplant for breast cancer.

We hope to bring the costs of healthcare down to something like half of its current cost, freeing up something like $1.4 trillion per year at today's rates. If we can just get rid of the $900 billion in waste, we are two-thirds of the way to our goal.

So why do we do these wasteful things? What is the economic model that is supporting the waste?

Doctors and hospitals do these wasteful things, even though they often know that they are wasteful, because we pay them to. Doctors will tell you about the many patients they have who demand an antibiotic when what they have is a cold, or the patients whose presenting condition is, "I need an MRI." That's like taking your car to a mechanic and saying,

---

Available at: http://www.cbsnews.com/stories/2009/09/24/eveningnews/ main5337931. shtml

Maugh T, "Overuse of CT Scans Will Lead to New Cancer Deaths, a Study Shows," *Los Angeles Times*, December 15, 2009. Available at: http://articles.latimes.com/2009/dec/15/science/ la-sci-ct-scans15-2009dec15

Numerous cites at the website of Dr. David Brenner of the Center for Radiological Research at Columbia University: http://www.columbia.edu/~djb3/

27 Prasad *et al.*, "A Decade of Reversal: An Analysis of 146 Contradicted Medical Practices," *Mayo Clinic* Proceedings, August 2013. Available at: http://www.mayoclinicproceedings. org/article/S0025-6196(13)00405-9/abstract

"Use your fanciest machine, that one right there," rather than saying, "How much does it cost for a tune-up?" Most doctors, most of the time, will give the patient what they want. If they don't, they'll lose the patient to a doctor who will do it.

What should we do instead? Pay for the results instead of the process. If we pay for healthcare differently, in ways that pay for the result we want rather than particular tests, therapies, and supplies, the waste goes away. Here is the gold mine at the center of healthcare: not paying for what is not necessary, paying more for what really works. That's $900 billion, lying there waiting to be picked up off of the ground.

But Hospitals Can't Just Charge Less. Running a Hospital Is Hugely Expensive!

True. Any hospital that reduced its income overnight by half would go bankrupt very quickly. Getting to better healthcare for far less money will be a difficult process, involving cutting out the waste, learning to be far more efficient at every process that makes up healthcare, and most importantly doing medicine — and getting paid for it — in revolutionary new ways. It will not be easy.

It is no longer a matter of opinion, though, whether hospitals, health systems, medical practices should learn to provide healthcare for far less. That debate is over. They now will be forced to get by on less money. Learning to provide healthcare for less is a matter of survival for them. It is not optional.

The task is extraordinarily difficult because no one has done it before. It's prototypes all the way down. Any inventor will tell you that the prototype is not even supposed to work perfectly. The purpose of the prototype is to show you what doesn't work. We are just at the beginning of that process in healthcare.

The biggest factor in the challenge, though, lies in the people who currently run healthcare institutions: Their skills, instincts, and training all lie in the old way of doing healthcare. To understand this, we need to understand some basic laws of behavioral economics — which I will now provide.

Joe Flower's Three Laws of Behavioral Economics

First Law:
People do what you pay them to do.
Too obvious? Maybe. Yet we often seem to forget it when we talk about healthcare, as if healthcare were somehow immune from this simple law. If you want to understand how people and organizations act, you have to ask yourself how they make their living.

Second Law:
People do *exactly* what you pay them to do.
If you apply the first law, and you still don't understand why people do what they do, you haven't been exact enough. Why do doctors often spend so little time with their patients? Many reasons, but not least because they are paid per visit. My Kaiser doc is not paid per visit. My appointments with her are four times longer than the national average, and they are power-packed. Each visit not only deals with every complaint, question, or concern that I bring in, it also touches on everything else in my medical history, knees to heart to vaccinations.

Third Law:
The population of individuals trying to decide whether to have a third drink consists exclusively of people who have already had two drinks.
People's judgment is tempered by their experience. Those who are now running healthcare institutions (or health plans, or pharmaceutical companies, or device manufacturers) are at the peak of their careers. They got there by learning the old way of doing things exceptionally well. Circumstances are demanding that they do things quite differently. But that is an invitation to be a beginner again, to take a huge risk with the organization they have struggled so hard to build and to command. It is no mystery when they are cautious. They will fully turn to the new ways only when they are fully convinced that the old ways will no longer work.

What does this look like in real life? To understand that, let's take a look at the conversation that has made healthcare so huge.

The Conversation

Scene: Hospital system CEO's office,
Gargantua Regional Medical Center
Decade: 1990s
Characters:

- **Hospital system CEO** (For actors playing this role, think of yourself as the head of a large business enterprise. Your motivation is to foster the survival and growth of your institution with its thousands of employees and its budget in the hundreds of millions to billions of dollars. Your personal career prospects depend on how well you do that. Here's what you know about this doctor: He is not on your payroll, but he has privileges in your hospital. In fact, he is a rainmaker — he brings a lot of business into the hospital. You're not sure why he asked for this meeting. Whatever he is about to suggest, you know that if he is not happy with your reaction he could just take his business across town to Massive Memorial or St. Henry the Virgin's. He could also quite comfortably start his own center and go into competition with you.)
- **Interventional cardiologist** (For actors playing this role, your motivation is to be not only a good doctor but a successful one — in fact, a very successful one. You've got kids to put through college, maybe a house on the lake, a retirement portfolio to build up. You are an independent businessman. You're just as aware as the CEO that you have options: You can take your business elsewhere, or you can find some investors and start up in competition.)

CEO: Come on in, Frank. Have a seat. Can I get you some coffee? Nancy, will you bring Frank a cup of coffee? How do you take it? Nancy, he says just one sugar. How's Donna? That little problem she had clear up?

Great. Great to hear, yeah, I hear Doc Robertson is a wizard with that kind of thing. So what can I do for you?

Doc: Thanks for the coffee. That is good. Listen, I just want to start a conversation about something that could be very big for you and Gargantua. You know I started doing stents here about 15 months ago.

CEO: Yeah, looks like you've done a pretty good business at it.

Doc: Well that's the thing. I've done a good business and I've brought a lot of cases into Gargantua. But it's all been sort of ad hoc. We could do a heck of a lot better business if you would build me a whole cath lab, like give me a whole floor of that new wing. We'll have all the latest equipment, have it set up for maximum efficiency, have the recovery area right across the hall. Any problems, we're right here in the hospital already. I'll bring in a few more interventionalists, and you contract with our group exclusively to do the whole thing. Of course, you provide the support, nurses, supplies, all that, as usual, and of course you're billing for all that, facilities fees and so on.

CEO: Pretty big vision for your first two sips a coffee! I'm sure this all pencils out for you, or you wouldn't be here. But of course I need to figure out if it pencils out for us.

Doc: I'm pretty sure it does. A lot of people are going this way. In fact, your concern should be more how fast you can jump on this, because as of now there is no big heart center in the state. It's a big market opportunity and I'm sure someone is going to do it soon. I've heard some rumors from docs at both Massive and St. Hank's. But I'm sure you could still scoop them if you act fast. We should name it something big, something regional. Like, "Intergalactic Regional Heart Center."

CEO: Can we do that much business? I mean, how many people need stents?

Doc: Actually, a lot.

CEO: Isn't it just something you do for people who come in with a heart attack?

Doc: Not at all. You do it for people who come in with heart pain — angina. You take a look at their cardiac arteries, you can see where there are blockages, narrowings. So you put 'em on the table, stick a stent in each one. Some people need one or two, some need five or more. They pink right up, pain goes away. So, yeah, it's a lot.

CEO: Really? But no hospital days, huh? Isn't this completely an ambulatory thing?

Doc: Ideally, yes, like six hours bed rest in the recovery area, then off you go. But most of them end up spending the night, a few two nights. They had the procedure late in the day, or we're waiting for the vitals to stabilize or to take another look and make sure everything's copacetic. So you've got some hospital days, some imaging, and the facility fees for anything. There's a whole patient flow protocol they've been working up. But look, I've got a consultant who has really run the numbers on this, based on what other places have found, how many cases we should be able to run if we built a big facility, how far we could draw patients from, the reimbursement flows, all that. I should bring him to meet with you, show you how it works out.

CEO: Okay. Okay, let's do that. Work with Nancy to arrange it. Has to be when we can get Barry, my CFO, in on it. And the VP of development, Cheri. Of course, eventually it will have to go before the board, because we are talking a capital issue here....

The Conversation (Annotated)

First: Is this realistic? Yes. Of course, it doesn't represent every such conversation. There are a thousand ways in which healthcare expands over time. But this captures the essence. I have been reporting on the industry, visiting hospitals, interviewing healthcare executives and clinicians, listening to presentations at conferences, speaking at conferences, consulting clients on their strategy, and running board retreats for 35 years. Yes, this is realistic. This is normal.

Here's what happens: Something new shows up, a procedure, a test, a protocol, a drug, something new you can do for a patient. It gets FDA approved, or it's a procedure that doesn't need approval. It looks like it helps some people with some problem, it gets a reimbursement code from CMS (Medicare/Medicaid), and then from the other payers, so physicians start doing it. If it looks like they could make money at it, they start doing it a lot, on everyone that they can argue qualifies for needing it.

The conversations that lead to enormous expansions in healthcare are not medical science conversations. They are business conversations.

They are just like the conversations that result in a manufacturer introducing a new product line, or a new big-box store being built in your town. These conversations ask, "Is this something we can do? How much can we get reimbursed for it? How much will it cost us to do it? What's the capital involvement? What's the incremental operating expense?"

The question, "Does this solve a medical problem for the patient?" is not asked, because the conversation assumes that the doctor knows what he's doing, that his specialty is adopting this procedure because it is medically a good thing. And besides, it has the FDA's blessing, and the CMS's blessing.

But nowhere at any level does anyone ask, "Does this solve a medical problem better, safer, more efficiently, more effectively, than other methods that cost less?" Each advance in medical science is seen first and foremost as a business opportunity. Whether it is stents to open up occluded vessels or precise, automatic insulin pumps for patients with type 1 diabetes, what you and I would look on as an opportunity to save lives and end suffering is looked on in the industry, in most of the conversations and planning and fundraising about it, as a way to grow the business and make more money.

In the Default Model of code-driven, fee-for-service payments, making a procedure more efficient just means that you can do more of them. Solving the problem in a way that incurs fewer costs (like whacking a Bible cyst with a really big book) is not a good business goal, because the Default Model will reimburse those costs. It will pay for your waste. It's good business to do wasteful, unnecessary procedures.

Making a procedure more efficient does not make the system more efficient. In fact, the way things are done now, it often adds costs to the system, because when you can do a procedure more efficiently, you can do more of them faster, and charge for every one.

So we get one fad after another of medical advances that help some people, even save some people, then are expanded to vast populations for whom they are inappropriate, costing all of us billions through insurance or taxes or our pocketbook.

Cardiovascular stents are a good example. They showed up in the late 1980s. A heart attack (acute myocardial infarction or AMI) means some piece of your heart muscle is dying. It has been starved of blood by a blockage in the artery serving it. To open up the artery and end the blockage, an interventional cardiologist performs a percutaneous coronary intervention or PCI (also called a coronary angioplasty). The doctor introduces a long thin tube (a catheter) into your arteries, usually through your groin or your wrist. The catheter carries a tiny balloon at its tip. The doctor steers it up through your blood vessels until it reaches the blocked spot, using angiography and ultrasound to watch the progress. At the occluded spot, the physician inserts the balloon through the blockage, then expands it, until the artery opening is the normal size. The physician withdraws the balloon and covers it with a small metal mesh device, the stent. The physician pushes the stent-covered balloon back into the blockage and expands the balloon again, pushing the metal stent into the artery walls and keeping them apart. Stents are now usually coated with drugs that keep the artery lining from re-growing over it. This is called a "drug-eluting stent." A long blockage may need several stents covering many inches of arteries. Cardiologists call this a "full metal jacket."[28]

This is a pretty neat trick. In fact, PCI is a triumph of modern medicine that developed in multiple stages over decades. It is inarguably a great thing for people who are actually having a heart attack, or who have "unstable angina," sudden or unexplained heart pain that can signal an impending heart attack. In these patients the treatment is considered mandatory: Get in there and open up the blood flow. But interventional cardiologists swiftly made PCI the go-to practice for anyone with heart pain, including "stable angina," the kind that shows up predictably when the patient is exercising or experiencing a strong emotion.

PCIs grew to dominate the cardiovascular market in the 1990s and especially in this century. In the past decade, some 7 million Americans have undergone PCIs at the cost of more than $110 billion.[29] Today, the U.S. medical system performs more than 700,000 PCIs per year, half of

28 "Coronary stent," Wikipedia. Available at: http://en.wikipedia.org/wiki/Coronary_stent; "History of invasive and interventional cardiology," Wikipedia. Available at: http://en.wikipedia.org/wiki/History_of_invasive_and_interventional_cardiology

29 Waldman P *et al.*, "Deaths linked to cardiac stents rise as overuse alleged," *Bloomberg News*, September 13, 2013. Available at: https://bangordailynews.com/2013/09/30/health/deaths-linked-to-cardiac-stents-rise-as-overuse-alleged/

them elective. It is estimated that two out of three elective stents are un-necessary — more than 200,000 per year,[30] at a cost of over $2.4 billion.

Since 2007, repeated long-term major studies have shown that for patients with stable heart disease PCI has no advantage at all over "medi-cal management" — drugs and lifestyle change.[31] And PCI, like any in-tervention, has risks of infection, scarring, and even puncturing arteries, which can lead to further disability and even death. In 2012 alone, car-diac stents were linked to 773 deaths, according to FDA reports.[32]

Yet since these major studies started coming out, PCIs have declined only slightly, about 20 percent. When the American Medical Association and the Joint Commission (the major hospital accreditation organiza-tion) convened a panel of experts last year to name the five most over-used procedures, PCI was one of them, too often providing "zero or negligible benefit to patients, potentially exposing them to the risk of harm."[33]

Why? These facts are not irrelevant: Hospitals make an estimated $25,000 from each PCI patient with private insurance, half or a third of that for Medicare patients. The physician nets a separate fee that averag-es around $1,000 — for a procedure that takes about 45 minutes.[34] The income of interventional cardiologists has soared to over three times that of primary care doctors. PCIs can easily form a significant fraction of a hospital's bottom line. In one documented case, a hospital attrib-uted one-sixth of its revenue to PCIs. When one particularly enthusiastic stenter left the hospital, PCIs dropped by 34 percent, costing the hospi-tal an estimated $15 million per year.[35]

30 Stergiopoulos K; Brown DL, "Initial Coronary Stent Implantation With Medical Thera-py vs Medical Therapy Alone for Stable Coronary Artery Disease: Meta-analysis of Random-ized Controlled Trials," *Archives of Internal Medicine*, February 27, 2012. Available at: http://archinte.jamanetwork.com/article.aspx?articleid=1108733

31 Stergiopoulos and Brown, *ibid.*
Boden *et al.*, "Optimal Medical Therapy with or without PCI for Stable Coronary Disease," *The New England Journal of Medicine*, April 12, 2007. Available at: http://www.nejm.org/doi/pdf/10.1056/NEJMoa070829

32 Waldman P *et al.*, *ibid.*

33 Quoted in Waldman P *et al.*, *ibid.*

34 Waldman P *et al.*, *ibid.*

35 Waldman P. *et al.*, *ibid.*

Medical management consists of counseling patients to change their diet, stop smoking, moderate their drinking, and get off such stimulants as methamphetamines or cocaine. The drugs prescribed might include aspirin, beta blockers, ACE (angiotensin-converting enzyme) inhibitors (all drugs that open up the arteries and ease the flow of blood), or statins which lower cholesterol levels in the blood. This style of treatment requires real effort and compliance on the part of the patient, at which many patients do not succeed — yet across whole populations it works just as well as PCI. Obviously, medical management is not only far less invasive, it is far less profitable for practitioners and healthcare organizations.

A lot of patients, of course, prefer something that requires no sustained effort or change in lifestyle or diet. They just want something done to them, and fast. But even counting those patients who don't do well with medical management and eventually have to have stents put in, trying medical management first has better outcomes than just packing in the stents.

Definitive comparative controlled studies take enormous time and effort. By the time such studies began coming out in the late 2000s, many of the 10,000 interventional cardiologists in the United States had built their career trajectories, their income, their mortgages and 401ks, even their marriages and status in the community, around the enormously profitable patient flows of this one procedure. Hospitals and health systems had similarly built their strategic plans, their capital acquisition efforts, their staffing levels and operating budgets around the patient and revenue flows of PCIs.

Review the third law of behavioral economics given above: The population of individuals trying to decide whether to have a third drink consists exclusively of people who have already had two drinks. By the time these big studies came out, both the cardiologists and the systems within which they worked were way more than two drinks into elective PCIs.

In a quote from a Bloomberg News investigative article:

"Stenting belongs to one of the bleakest chapters in the history of Western medicine," said Nortin Hadler, a professor of medicine at the University of North Carolina at Chapel Hill. Cardiologists "are marching on" because "the interventional cardiology industry has a cash flow comparable to the GDP of many countries."[36]

This is a snapshot of how medicine in the United States became the rampaging economic monster of our nightmares.

How Do You Change a Whole System?

Changing this whole system seems like an impossible task, and it is. On the other hand, we don't have to change the whole system for the whole system to change, we just have to push it to the tipping point.

How does that work? How does a system come to have a tipping point?

Let's pull in some concepts from systems thinking and game theory. Before 2010, the U.S. healthcare system was stuck. The nature of its stuckness is best described by a concept called the Nash Equilibrium.

Do you remember the 2001 film *A Beautiful Mind,* in which Russell Crowe played the crazy genius mathematician John Nash? This was one of Nash's brilliant concepts.

In a Nash Equilibrium, all of the various players in a game have worked themselves into a "local optimum," that is, they are optimizing their circumstances as best they can given the rules of the game and the various inputs of energy they have available to them.[37] They have nothing to gain in their immediate situation by changing their own strategies. They could maybe imagine an even better circumstance to be in, but to attempt to get there they would have to give up their present good circumstances. They are like people marooned on an island in a river in the middle of a flood. They would be better off on shore, but they would have to jump off their safe island and brave the raging river to get there. So they are stuck, even if their present circumstance looks untenable in the long run. They can't change anything without being worse off, at least for a while, and risking that they will be permanently worse off.

---

36 Waldman P. *et al., ibid.*

37 "Nash equilibrium," Wikipedia. Available at: http://en.wikipedia.org/wiki/Nash_equilibrium

So they are stuck **unless something changes** — different rules, different inputs of energy. Maybe the flood level drops. Maybe a loose boat happens to float down the river and bump up on their island.

So think about a system that is stuck in its current configuration. There might be a different configuration that would be more efficient, that would work better for almost all the players. But they can't get to that more efficient configuration. Now imagine that something changes: new rules, new inputs of energy, new players. Not only is change now possible, once the system starts to change, there will come a point at which change is rapid, and the system will snap into place in the new configuration.

For instance, imagine that some change means that some portion of the organizations providing artificial knee operations can provide them for 25 percent of the previous average cost. Imagine another change means that the market now cares about what the price is and can choose based on it. Ask yourself: What percentage of the providers have to move to the new, lower cost structure before suddenly all of them have to offer much lower costs or get out of the market for that procedure?

Where is the tipping point? Is it 10 percent? Twenty percent? Who knows? But we know absolutely it is not 100 percent. At some point, the lower price range becomes the new normal, and organizations that can't compete at that level give up on it.

Imagine this happening across healthcare, in micro-markets defined by region, by constituency (Low income? Luxury market?), by procedure type (Colonoscopy? Birth? Tumor excision?), by delivery method (Mobile? Distant medical center? Local clinic?), by payment method (Capitated? Self-insured company? Preferred provider "narrow network"?).

Imagine that in each of these micro-markets some percentage of existing competitors or new ones manage to break the price/quality barrier of the previously stuck system and offer better service for vastly lower price. At some point in each micro-market and competition situation, the lower cost for higher quality becomes the new normal, and those who cannot compete at that level fall away, and turn their efforts to some remaining parts of the market that the change has left to them.

In the end, we will get what systems theorists call "order for free," that is, after massive efforts trying to cause change, past a certain point things just snap into place. They reconstitute themselves into a higher-efficiency system.

Some parts of healthcare are more amenable to this systemic change than others. And in some parts of healthcare the decision-making is different. For instance, when they scrape you off a highway and cart you off to some emergency department to try to patch you back together, you are in no position to make any kind of market decision. This scenario is routinely cited by people who are trying to argue that market forces cannot have any affect in healthcare. But there the market decision is made at other levels, the levels of the system's decision whether to have an emergency department (ED) at all, and decisions by local and state authorities about how to support and pay for emergency facilities, as well as decisions by payers and the federal government how to support and pay for emergency facilities and procedures. The systemic market effects are there in every part of healthcare, but will operate more strongly and immediately in some parts than others, and sometimes the locus of decisions will be different, not always located with the customer/patient or his or her family.

This tendency for the system to snap into place around the new normal will be exaggerated in healthcare simply because many of the changes needed to effect one particular outcome in fact extend across the system. If you wish to offer a lower price and higher quality for diabetes care or skin cancer care, you will likely have to change your financial ability to carry risk, your IT structure (especially its ability to track real costs and effectiveness), your staffing methods, your team organization — all kinds of changes that make the whole organization more efficient, more capable of carrying risk, more flexible, at a lower cost basis.

What this means is that we do not have to change all of healthcare for all of healthcare to change. If we can change it here, there, in this micro-market and that one, there comes a point in each micro market at which things snap into a new configuration. And there comes a tipping point at which all of healthcare slides fairly rapidly out of the old configuration, out of the Default Model, and into one or more new configurations that make it vastly cheaper and better. This means, in the end, that each success we have in changing the system will eventually have a magnified, highly levered effect on the whole system.

So What Can We Really Do?

More than you might think. Now that we have laid out some basic understandings, we can cast about for what can be done. What works? What has been shown to work? What tools are available that we might not have realized we had? What strategies will magnify the effects? What are the points of leverage where a reasonable amount of force will shift the whole system? They are there. There are seven of them.

Over the coming pages we will visit all seven:

1. Shopping
2. Transparency
3. Results
4. Prevention
5. Targeting
6. Trust
7. Tech

In each of these seven areas, we will call out specific opportunities and to-do lists for each of the specific groups that can actually revolutionize healthcare:

- Employers and other purchasers
- Consumers
- Health plans
- Entrepreneurs, inventors and investors
- Hospitals, physician groups and healthcare institutions
- Government — legislators and policymakers at the federal and state level

For all of us, there is important work ahead.

Section 2: The Levers Of Change

Lever 1: Shopping

The Problem

WITHOUT THE ABILITY to shop for the best product at the lowest price, we end up paying for things we don't need at extravagant prices and no guarantees. Healthcare as we have known it provides us with no ability to shop for the best product at the lowest price.

The Solution

Understand what shopping actually is, and find new business models that allow healthcare purchasers and consumers to shop for the best product at the lowest price.

Ahmed Buys a Rug

Ahmed wakes up one morning and finds a stain on the rug in the foyer, some red wine that a guest spilled during last night's party. The rug was old anyway, so he decides that today is the day to replace it. He gathers up the old rug, to make sure he gets the size right, and heads to the bazaar.

In the street of the rug sellers at the bazaar he finds a dozen merchants hawking their wares. He can see the rugs on display, feel their weave, read what the labels claim about what they are made of and where they come from. He can read the prices on the tags, listen to each merchant try to outdo his neighbors with their calls of: "Fabulous discount, just for you, Ahmed, since you are such a longtime customer and dear to me and my family." He can judge the character of the merchant, and have some idea how much each will stand behind his product. He selects a rug that is the right size and color for his foyer, haggles over price, pays the man, and carries the rug home on his shoulder.

Imagine now that Ahmed dreams again the following night, but this time, it's about a healthcare rug. He dresses and shaves, gathers up the old rug, and heads out to the healthcare bazaar. Instead of a street full of merchants, there is only one. In some versions of the dream, there are two, but they are so alike they and their booths might as well be twins. In this version of the dream, there is only one healthcare rug merchant, and he has no rugs on display.

"You sell rugs?"

"Yes, that's what the sign says. I sell rugs."

"But where are they?"

"You can't see them."

"How can I choose one?"

"Trust us. We will send a team to examine your situation. There will be a charge of course for the examination. But once it is done, you can be assured that we will choose and install the perfect rug for you. You will see it once it is installed, and you will be very happy with it. Trust us."

"Oh. Okay, if that's the way it is, I guess. So how much will all this cost?"

"That depends on many factors that are yet to be determined."

Ahmed considers this. "Such as the size of the rug, how nice it is, whether it is silk of wool, whether it is hand or machine woven?"

"Yes, and also what your rug-buying arrangement is. The rug may actually cost you nothing at all. It may cost you a few silver drachmas. It may cost you everything you have set aside in your special rug-buying fund plus a sackful of gold florins. It may cost you everything you own, your house, your job, all your savings, all you can earn for the rest of your life, and the patrimony you hoped to leave your children. Maybe. We can't tell just yet."

"That's nuts! If that's the way it is, I'll just do without a rug! I don't have to enter into such a crazy transaction with you or anybody!"

"Actually, you do. You actually do have a stained and tattered rug. It's right there on your shoulder. It must be replaced. The penalty for not replacing it is death — and a slow, agonizing death at that."

Shocked, Ahmed wakes from his nightmare, and rushes to the foyer, gratified to see the nice new rug he actually bought yesterday.

A crazy story? Of course. But that's healthcare the way we have practiced it in the past.

Healthcare without Shopping

Shopping brings us lower prices. For most of the things we pay for, shopping — the ability to choose among alternatives, to know what the price is, and to have some idea how good the quality is — keeps prices competitive, brings new products to market, and allows new businesses to flourish.

The traditional way we have paid for healthcare for older people is through a government bureaucracy that must by law spread the business to anyone legally qualified to provide healthcare. There are some price controls involved, but they are mostly set by commissions that represent the industry. There is no real shopping involved.

The traditional way we buy private healthcare (as consumers or as employers) is through a middleman, the insurer. In markets where there is actual competition, there is some incentive for the middleman not to be the highest-priced competitor. The highest-priced middleman will lose market share to cheaper competitors. But there is also little incentive to be the lowest-priced competitor, because healthcare customers who shop for the lowest price alone are considered the worst kind of customers — not loyal, and more likely to be really sick and need a lot of healthcare resources.

At the same time, how do these middlemen make their money? Their profit is, in effect, a percentage of the total cost of healthcare for their customers. Under the ACA, that percentage is limited: Depending on the type of plan, the insurance company must pay out either 80 percent or 85 percent of all its income to pay for medical care for its customers. It gets only 15 percent or 20 percent for administration, marketing, and profit. So while these middlemen don't want their premiums to be the highest in the market, they actually have a huge incentive to keep the overall cost of healthcare high because they get a percentage. Healthcare that costs half as much would automatically mean a health insurance industry that is half as big, half as powerful, and half as profitable.

Health plans that want to lower their premiums by paying lower prices to healthcare providers often have little leverage. Eighty percent of Americans in the private market are in "preferred provider organizations" (PPOs) that were designed to lower prices by bringing more customers to healthcare groups that would make a deal for lower prices.[38] That should work in markets of healthcare providers that are truly competitive. But fewer and fewer are. In recent years medical organizations have been massively consolidating, with chains and alliances growing ever larger. Any medical organization that is large enough in a given area becomes a "must have:" If a health plan doesn't cover services there, it's hard to sell that health plan to employers and consumers. The health plans simply have to knuckle under to the high prices.

So there has been little real, aggressive, incentivized shopping in most of healthcare. None of the middlemen in healthcare have any serious incentive or leverage to fight back against the outrageous costs and waste in healthcare.

Healthcare with Shopping

There are two groups of healthcare buyers who have the incentives and the power to be real shoppers: employers and consumers. For employers, the incentive is obvious: Healthcare expenses have been an ever-increasing burden. For employers whose health coverage is self-funded, any savings drop straight to the bottom line. The new rules under the ACA do not allow companies to easily escape the burden. In any case most employers do care enough about their employees to make sure that they get good healthcare. And most seem aware that a healthier workforce means less absenteeism, lower turnover, and higher productivity.

---

38 Rosenberg T, "The Cure for the $1,000 Toothbrush," *The New York Times*, August 13, 2013. Available at: http://opinionator.blogs.nytimes.com/2013/08/13/the-cure-for-the-1000-toothbrush/

So employers have a big incentive to find their employees good health-care at the lowest possible cost.

One more big incentive looms over employers: Starting in 2018, the federal government will impose a 40 percent excise tax on health plans in every year that their annual premiums exceed $10,200 for individuals and $27,500 for families. This is what has been called the "Cadillac Tax." So if your company is paying on the high end for healthcare, it could suddenly get 40 percent higher in just a few years. For some of America's largest corporations, that tax could pull as much as $1 billion off of their bottom line per year. The big health plans have been assuring their big customers that they aren't going to pay the tax, not because the insurers will flout the law, but because they will do whatever it takes to rein in costs. The old way they did that was by shopping for the lowest insurance premium. That has clearly not worked, and is not enough to keep costs down.

Then there are consumers, who increasingly have to pay more of the cost themselves. More employees on commercial plans and all of the newly insured coming into the system through the ACA's exchanges "participate;" that is, they pay deductibles, co-pays, and coinsurance and thereby share some of the burden for the total cost of healthcare. For people on the Bronze and Silver plans under the ACA, those deductibles, co-pays, and coinsurance can be quite large. Often people with these plans are paying almost all of the first $1,500 to $5,000 per year right out of their own pocket.[39] So more and more of the healthcare consumers who in the past would have gone for what they believed was the best treatment, or simply followed their primary doctor's recommendation, are now suddenly asking shoppers' questions: How much will this cost me? How good is this? How do we know? What are the alternatives?

These two powerful cadres of shoppers — employers and consumers — are the shock troops in the healthcare revolution. Consumers are just out to get a good deal, to pay an honest dollar for an honest result. Employers are out to explode the business model of healthcare.

---

39 Herman B, "High-deductible plans dominate next open enrollment," *Modern Healthcare*, November 13, 2014. Available at: http://www.modernhealthcare.com/article/20141113/NEWS/311139966

What Employers and Other Large Purchasers Can Do

After the federal government, employers and pension plans are the largest buyers of healthcare in America. Their strategy to get more for less calls for them to explode the business model of healthcare — by paying for it differently. They can do this in seven specific ways:

Private exchanges: At the first level of cost control, many employers are joining private insurance exchanges — about a third are considering it now, and half are considering it over the next few years.[40] Private exchanges work just like the Obamacare public exchanges: Insurance companies compete on them transparently, with similar offerings and real prices. The plans on them are designed to comply with the ACA. This saves money in two ways: The health plans have to offer competitive premiums and packages. And most employers find that employees actually tend to pick plans that are not as rich and expensive as the employer might have picked for them.

Private exchanges can help keep premiums down and force health plans to compete for customers. But they are not, by themselves, the key to drastic price drops, since they leave the health plans in the middle.

Self-fund: About one-third of all U.S. employees with healthcare coverage don't actually get it through an insurance company. Instead, the employer uses the insurance company only to administer the claims. The employer pays the claims itself, while taking out a backup insurance policy to take care of any really large claims. This is called being "self-insured" or "self-funded." Self-funded employers never have to argue with the insurance company about whether the premiums are too high. More importantly, self-funding means that the employer can cut out the middleman and become the direct buyer of healthcare. The employer can treat healthcare as it would any other supply stream. The employer can shop for alternative sources of the supply, evaluate its quality, negotiate for package deals, and work aggressively toward the highest quality available for the lowest price.

---

40 Mercer survey: "Employer Plans for Dealing with Healthcare Reform Evolving As 2014 Draws Closer," June 12, 2013. Available at: http://www.mercer.com/press-releases/health-reform-plans

Since self-funding is the first step in directly getting a grip on health-care costs, more and more employers are turning to it — particularly over the last five years. Over that time the actual costs of healthcare in America have moderated, as we have seen, often showing less than two percent inflation per year. Yet over those same five years, many employers have found themselves facing huge annual rises in their premiums — up to 75 percent or more per year. Many have felt that it's time to put themselves in charge.

Self-funding has traditionally been something really large employers did. With their size they can spread the risk across a larger population. Now, more, smaller employers are going for it. Some insurance commissioners across the country are putting rules in place that raise the deductible for small employers before their backup insurance kicks in, effectively making self-funding impractical for them. In response, some smaller employers are joining together in multi-employer groups to self-insure.

At the same time many large insurers have begun to offer self-insurance packages: The insurer administers everything, but the employer takes the risk. These types of plans will not have the profound affect on healthcare prices that direct self-insurance will, because they leave the middleman in the middle, deciding what is covered and negotiating prices.

Once the employer and the third-party administrator representing it get their hands directly on the bills, prices can drop dramatically. In one extreme (but not all that uncommon) case[41] an employer realized it had been paying an extortionate $10,000 per visit for dialysis patients. The new price? $975 — over 90 percent lower. Overall costs went down so much that the company was able to expand coverage, offer a lower premium, and open an onsite primary care clinic. Companies that offer self-insurance packages to get the employer "out of the PPO trap" claim that their clients often experience a 15 to 20 percent drop in costs the first year (more if their employees have been in the hospital a lot), and that costs stay close to flat after that.

---

41 Rosenberg, *ibid.*

Employee risk: Employer shopping works better if you can turn the employees into shoppers as well by making them pay part of the cost. The most typical set-up combines a consumer-directed health plan (CDHP) with an attached health savings account (HSA) or other similar tax-deductible account. The CDHP is like the plans offered through the Obamacare exchanges: They have high deductibles, co-pays, and coinsurance for everything except a few preventive matters. Both the employer and employee can put pretax money into the HSA to help cover these costs.

More and more employers are pushing their employees into such plans. By 2012, some 31 percent of employers offering health insurance offered CDHPs[42] — some 15 percent of the total private market.[43] All of the newly insured coming into healthcare through the ACA exchanges are in such plans.

Co-pays and coinsurance both call on the employee to participate in the cost of their own healthcare, but they give the employees different incentives. A co-pay is a flat rate — $50, for instance, for a doctor visit. The employee has some reason to wonder whether the visit or test or procedure is really necessary, but no reason to wonder what its full price might be. Coinsurance is a percentage, say, 20 percent of the full price. With coinsurance the full price makes a big difference when the employee becomes a healthcare shopper.

Nobody likes having to pay part of the cost, and consumers are really hitting the wall on how much of their paycheck they can dole out for healthcare, even after the passage of the ACA. At the same time, making them pay too much of the cost is also medically counterproductive. With high deductibles and co-pays and co-insurance, many people will simply do without treatment — even for life-threatening conditions.

At the same time, involving the employees as shoppers is very important for bringing down the cost of healthcare, because suddenly those

---

42 Henry J. Kaiser Family Foundation, Health Research and Educational Trust. 2012 employer health benefits survey [Internet]. Menlo Park (CA): KFF; September 11, 2012 [cited July 8, 2013]. Available at: http://kff.org/ private-insurance/report/employer- health-benefits-2012-annual-survey/

43 Employee Benefit Research Institute, "Who Contributes —— And How Much — To Health Accounts?" press release, February 12, 2014. Available at: http://www.ebri.org/pdf/PR1062. HSAs.12Feb14.pdf

millions of employees and customers become hyper-aware of price. Look at the map in the previous chapter showing the wild variation in prices for an ankle MRI mere miles or blocks apart. No one who is paying a piece of the cost and has a choice and knows the price is going to buy the $2,200 model when they could buy the $700 or $400 model a subway stop away.

Build your own ACOs: As one other way of cutting out the middle-man, some employers are working directly with healthcare providers to create accountable care organizations in their areas — affiliations of medical groups who are paid in a way that gives them the incentive to provide better, less expensive, less wasteful care. These are offered to employees as an alternative to traditional health plans, with the goal of giving the employees better, more coordinated care that meets quality goals, all at a lower price. The pioneer in this is Boeing, in its Seattle, St. Louis and Chicago markets.[44]

Audit the bills: All businesses audit their invoices. They buy parts and raw materials, they hire subcontractors — and when the invoice is presented, they audit it. They match up the delivery list with the pieces on the pallet and the purchase order. They look for double billing, added charges, wrong prices, substituted product. If the bill is wrong, they don't pay it. If the parts don't work as promised, they reject the lot and refuse to pay for them. They work out the adjustments with the supplier. If the supplier is unreliable, they change suppliers.

How much of this do we do traditionally in Default Model private healthcare? Zero. Insurance companies often deny claims, sometimes for no real reason, forcing the physician or hospital into a complicated appeals process. Medicare does automated mass audits of hospital bills, looking for "upcoding" (billing for something more complicated and expensive than the patient presented) or outright fraud, and has recovered hundreds of millions of dollars. But in the private market almost no one really audits healthcare bills on a regular basis.

It can be difficult or impossible for employers to even find out what the bills actually are. The healthcare privacy law (the Health Insurance

---

44 Potter W, "Taking insurance companies out of healthcare," *Public Integrity*, September 15, 2009. Available at: http://www.publicintegrity.org/2014/09/15/15524/taking-insurance-companies-out-health-care

Portability and Accountability Act or HIPAA) forbids employers from seeing them. The contracts that insurance plans and administrators make with hospitals often have "gag rules" in them that actually forbid either party from disclosing either the amounts agreed to beforehand, or the amounts actually paid for any particular item.

Now that's changing. Self-funded employers are hiring third-party companies such as the Atlanta company Advanced Medical Pricing Solutions, or AMPS, and the Philadelphia-area company ELAP Services. These companies employ doctors to audit the bills line by line and push back on wrong charges, upcoding (giving an item a price code for something actually more expensive), double billing, questionable charges, routine hospital charges for doctors who may have peeked at the patient but contributed nothing to the case, and on and on.

Go cost plus: ELAP is one of several benefits companies pioneering a radically different method of reimbursing hospital bills: Self-funded employers, under such a system, just pay the hospital its cost plus a percentage for profit. Some benefits companies define this as "Medicare +40 percent."

Medicare now publishes what it pays each hospital. Hospitals don't typically know their own costs for any particular item very well, let alone how much of that cost is covered by the Medicare payment. Medicare reimbursements are all over the map: Some items (such as, say, a diabetes nutritional consultation) are clearly under-reimbursed, while other items (such as implanting cardiac stents) are clearly wildly profitable. Overall, hospital executives commonly believe that Medicare pays them less than their costs. The common industry-wide estimate is that Medicare pays something like 91 percent of actual costs. If this is true, Medicare +40 percent would give hospitals their cost plus 31 percent. Most companies would call that a pretty decent margin over costs.

> **Employer Alert! The phantom, nobody-pays-this chargemaster rates are often three or four times Medicare rates, or even greater, so a 50 percent discount from chargemaster rates still leaves you with stratospheric costs. Paying from Medicare up rather than chargemaster down puts you in far more reasonable and negotiable territory.**

Some benefits companies have claimed significant successes with cost plus plans. Kathy Enochs, chief operating office of GNP, a Dallas third-party administrator that works with ELAP, says that only 15 percent of patients get hit with balance bills — and in those cases lawyers from companies like ELAP and AMPS fight back. They win, according to Steve Kelly, the president of ELAP, "98, 99 percent of the time."[45] Since charge-master rates vary wildly even within the same market and have no relation either to what most payers pay, or to the hospitals' actual costs, they are hard for the hospital to defend in court as "reasonable and customary" as required by law. Enochs claims that so far no patient under a GNP cost plus plan has had to pay a balance bill.

> **Hello! Calling all employers and consumers! Ladies and gentleman, we interrupt your regularly scheduled book to direct your attention to the nugget buried in the quote in the previous paragraph: When hospital bills are directly challenged by lawyers from benefits companies, the hospitals back off or lose almost every time, because it is hard for the hospitals to legally defend what they charge as "reasonable and customary."**
>
> **I am not a lawyer, this does not constitute legal advice, and legal experience here is still thin on the ground. But the experience that exists does suggest, once again, that any strategy for dealing with major medical bills should not start with the assumption that they are anything but phantom numbers made up for the occasion.**

Similarly, the Cincinnati firm Custom Design Benefits shows small- to medium-sized employers paying 7.7 percent to 67 percent less in overall costs compared with the renewal quotes they had received from traditional insurers in their market. The percentages of claims subject to balance bills were miniscule — 0.2 percent to 0.7 percent of total claims.[46]

---

45 Rosenberg *ibid.*
Hancock J. "Beat High Hospital Bills by Setting Your Own Price," Kaiser Health News, May 14, 2015. Available at: http://time.com/money/3857428/hospital-bills-set-your-own-price/
46 Case studies provided by Custom-Designed Benefits.

Reference pricing: Let's refer once more to the map in the introduction showing prices for an ankle MRI in the Washington, D.C., area. All the prices were from organizations that had been rated for quality. You'd be happy having your procedure done at any one of them. There were a cluster of prices between $400 and $730. Then there were outliers at around $1,200, $1,800, and $2,200.

Imagine an employer (or a group of self-funded employers working through an insurance company or other benefits administrator) advising its employees: "For this item, there are number of quality providers of ankle MRIs in the area for less than $700. We will call that a 'reference price.' You can go to any covered provider you wish. If the charge is less than $700, your co-pay is $0. If you choose the one that charges $730, your co-pay is $30. Choose the one that costs $2,200, and your co-pay is $1,500."

What effect do you think that would have on the price of that item in that market?

We don't have to speculate. We have some pretty good test cases.[47] For instance, CalPERS, the California Public Employees' Retirement System, which is one of the nation's largest buyers of healthcare, tried this idea out on replacement hips and knees. It found that among high-quality California hospitals the actual amount it was paying varied between $15,000 and $110,000, with a median price of $43,000. This was for the hospital's "allowed charges," not including the charges of the surgeons, anesthesiologists and such who could bill separately. CalPERS found that those outside charges didn't vary that much, but the hospitals' charges varied enormously. In January 2011 CalPERS set a reference price of $30,000 and got 46 of California's hospitals, including a number with the highest reputations, to agree to do replacement hips and knees for that price or less. Within the following year, the median price for replacement hips and knees for CalPERS members dropped from $43,308 to $28,465 — a 34 percent drop, magically just below the refer-

---

47 Robinson JC, Brown TT, "Increases In Consumer Cost Sharing Redirect Patient Volumes And Reduce Hospital Prices For Orthopedic Surgery," *Health Affairs*, August 2013, pp. 1392–1397. Available at: http://content.healthaffairs.org/content/32/8/1392.abstract;

Abelson R, "Employers Test Plan to Cap Medical Spending," *The New York Times*, June 23, 2013. Available at: http://www.nytimes.com/2013/06/24/health/employers-test-plan-to-cap-medical-spending.html

ence price. These price drops prompted by one payer echoed across the system in a prime example of the systemic shifts that can happen when some percentage of the market changes. In the years since 2011, prices for replacement hips and knees across all California hospitals for all buyers have narrowed considerably, and average prices have dropped. In this market for these products, CalPERS established a new normal, and the market re-organized around it.

Similarly, when Safeway discovered that California prices for colonoscopies varied from $848 to $5,984, it set a reference price of $1,300 — and found that its employees had no trouble finding doctors and surgery centers willing to take that amount.[48]

Some hospital executives argue that this price is a loss leader, that hospitals who cut their prices could not sustain such price cuts across a wide variety of products,[49] and would simply offset one price cut by price rises on other products. But that has not happened in California in the several years since CalPERS started reference pricing, and began expanding it to other products.[50] And the fact that such a wide variety of hospitals took such deep cuts on two of their most profitable items — including orthopedic hospitals for which those items represent a significant part of their business — argues that $28,000 is actually significantly closer to a true market price than the previous ridiculously wide array of prices.

Shopper alert! When you can establish a mechanism for a true market price to emerge, the range of prices narrows, and the median price drops. The price doesn't narrow to the previous median price. Rather it narrows and drops to something around what was the previous 25th percentile for that product in that micro market.

Reference pricing works best of course for items that are shoppable, that is, discrete items of healthcare that you can schedule ahead of time and

48 Rosenthal E, "Colonoscopies Explain Why U.S. Leads the World in Health Expenditures," *The New York Times,* June 1, 2013. Available at: http://www.nytimes.com/2013/06/02/health/colonoscopies-explain-why-us-leads-the-world-in-health-expenditures.html

49 Personal conversations with author

50 Robinson *et al.* 2013, *ibid.*

that are offered by a variety of high-quality providers at widely varying prices. This does not describe all of healthcare by a long shot, but it does describe a surprising amount of it, especially the most profitable and overpriced parts.

Reference pricing targets extremely high cost variations on procedures for which a reasonable level of quality can be established across many providers. Unlike coinsurance, it does not encourage the patient to question whether the surgery or test is appropriate or necessary at all.

Reference pricing is not limited to self-funded employers. Some health plans are experimenting with it in their PPO products. Medicare Advantage plans (health maintenance organization style plans offered under Medicare) can offer it, and under the ACA, Medicare is experimenting with it under other types of plans. According to an Aon Hewitt survey, while only some eight percent of employers used reference pricing in 2013, 62 percent intend to try it.[51]

Centers of Excellence: Reference pricing still leaves the employee or consumer lots of choices, and lots of responsibility to choose the best quality. As long as you go to a provider whose in-hospital costs are below the reference price, the payer will cover it.

Here's a different tactic: For any given high-cost procedure (birth, cardiac stenting, lung transplant), the payer evaluates all the providers within any one region, finds a few that can show top quality, and then negotiates for the lowest price among them. Whichever of the top-quality providers comes in with the lowest bid becomes the Center of Excellence[52] for procedures of that type and wins an exclusive contract — employees are not covered for those procedures at any other facility. The prices are more often bundled prices, that is, they count everything, including the surgeon, the anesthesiologist, the extra MRI, all that. The contract can be re-negotiated every year. To keep the contract the provider has to demonstrate continued high quality and keep the price low.

---

51 Aon Hewitt, "Employers plan pay tactics to cut costs: Companies weigh performance pay, value-based pricing," June 10, 2013. Available at: http://www.healthcarefinancenews.com/ news/employers-plan-pay-tactics-cut-costs

52 Robinson JC, MacPherson K, "Payers test reference pricing and centers of excellence to steer patients to low-price and high-quality providers." *Health Affairs* (Millwood). 2012;31(9): pp. 2028–36.

Shopper alert! Since, as we have seen, there is little to no relationship between quality and price, it's a smart tactic to narrow the choices to providers that can prove high quality, then negotiate the price.

These tactics are growing in popularity. In a survey, 59 percent of employers told Aon Hewitt that they intend to "steer participants to high-quality hospitals or physicians for specific procedures or conditions."[53]

Hospitals negotiate hard against this. The reason hospital ownership is becoming more concentrated is expressly to give the hospitals more regional market power against buyers. **The buyers' Centers of Excellence strategy breaks the hospitals' concentrated-ownership strategy by bargaining for particular services at particular hospitals à *la carte*, separately from everything else that their network of providers offers — and it does that for their most profitable items.** The hospitals want to be able to insist that the buyer (the health plan or employer) can buy only their whole system, that they can't be in-network for some things and not other things.

We are used to thinking of healthcare providers and hospitals especially as the good guys, rescuing us in our most vulnerable times, being there for us when we need them. And in many ways this is true. But it is not true in these power games played in the healthcare market. If you are inclined to feel bad about busting their chops over price, it is worth noting that monopolistic practices and restraint of trade are exactly why we have a century-old body of antitrust law in this country. In many regions of the country, increasingly concentrated ownership of health systems is resulting in exactly such monopolistic practices and restraint of trade. Playing hardball in breaking such practices is more than just okay, it's what we must do to make healthcare better and cheaper for everyone.

Medical tourism: Two years ago Wal-Mart suddenly put every hospital and facility in America that does transplants, orthopedic, spinal, or cardiac procedures in direct competition with some of the best and largest medical institutions in the country, including Mayo and the Cleveland Clinic. How did they do this? You might call it Centers of Excellence + travel. You might call it medical tourism. Wal-Mart signed direct contracts

---

53 Aon Hewitt, *ibid.*

with six top medical institutions to provide specific medical services for its 1.1 million full-time employees and dependents.[54] If you are one of those covered and you need a new knee or cardiac procedure, you take it to the designated facility — and Wal-Mart not only covers the medical expenses, it covers the travel expenses for you and your companion.

A number of major companies are doing the same thing. Lowe's sends all its employees needing heart surgery to the Cleveland Clinic, as does Boeing.[55] If any of PepsiCo's 250,000 employees need complex joint surgery or cardiac intervention, they can opt to get whisked off to Johns Hopkins in Baltimore.[56] Kroger, the grocery chain, offers any employee needing hip, knee, or spinal fusion surgery a benefit to get it done at any of several hospitals across the United States, including Hoag Orthopedic Institute in Irvine, California, as does the newspaper publisher Stevens Media.[57]

These are primary examples of the idea that better medicine can cost less. The Cleveland Clinic doctors, for example, are on salary. They don't get paid per procedure, so they have no incentive to do more just to pump up the volume. Michael McMillan, executive director of market and network services for the Clinic, said of the Lowe's deal, "The thing we will want to demonstrate together is that by an employee traveling to a place with better outcomes, fewer re-operations and lower complication rates, over time it will lead to lower costs."[58]

Take a look at the brand names here: Mayo, Cleveland Clinic, Johns Hopkins, Hoag Orthopedic. These are not Crazy Eddie's Discount Chop

54 Diamond D, "Wal-Mart Could Transform Healthcare. But Does it Want to?" *California Healthline*, May 8, 2013. Available at: http://www.californiahealthline.org/road-to-reform/2013/wal-mart-could-transform-health-care-but-does-it-want-to?

55 Spector H, "Lowe's will bring its workers to Cleveland Clinic for heart surgery," *Cleveland Plain Dealer*, February 17, 2010. Available at: http://www.cleveland.com/healthfit/index.ssf/2010/02/post_27.html;
PWC Health Research Institute, "Medical Cost Trend: Behind the Numbers 2014," June 2013.

56 Walker A, "PepsiCo to pay for employee surgeries at Hopkins," *The Baltimore Sun*, December 11, 2011. Available at: http://articles.baltimoresun.com/2011-12-11/health/bs-hs-hopkins-pepsi-20111209_1_surgeries-pepsico-mercer-health-benefits

57 Terhune C, "Companies go surgery shopping," *Los Angeles Times*, November 17, 2012. Available at: http://www.latimes.com/business/la-fi-bargain-surgery-20121117,0,7716044.story

58 Spector, *ibid*.

Shop and Body Part Emporium. They are the best in the business. Yet their package prices are typically set either at the national median or as much as 15 percent lower. The buyers deny that they are just looking for lower costs, but the combination of lower costs, fewer mistakes and do-overs, and all-round better medicine is so attractive that the buyers typically not only pick up the travel expenses and co-pays, they often offer employees bonuses of up to $2,500 to get on the plane to Cleveland or Baltimore — or John Wayne Airport in sunny Orange County, California.

Smaller companies may find the research, negotiation, and logistics of getting into such medical tourism daunting. But **there are now firms that specialize in arranging such deals**. These include the healthcare consultant Mercer and the Denver company BridgeHealth Medical, which has arranged packages with 45 institutions — including complete knees for as little as $19,000.[59]

The *Los Angeles Times* described the experience from one patient's point of view:

> At Kroger, employees may pay 10 percent out of pocket if they choose one of the company's 19 select hospitals, compared to 25 percent to 50 percent out of pocket for other nearby medical centers.
>
> Carol Vogel, a 64-year-old writer in Minden, Nev., said she was skeptical about flying to another state for surgery until the human resources manager explained how much she stood to save.
>
> In Newport Beach "this was 100 percent paid for," Vogel said. If she stayed closer to home in Nevada, "I would have been out $8,000 or $9,000 easy on my insurance."
>
> She said she's pain-free in her left hip for the first time in years, so she scheduled an implant for her right hip later this month, followed by a free stay at Island Hotel, an oceanfront resort in Newport Beach.
>
> "This is like the honeymoon we never had," she said. "Are you kidding me?"[60]

---

59 Terhune, *ibid.*
60 Terhune, *ibid.*

As Chip Burgett, an executive vice president at BridgeHealth told the *Los Angeles Times,* "There is a lot of excess margin in healthcare and plenty of room in the pricing of these hospitals. Hopefully this drives true competition in healthcare that's not just based on how many helicopters a hospital has."[61]

Employer buying groups: In some areas small employers have joined together in healthcare buying groups, realizing that collectively they have significant leverage in bargaining with the healthcare providers in their area. For instance, the Savanna Business Group, founded in 1982, comprises area firms with some 16,000 employees and altogether more than 35,000 covered lives. It does more than gather data, share experiences, and hope that the local providers will reform. Instead, it forces the providers in the area to compete for the exclusive business of those 35,000 covered lives. The results are impressive. Between 2000 and 2010, as premiums nationwide increased 90 percent, the average cost per employee for group members rose less than half as much — 44 percent. To compare two similar employers: In 2010, the City of Savannah, a group member, paid $7,007 per employee in healthcare costs. Chatham County, a nonmember, paid $12,619 per employee — 80 percent more.[62]

According to Aon Hewitt, some 21 percent of employers already participate with other employers in some kind of group purchasing arrangement — but another 38 percent intend to take up the practice in the coming three to five years.[63]

Onsite clinics: Increasing numbers of companies are building medical clinics right into the work sites, whether they are in office buildings, warehouses, or factories. PepsiCo, for instance, has them at many facilities, including 38 that are run by Johns Hopkins.[64]

---

61 Terhune, *ibid.*

62 Klepper B, "When Employers Get Serious About Managing Healthcare Risk," *Care and Cost,* April 7, 2013. Available at: http://careandcost.com/2013/04/07/when-employers-get-serious-about-managing-health-care-risk/
Klepper B, "When Employers Collaborate to Manage Healthcare Costs," Eau Claire, Wisconsin *Leader Telegram,* December 9, 2012. Available at: http://brianklepper.info/2012/12/09/when-employers-collaborate-to-manage-health-care-costs/

63 Aon Hewitt, *ibid.*

64 Walker, *ibid.*

These are not your father's company doctor, who was there just to patch up injured workers and get them back on the line. Today's on-site clinics are typically full-service primary care practices. Employees can stick with the old routine and wait for an appointment with their usual doctor, take an afternoon off, and pay the co-pay or co-insurance. Or they can pop downstairs as a walk-in at the onsite clinic, skip the co-pay, and even get most prescriptions filled free on the spot.

The company does not own the clinic, employ the doctors, or get any information about who is getting treated for what condition. The clinic is run under contract by an outside medical institution, or by one of the companies that specialize in building and running such clinics. The company gets a single bill per month for the actual costs of running the clinic plus a contracted fee.

Risk contracts: Some employers have special needs. Think, for instance, of a large warehousing concern with an unusually high number of employees with back problems. Rather than sending them to a spine and pain clinic for back operations paid for on a fee-for-service basis, some employers might contract with the clinic for a set per-employee, per-month amount, to pay for all back care, with bonuses based on fewer employees complaining of back pain or taking time off work for back problems. Suddenly the incentives of the back experts are reversed: Instead of seeing how many operations they can fit into a day, they are down on the warehouse floor arranging for free yoga classes and ergonomic lifting classes, and buying weight belts.

Mental health: Include a strong mental health component to any benefits program (see below — Special Focus: Mental Health). Do this not just to be nice, or to comply with the Americans With Disabilities Act (ADA) and the parity provisions of the ACA. Do it because **a successful behavioral health program will drop absenteeism, workplace accidents, and your overall healthcare costs**. Remember, your employees will be dealing with a third party; there are ways of designing these services so that you and they will have the privacy you need.

Employers these days seem to be the lion that has awakened. Most of these techniques were little heard of only a few years ago. Now they are spreading. Typically when I work with a state association of employers, I can pull examples of the use of these tactics from employers in their own association, even small and medium employers. Surveys now show that most employers are considering them, trying them out, spreading their use. In a survey of nearly 800 large and midsize U.S. businesses, 53 percent of the respondents told the human resources consulting firm Aon Hewitt that they were "moving toward provider payment models that promote cost-effective, high-quality healthcare results."[65] Nap time is over.

What Consumers Can Do

Some people hate being called "consumers" of healthcare. But we are talking here about economics, and what it takes for the healthcare system to offer you true value for your money. You are a "patient" when you're sick, or when you are talking with your doctor about the condition of your body. When you are making decisions about how and where to spend your healthcare dollar, you're a consumer.

This is supposedly the great era of consumer empowerment in healthcare. But as my friend and colleague Ian Morrison puts it, "When you hear the word 'empowerment,' it's code for 'You're on your own, pal.'"[66]

Even under Obamacare, consumers have pretty much hit the wall on how much they can spend on healthcare. As Morrison points out, "The average family can't afford the average premium. On top of that, each year the share of the premium that workers have to pay continues to rise."[67] As do the deductibles, the co-pays, the co-insurance.

As a consumer, though, you can get a better deal for yourself and your family, and at the same time actually help change healthcare for the better. You can do this by taking two steps:

---

65 Aon Hewitt, "Employers plan pay tactics to cut costs: Companies weigh performance pay, value-based pricing," June 10, 2013. Available at: http://www.healthcarefinancenews.com/news/employers-plan-pay-tactics-cut-costs

66 Morrison I, "The American Health Care Consumer," *Hospitals and Health Networks Daily*, January 6, 2015. Available at: http://www.hhnmag.com/display/HHN-news-article.dhtml?dcrPath=/templatedata/HF_Common/NewsArticle/data/HHN/Daily/2015/January/morrison_consumerism_obamacare

67 Morrison, *ibid.*

1. Become a shopper
2. Become a fierce shopper

You become a shopper for healthcare by opting for a lower premium health plan in which you pay part of the cost through deductibles, co-pays, or coinsurance. (To remind you, a co-pay is when you pay a set dollar amount for each visit to the doctor, for instance. Coinsurance is when you pay a percentage of the charges.) You become a better shopper, even a fierce shopper, by doing all the things that you would do in buying any other high ticket items, such as a car, a home entertainment system, or a new coat of paint for your house.

Coverage: Get insured. If you do not already have coverage through your employer, get covered either through the ACA exchanges or out-side the exchanges directly from an insurer. Under the ACA, insurers have to take on anyone who shows up — but they don't have to do it whenever you feel like showing up. You can sign up during the open enrollment period at the end of each year, or at other times if you have a "triggering life event" such as getting married or divorced, or losing your job.

Some people avoid paying for healthcare insurance because of the cost — along with the guess or the hope that they will never get seriously sick. So rather than pay hundreds of dollars per month for insurance, they figure they will just pay out-of-pocket for ordinary doctor visits and hope for the best.

A couple of thoughts: First, a lot of people greatly underestimate how much healthcare can cost. They may be stunned to learn that a serious infection that puts them in the hospital for a couple of weeks can cost as much as a house, as can a premature baby, or some injuries from a traffic accident — **even if they manage to bargain the hospital down from chargemaster prices.**

Under the ACA exchanges, the cost of the premiums are capped at a percentage of your income if you make less than four times the federal poverty level. Here are the extremes: If you are a single person making just over the federal poverty level of $11,490 per year, your premium level is capped at two percent, which comes to $20 per month. For a family of four with a household income just under $94,200 (four times the federal poverty level) your cap would be 9.5 percent of your income, or $747 per month for the family policy.[68]

It is true that many of the less expensive plans have high deductibles — high enough that you may well end up paying out of pocket for all of your ordinary healthcare if you don't get really sick or have a serious accident. But there is an important hidden benefit to having insurance: Even when you are paying the bills yourself, you will be paying them at the rates the insurance company has negotiated with the hospital or the doctor, far lower rates than the "charge master" rates they charge to people with no insurance.

> **Shopper alert! When you buy health insurance, even with a high deductible, you're insuring against a major medical event becoming a life-changing financial catastrophe as well — and you're also buying the right to be treated at the much lower insurance company rates.**

Shopping for insurance: Henry J. Kaiser built his vast combine of steel, aluminum, shipbuilding, concrete, and other industries on one motto: "Find a need and fill it." And boy howdy! Is there one huge need in helping consumers buy healthcare insurance! PhDs, MBAs, CPAs, actual rocket scientists — doesn't matter who you are, it's tough to figure out. In the old days your employer bought it for you, or you had a few choices, or you just got a Medicare card, or a Medicaid enrollment. There wasn't much choosing involved. Today you may have scores of options and hundreds of decisions to make.

Luckily, some companies have found that need and are filling it.[69] Gravie.com and Benefitter.com create dashboards for you that bring all your options, for you in your situation in the place where you live, into one place. They handle all the transactions and answer your questions. How much do they cost? Zip. They make their money from fees from

---

68 Fernandez B, "Health Insurance Premium Credits in the Patient Protection and Affordable Care Act (ACA), Congressional Research Service, March 12, 2014. Available at: https://www.fas.org/sgp/crs/misc/R41137.pdf

69 Hixon T, "Startups Are Rebuilding The Healthcare User Experience," *Forbes*, March 3, 2015. Available at: http://www.forbes.com/sites/toddhixon/2015/03/02/start-ups-are-rebuilding-the-healthcare-user-experience

the insurance companies. But they make the same no matter which company you choose, so their interest is in serving you. They specialize in helping employers transition their employees to the exchange market.

Healthsherpa.com is a user-friendly interface for the ACA exchange websites. Think of it as TurboTax for Obamacare.

HMOs' hidden benefit: Kaiser Permanente, Group Health of Puget Sound, and others like them are true staff model health maintenance organizations. That is, the doctors and nurses all work for the same organization that provides the insurance, and the hospitals are all owned by the same organization. This is an important factor in choosing your health insurance.

Here's why: Suppose you research the different health plans and find one whose network (according to the health plan) includes the hospitals you think are important, or the oncology team that has been treating you for years, or your favorite primary care doc. So you sign on the dotted line. Here's the kicker: The health plan does not actually guarantee that those institutions and doctors are in the network. People often report discovering that they are not when they try to use their health insurance. There is certainly no guarantee that they will be in the network next year, or that no out-of-network practitioner will get sneaked into the case, or that they will not find some reason in the fine print that they don't cover your particular variety of brain tumor. (See "Lever 6: Trust" for a full discussion of this.)

Opinions vary about the quality of these institutions (Personally, I am a longtime member of Kaiser of Northern California, and a big fan of their quality, except for mental health) but there is no argument about one aspect of staff model HMOs: What you see is what you get. They are not going to suddenly stop treating brain tumors just when you get one. If you find you like one of their primary care practitioners, that doctor is not arbitrarily going to be knocked out of the network next year. They are not going to invite some high-priced outside surgeon to assist on your hysterectomy and then sock you with a huge bill.

Trust (again, see Lever 6) is of enormous importance in healthcare. That includes the financial arrangements that connect you to your healthcare provider. In the modern narrow-network versions of the Default Model, that trust is not there. **If your plan is described as a PPO (preferred provider organization), you have a "narrow network" plan.**

What is "preferred" about these providers is not that they are special in any way. Rather, they have agreed to charge a discount. Since this agreement is re-negotiated every year (and sometimes more often) the health plan cannot guarantee that it will provide what it claims to provide. Staff model HMOs can guarantee that, because for them, those doctors are not just in some nebulous and changeable network, they are on the payroll.

> Use this book! If you are employed and insured through your employer, talk to your employer or the human resources department about this book. Get them a copy. If cost is a problem, contact me through my website, ImagineWhatIf.com. Many of the things that can drive down costs for an employee have to be done by the employer.

Cost: Find out how much something is going to cost before you agree to it — not how much the phantom charges might be, or what it cost other patients on average over the last year. To the extent you can, find out how much the whole thing will cost you. This is not easy. Check the next chapter ("Lever 2: Transparency") and the resources in the appendices at the end of the book for the best sources of information. To the extent that you can, never agree to anything until they tell you how much it's going to cost you.

Shopper alert! Make no assumptions about cost.

- Yes, removing a tiny wart-like bump on your cheekbone can result in a medical bill of more than $25,000.[70]
- Yes, you can be billed thousands of dollars for services you specifically declined.
- Yes, you can take your child to a hospital that is in your insurance network — and only later find out that the doctor attending the child in the in-network hospital is an out-of-network doctor,

---

70 Rosenthal E, "Patients' Costs Skyrocket; Specialists' Incomes Soar," *The New York Times*, January 18, 2014. Available at: http://www.nytimes.com/2014/01/19/health/patients-costs-skyrocket-specialists-incomes-soar.html

whose attentions saddle you with a bill for tens of thousands of dollars. Yes, they can do that.

Quality: Make no assumptions about quality, either. Most Americans believe that cost is a proxy for quality in healthcare: The more expensive the hospital or surgical service, the better it must be. After all, this is at least roughly true in other fields. Buying a $50,000 car will get you a better car than buying a $10,000 car. This is not true in healthcare. **The relationship between cost and quality is not completely random, but close enough.** You can get high-quality healthcare for less — much less — but you have to be a fierce and diligent shopper to get it.

"They have a great reputation" is an even tougher assumption to challenge. Reputation is not necessarily deserved. The big name-brand hospitals, systems, and medical centers may or may not have better quality and better outcomes than less-well-known places. **Those "Best Hospital" lists and rankings? They are all based on reputation, that is, on surveys of opinions, not on successful outcomes.** Even places with worldwide reputations and Nobel Prize winners on staff, such as Johns Hopkins, Stanford, or the Harvard hospitals, do not necessarily have the very best outcomes, the fewest problems, and the lowest infection rates even in their local area for your particular problem.

Testimonials are equally worthless. Everybody has at least some customers who were ecstatically satisfied, because everything worked out great.

You need to build a trusted relationship with a regular primary care provider. If you deeply trust your primary care provider, he or she can be your best ally in finding high-quality specialists and other providers. If you don't have that sense of deep trust, then be at least a little skeptical about your doctor's recommendations. After all, the doctor is talking about colleagues in the same town, with whom he or she might play golf, and might see socially. If the doctor is recommending someone in the same multi-specialty practice, he or she has a business relationship with that physician. If your doctor is recommending a particular lab, imaging center, or other testing service he or she may well have an ownership interest, despite federal laws that attempt to make such interests illegal.

And of course, pay no attention to anything that any staff member says about the practitioner, who is after all in one way or another the boss. You call or show up to inquire about a particular doctor, and the assistant says, "Oh, Dr. Burgess? He's wonderful. His patients really like him." Well, what else is she going to say? Is she going to wrinkle her nose, raise her eyebrows, run screaming from the room?

For any service or provider, try to find out the real numbers, the definitive markers for quality, such as infection rates, readmissions, and unnecessary complications. If you're having a particular procedure done, it also matters how often this particular team does it. Everybody has to have learning experiences, but you don't want to be theirs. **If some surgical team is going to open up your heart and tinker around inside, you want a team that does that same thing together at least 250 times a year. Experience counts. Outcomes matter.**

Question the conventional wisdom: According to the conventional wisdom, dealing with your health has four steps:

1)   Wait until you're sick.
2)   Go to the doctor, clinic, or emergency department.
3)   Do whatever they tell you.
4)   Try to cope with the cost.

Call that the "medical box." Outside that box is a world of other ways to deal with your health. Some methods are very effective for some things, and almost all of them are significantly less expensive than mainstream medical care. When you have a high-deductible plan and are paying part of your healthcare costs, you need to be on the lookout for cheaper ways of getting fixed up. We are talking about complementary and alternative medicine, and functional medicine. Complementary and alternative practitioners include chiropractors, acupuncturists, naturopaths, even some hypnotherapists, and others. Depending on the nature of your problem, they may be just the thing for it. No, you don't take your broken leg to an acupuncturist. But back pain? Joint inflammation? It is worth trying. There is significant literature showing the usefulness of these methods. Learn what tools are available and use them wisely.

In states where it is legal, consider medical marijuana. It is one of the more effective drugs available, especially for chronic pain management, sleep problems, and stress, with far fewer side effects than many alternatives when used conscientiously.[71] Mainstream healthcare still shies away from this very effective tool because of federal drug laws. We will likely see that change in the coming few years.

Functional medicine is a rising new field that looks at health problems at an earlier stage in their development. The Cleveland Clinic, one of the most respected medical systems in the United States, has now opened its Center for Functional Medicine under the direction of Mark Hyman, M.D., author, founder of The UltraWellness Center in Lenox, Massachusetts, and chairman of The Institute for Functional Medicine.[72] Instead of asking, "In what way are you sick? How can we fix that symptom?" functional medicine asks, "How is your system out of balance? What can we do to put it back in balance? What can we learn from conventional tests and new kinds of tests at a much earlier stage of illness, so that we can fix the problem before it becomes full-blown disease?"

In conventional medicine, by the time we reach the conventional criteria for diagnosis, we may already have lost up to 70 percent of function. Functional medicine studies illness when the losses are still relatively low, and draws from a range of fascinating research through the last decade or so including research on the role of inflammation, the key role of digestion, and the complex interactions between digestive functions and brain function. Look in the Resources for ways to investigate how functional medicine might provide you with more tools for your health.

Payment: The number one thing not to do if you get sent a big medical bill? Pay it.

Shopper alert! The number one thing *not* to do if you get sent a big medical bill? Pay it.

---

71 Really? You looked at a footnote to find out how I know this?

72 Cleveland Clinic, "Cleveland Clinic Opening Center For Functional Medicine," press release, September 15, 2014. Available at: http://my.clevelandclinic.org/about-cleveland-clinic/newsroom/releases-videos-newsletters/cleveland-clinic-opening-center-for-functional-medicine

If you are being billed because you are uninsured, it is a near certainty that the bill is inflated and is far higher than any bill the folks at the hospital would have sent to an insurance company, much less Medicare. It is also a near certainty that, whatever the price, and whether you are insured are not, there are numerous items on the bill that they should not be billing you for.

They will assure you that those are just the standard prices, and that the bill has been audited and is correct. None of this is true. There are no standard prices in healthcare, and there are almost no perfectly clean bills. You could easily go bankrupt trying to pay bogus medical bills.

Surprisingly, many of what you may think of as the nicest not-for-profit organizations, even some religious-based organizations with a charity mission, are perfectly willing to go after people's houses and retirement funds, or sell the unpaid bills to bill collectors who will do it for them.[73] You need help. You need someone on your side.

The same is true if you are insured, but receive bills for out-of-network services, or bills for an unpaid balance ("balance bills") in which the doctors or hospitals are claiming that the insurance company did not pay them enough.

Who can you get on your side? If you are insured, try the insurance company. Many of them will fight balance billing for you, and can try to get out-of-network bills reduced. Otherwise, or if you are uninsured, you will likely find a medical claims advocate helpful. You will find some ways to look for a medical claims advocate in the Resources Appendix.

Keep in mind the negotiators' adage: You don't get what you want. You don't get what you deserve. You get what you settle for. For far too long we, the customers of healthcare, have been settling for paternalistic reassurances about quality and blatant secrecy about cost. Don't settle for it. It's your money and your body. Get it done right.

Resources: Please refer to the Resources appendix at the end of the book for a wealth of resources to help you be a fierce shopper.

---

73 Hebert S, "When Nonprofit Hospitals Sue Their Poorest Patients," ProPublica for National Public Radio, December 19, 2014. Available at: http://www.npr.org/2014/12/19/371202059/when-a-hospital-bill-becomes-a-decade-long-pay-cut

Results already showing up

Where might we first expect to see the results of more consumers, employers, and other purchasers of healthcare getting the shopping bug? We would expect to see a fall-off in the use of the highest-cost services, such as in-patient hospital days, and a rise in less expensive ways to access healthcare, such as outpatient procedures, clinics, primary care, urgent care, and retail care.

That's exactly what we have been seeing over the last five years as more employees have been absorbing some of the cost of their healthcare and then in 2014 when the new Obamacare exchange plans with their high deductibles and co-pays came into full use. Many hospitals across the country are shrinking, closing wings and decommissioning beds, exporting more patients to outpatient clinics, in some cases closing the hospital itself in favor of an outpatient surgery and expanded primary care. The trend is slight so far — there were 5,101 community hospitals in the United States in 2008, and by 2014 that had dropped to 4,974 — but the trend is definite and strongly felt within the industry. As Karin Henderson, executive director of strategic management for six-hospital Cone Health in Greensboro, N.C. told *Modern Healthcare,* "Patients are shopping. It is a new day in healthcare."[74]

> **"Patients are shopping. It is a new day in healthcare." — Karin Henderson, Cone Health, Greensboro, N.C.**

What Government Can Do

Government can support shopping in many ways. Federal and state governments especially can clear away legal restrictions that actually are designed to make the market more comfortable for the current players. There are a wide variety of these, including:

---

74 Evans M, "Hospitals closing, shrinking as outpatient care grows," *Modern Healthcare,* February 21, 2015. Available at: http://www.modernhealthcare.com/article/20150221/MAGA-ZINE/302219988/hospitals-face-closures-as-a-new-day-in-healthcare-dawns
"Fast Facts on U.S. Hospitals," American Hospital Association: http://www.aha.org/research/rc/stat-studies/fast-facts.shtml

"Scope of practice" laws: Scope of practice laws dictate what can be done by a nurse, nurse practitioner, pharmacist, or other professional, and which are reserved only for physicians. Can a nurse practitioner prescribe medicine, for instance? Can a pharmacist give a flu shot? These laws are really guild rules designed to make sure that doctors have enough work, and are typically much more restrictive than licensing laws. We no longer need to make sure doctors have enough work. Instead we are desperate to find professionals to do medical care, especially primary care. If people are going to shop for basic healthcare, they need to have a lot more alternatives. The members of each profession should be allowed to do whatever they are trained and licensed to do.

"Corporate practice of medicine" laws: Most states forbid other business entities from directly employing doctors. So when a hospital or health system buys up practices, it typically puts them into a medical group that is owned by the hospital's captive foundation. When Walgreens puts in a retail clinic, or Disney puts in an employee clinic, the physicians are typically in a contracted medical group, not directly employed by the company. The main result of such laws is to make it somewhat more difficult for new competitors to show up in healthcare. They are, in other words, in restraint of trade, and should be abolished.

"Certificate of need" laws: Some states adopted "certificate of need" legislation that force all hospitals and health system to submit any plans for offering new services or building a new building to a commission, which would decide whether the facility was really needed. But the main criterion for "Is it needed?" has usually been "Can you get customers for it?" To which the answer has usually been, "If you build it, they will come." There is no evidence that the certificate-of-need process has kept costs down in the states that use it. There is plenty of evidence that it has kept competition down and impeded new entrants to the market. In other words, like the others, these are in restraint of trade and should be abolished.

Special Focus: How Medical Education Costs Distort The Healthcare Market

T HE EDUCATION OF a healthcare futurist happens in conversations, thousands of them, over months and years and decades. The thousands of articles read and catalogued, the databases assembled, the presentations absorbed at hundreds of conferences — these all provide data and background. But it's the conversations that make it real, that put things in context, that shape the data into a narrative that tells the story of where healthcare is going and why.

I was in Cleveland to present the Ken Lee Memorial Lecture in Grand Rounds at the rather amazing Cleveland Clinic. The evening before, my hosts invited me to a small private dinner at District, an exceptionally fine Cleveland restaurant, with some of the Clinic's top physicians and surgeons. The dinner was held partly to honor the work of a fine young doctor who was on the point of leaving Cleveland Clinic to go on to her residency elsewhere.

Over the tapas and an extraordinary Napa vintage, I asked about her experience at Cleveland Clinic. She was full of praise and enthusiasm for the efficiency and effectiveness of its unusual atmosphere, the collegiality of its doctors, the intelligence of its processes. So when she was finished with her residency, I asked, she might be hoping to come back to the Cleveland Clinic to practice? Her face clouded. Oh no, she couldn't possibly do that. She couldn't afford to. One of the ways Cleveland Clinic is able to offer efficient and somewhat less expensive healthcare is that it does not pay its doctors top-of-the-market rates. Given the great costs of medical education and the debt she had run up to pay for it, she would have to look for something much more lucrative.

The future of healthcare demands many different ways of providing the highest quality healthcare in ways that cost far less than today's healthcare. Yet we are educating our doctors in ways that force them to seek the most lucrative work just to pay off their debt. Do you see the problem here?

A full discussion of the costs of medical education does not belong in this book, as it is not something we outside of government can do much about. But I will make a specific argument about it. This handbook is essentially a guide to the unusual market economics of healthcare, and how we can affect them. The costs of medical education are one of several big distortions in that market that are peculiarly difficult to change without major intervention on the federal level.

Physicians — smart, deeply educated and continually re-educated, dedicated, compassionate, insightful, thoughtful — are the backbone and sinews of our healthcare system. They are a national asset. They are as much a part of our national infrastructure as are our Interstate Highways, or our military. We have become obsessed with national security since 9/11. If our number one obsession is our physical security and safety, why don't we see doctors as among our major assets in that struggle?

Let's take a moment to compare the costs of two national security assets: physicians and fighter planes.

What's it cost to become a doctor? About $250,000.[75] It makes a difference whether the school is private or public, whether the doctor goes on to study for a specialty, all that. But it averages about $250,000, and most of that cost is paid through student debt. The newly minted doctor starts commercial life owing something close to that amount.

For comparison, consider the new (and still evolving) F-35 Joint Strike Fighter. The cost per fighter, according to Department of Defense estimates? About $250 million. That's per individual plane. (Yes, these

75 Lorin J, "Medical School at $278,000 Means Even Bernanke's Son Has Debt," *Bloomberg News*, April 11, 2013. Available at: http://www.bloomberg.com/news/2013-04-11/medical-school-at-278-000-means-even-bernanke-son-carries-debt.html

are estimates, it depends on the type, there are lots of ways of juggling the books, it's a political hot potato, but still ... this is the best guess of outside defense analysts.)[76]

So, roughly speaking, one F-35 = 1,000 new doctors. We pay for the fighters out of general tax revenues. We make the doctors pay for themselves.

The argument, of course, is that doctors make a good income, so of course they should pay for this investment in a lifetime of good income. True. But flip that around: What does this debt do to the system, and to us as patients? It makes doctors seek out the most profitable livings, no matter what their feelings of civic responsibility and dedication to the patients, because they start out so far in the hole. This is a huge distorter in the market for less expensive, more effective and efficient healthcare.

Most other countries find ways to pay for doctors' education other than making them pay for it with loans. There are many ways to accomplish this, once we build the political will to look on physicians as a national asset and a part of the national infrastructure, rather than just as entrepreneurs who are on their own for their founding costs.

They Roll Up Together

These seven levers are systemic. Each one needs the others. Each one magnifies and potentiates the others. They work together. We will not see the cascade of massive changes in healthcare until we see these seven begin to link up across different parts of healthcare.

So, if we imagine that we have gotten the purchasers of healthcare, both the large purchasers and the individual consumers, acting like real shoppers, what do they need? They need information. For that we need the second Lever: Transparency.

---

76 Wheeler W. "Different Planes, Common Problems," *Time*, June 6, 2013. Available at: http://nation.time.com/2013/06/06/different-planes-common-problems/

Shopping: The To-Do Lists

Purchasers (Employers, Pension Plans, and Other Purchasers of Healthcare):

- **Self-fund and reinsure:** Take control of your costs by taking control of your risk.
- **Risk:** Offer employees lower-cost plans in which they share a titrated level of risk so that they get rewarded for good shopping decisions.
- **Audit:** Use medical auditing companies to make sure you pay no unaudited bill.
- **Cost+:** Research whether you can use a third-party administrator who is willing to bargain for "cost plus" contracting with healthcare institutions in your area.
- **Reference pricing:** Work with the insurance company or third-party administrator that administers your self-funded plan to set bundled reference prices for all big-ticket, shoppable tests and procedures.
- **Centers of Excellence:** Work with the insurance company or third-party administrator that administers your self-funded plan to negotiate exclusive or preferred contracts for major tests and procedures with the highest-quality medical providers who will offer the best price.
- **Medical tourism:** Find out whether you can save money and get better medical care for your employees by sending them out of the area for big-ticket, shoppable tests and procedures. Resources for arranging such "medical tourism" deals are

evolving constantly, and becoming more available to medium and small-sized employers. Check the Resources appendix for some that are available at this writing.

- **Onsite clinics:** Research the cost and possible benefits of contracting for primary care clinics in each of your major workplaces.
- **Employer buying groups:** If you are a small employer, consider joining an employer buying group to give yourself more market leverage with medical providers.
- **Export the problem to the ACA exchanges:** If your work force is primarily low wage, you and they may be better off if you provide them some cash and help them sign up on the ACA exchanges. Use Benefitter.com or Gravie.com to navigate the transition.
- **Functional medicine:** A functional medicine component in your benefits program may help your employees intervene earlier and more cheaply in any developing health conditions. Functional medicine practitioners are available in most major markets. The Cleveland Clinic now offers a department of functional medicine.

Consumers:

- **Get insured:** Even the costs you pay yourself (such as co-insurance or costs below the deductible) will be at insurance company prices.
- **Get help to get insured:** Use HealthSherpa.com as a customer-friendly interface to the ACA exchange that is available in your state. Or use Gravie.com as your dashboard for health insurance, whether on the private market or through the ACA exchanges.
- **Lower your premiums:** Opt for a health plan in which you pay part of the costs.
- **Lower your out-of-pocket costs:** Be a careful shopper. Plan ahead. Find out how much things will cost, using the information sources in the Transparency chapter.
- **Get your meds cheaper:** Ask your doctor if there is a cheaper alternative. Shop for drugs from online pharmacies, especially from countries with strong quality regimes, such as Canada.

Investigate whether your drugs are included in the low-cost pharmaceutical programs of such big-box retailers as Wal-Mart and Target or major drugstore chains such as RiteAid, CVS, or Walgreens. If you have been prescribed a particular drug that is very expensive, go on the drug company's website. Many of them have hardship programs that may allow you to get the drug for much lower cost or even for free.

- **Go retail:** Shop for primary-care-based convenience, access, and transparency. Right now, those are mostly being offered in the emerging full retail clinics offered by Walgreens and CVS drugstores, by The Little Clinic in grocery stores, and by Wal-Mart in some markets — nearly 2000 altogether across the country. Act like a consumer. Here is a recent tweet from a satisfied customer of a retail clinic: "Walgreens healthcare clinic: Saturday, two kids, scheduled appts, full exam room, no copay, out in 30 min. Hard for old model to compete." The kicker? That customer is a doctor herself.[77]

- **Don't buy blind:** Obviously, in emergencies, traumas, and rapidly developing illnesses, we usually do not have much choice about where and how we are treated. But much of the rest of the time, we do have choice, often more than we realize, certainly more than we usually exercise. As much as you can, don't agree to any procedure or test or service without being told how much it will cost you. Take along an advocate if you are not good at asking questions and insisting on answers.

- **Be very clear that cost does not equal quality:** Higher price is not a marker for better quality in healthcare.

- **Be very clear that reputation is not a guarantee of quality:** The big name brands in healthcare may have better quality than lesser-known places. Or they may not. And their quality for, say, cancer treatment is not a marker for their quality in anything else, like appendectomies or allergies. Make them prove it in their outcomes numbers.

---

77 Bielamowicz L, "Traditional primary care, meet next year's model," Advisory.com, November 20, 2014. Available at: http://www.advisory.com/research/health-care-advisory-board/blogs/at-the-helm/2014/11/next-years-primary-care-model

- **Bargain:** Do bargain. Even if it is against your nature. If you find you need to pay for something that is out of your network, don't just say yes to whatever the price is. Talk to them beforehand, tell them your situation. Ask if they can give you a discount for paying cash. Remember, all healthcare prices are vapor. They may tell you all kinds of things about the actual cost of doing business, or Obamacare mandating it, or whatever. They may even believe that these things are true. None of these things are really true. All prices are based on nothing but what they can bargain the payer up to, and what the payer can bargain them down to. Most payers are big, and have leverage over the provider. The individual is not so big and the provider knows that, and has little reason to bargain hard for this one individual. So put on the pressure yourself or have an advocate do it, tell them your tale of woe, and why you value this particular doctor or treatment.
- **Payment:** If you do get a huge medical bill (if you are uninsured) or a balance bill or out-of-network bill (if you are insured), don't just pay it. Get help to fight it or negotiate it down. Look for the help you need in the Resources appendix.
- **Get a partner, get a posse:** We want to think that this should be easy, that "they" should take care of us — the government, the doctor, the health plan. You pay your money and then do what they tell you. Sorry to say, it's not that simple. You need help. We all do. You especially need help if you are more vulnerable than average — if you have multiple chronic problems, if you are old, if you have young children, or are in some other high-risk category. You need to work on your health and shop for the right healthcare with someone else. If you have an intimate partner, hopefully that person can be your partner in this as well. Across the country, many older people are forming health posses to help each other keep track of their conditions and medications, go to the doctor with them to listen, ask questions, and take notes.
- **Mental health:** Pay as much attention to your mental health as your physical health. Shop for an insurance program that includes behavioral health. Get help when you need it.

- **DIY:** The most important advice is: Do it yourself. Be the active manager of your body and your health. Carefully explore methods for maintaining your wellness and catching illness before it becomes full-fledged disease. Use functional medicine; exercise; careful diet; a host of alternative and complementary methods that are less invasive, less expensive, and useful early in the process of health imbalances. More than ever before, in this next chapter of medicine in the United States and globally, what I call the Next Healthcare, it's your bank account that many medical costs will come out of. Protect your savings and your health by making use of the wealth of knowledge out there now about how to take care of yourself and your family.

Health Plans:

- **Enhance self-funded offerings:** Create and market packages of services for self-funded employers that go far beyond merely administering claims. Incorporate many of the strategies mentioned here, such as creating on-site clinics, contracting for medical tourism, auditing bills, and helping employees choose services wisely. Do this to gain market share and avoid losing it to new entrants who are already beginning to package such services.
- **Work with the dashboards:** Work directly with companies like Gravie.com that work as the customer's dashboard for health insurance, whether on the private market or through the ACA exchanges.

Entrepreneurs, Inventors, and Investors:

Over the coming few years we will see a crying need (read: a burgeoning market) for expertise, services, and apps that can help employers and consumers become fierce shoppers, choose services wisely, and negotiate bills. This is a much bigger need and a vastly larger market than fitness tracking devices and apps like Fitbit. Prime examples mentioned in this chapter include Castlight, which provides cost and quality information tailored to the individual's health plan and deductible arrangement; Gravie.com which work as the customer's dashboard for health insurance; the similar Benefitter.com which specializes in helping employers transition their work force to the ACA exchanges; and HealthSherpa. com, which provides a customer-friendly interface to the ACA exchange. These kinds of apps and services will represent a much larger market than fitness and wellness apps and services. See "Lever 7: Tech" for a full discussion of the kinds of apps and devices that will likely dominate the future of healthcare.

Hospitals, Physician Groups, and Healthcare Institutions:

- **Decide who you are:** We are moving into an era of much greater differentiation. Any smart strategy for these coming years will be based not on continuing to try to be all things to all people, but on understanding and capitalizing on your system's place in the developing ecology. It's time to settle on your strategic destination.
- **Know your customers. Seriously:** You may think you know your customers, but you probably don't. Most of healthcare is customer blind, has difficulty even identifying their true customers (Patients? Physicians? Employers? Insurance companies?), let alone what they can do to have the best, most profitable, most efficient relationship with them. It's called customer relationship management, and it's a skill that most healthcare institutions, from the C-suite to the physicians to the people answering the phones, simply do not understand at all.
- **See what someone else is doing:** Search the literature, your consultant relationships, and your networks for organizations that seem to be evolving in similar strategic directions in similar markets who might be doing something worth trying. Email me or find me on LinkedIn for help.
- **Get the facts:** Invest in the "Big Data" style analysis that you need to understand your market — and your possible markets, which may be much larger than your current one.

- **Run phantom financials:** Continually run projections that assume, for instance, that all of your fee-for-service revenue comes in at Medicare rates; or that all of your shoppable procedures are bundled and sold at 15 percent below the national median; or that you can grow new income streams beyond fee-for-service; and that you can combine the growth of these new revenue streams with their possible effect in lowering demand for ED services, surgery, and other high-intensity procedures. In other words, attempt continually to model your financial future.
- **Go to the table:** Negotiate directly with self-funded employers for parts of their business. Negotiate for cost-plus contracts.
- **Look for new revenue streams:** Consider taking on risk contracts, and building on-site clinics and retail clinics. Get into all the new revenue streams that are emerging.
- **Compete in retail:** Do it right, offering real, appropriate care, with full price transparency (on the wall, like the price of hamburgers), online scheduling, weekend and night availability, electronic health record (EHR), touch-screen check-in. Among many others, both Kaiser Permanente and Novant Health are partnering with Target to build walk-in clinics at Target stores in different locations. Temple University Health System has a chain of ReadyCare Clinics in Philadelphia.[78]
- **Be a destination:** Consider whether you are good enough (and efficient enough) at some particular processes to become a medical destination yourself, offering bundled products that pull in patients from across your region or even the country. Compete for Center of Excellence contracts within your region.
- **Be your own payer:** All this makes more sense with your own insurance arm. This can be expensive and difficult to build. Health insurance is a significantly different business. The risks of getting

78 Packer-Tursman J, "Consumerism increases retail opportunities and access to coverage and care," *Managed Healthcare Executive*, February 9, 2015. Available at: http://managed-healthcareexecutive.modernmedicine.com/managed-healthcare-executive/news/consumerism-increases-retail-opportunities-and-access-coverage-and-care
Patel C, "The New Frontier Of Telemedicine Is Drug Stores," TechCrunch, March 4, 2015. Available at: http://techcrunch.com/2015/03/04/the-new-frontier-of-telemedicine-is-drug-stores/

it wrong are large. But it allows you to operate as a much more integrated business, and reap profit from your savings. Many of the most progressive healthcare organizations have done this, including Sharps, Sutter, Intermountain, Geisinger, and Scripps. Some organizations, such as Nebraska Medical Center and Methodist Health System in Omaha, have joined together to build regional insurance companies.[79]

Federal and State Legislators and Policymakers:

- **Abolish laws that act in restraint of trade:** We need more competition for providing actual healthcare services in all the different ways people want to buy them. Much of the ossification of the current healthcare marketplace is built on a web of laws and regulation designed to make the legacy players comfortable.
- **Expand Medicaid:** Those states that have not expanded Medicaid under the ACA are missing a big opportunity not only to have their poor get better medical care, but to bring more medical jobs to their state.
- **Re-design Medicaid programs:** The inside-of-the-box approach on how to save money in Medicaid is to severely restrict choice and make it difficult for recipients to actually use their Medicaid benefit. What is the outside of that box? Redesign the program to give them for more opportunity to use healthcare, at the same time that they can become smart shoppers about it — using fewer emergency services, for instance, and more low-price retail services and federally qualified clinic services. Some of the most successful preventive programs and "super user" programs (see the section on Targeting) are actually Medicaid programs.

---

79 Herman R, "The Risks of Provider-Operated Health Plans: Are the Rewards Worthwhile?" *Beckers Hospital Review,* January 31, 2014. Available at: http://www.beckershospitalreview.com/ payer-issues/the-risks-of-provider-operated-health-plans-are-the-rewards-worthwhile.html

Lever 2: Transparency

Problem

YOU CAN'T HAVE a market without price tags and quality ratings. Any talk of consumer-directed healthcare is just so much
smoke and hokum until the actual chooser knows how much the
thing costs, and how good it is — and has reason to care.

Solution

Find ways to give purchaser and consumers the information they need:
actual prices for different parts of healthcare, and realistic measures of
the quality of outcomes they can expect.

Pricing

Healthcare pricing has always been opaque. Pricing has been so frag-
mented and so bound up in contractual secrecy, complexity, and ongoing negotiations that nobody could tell you how much something was
going to cost beforehand. Even the people who are providing you the
service can't tell you how much the whole thing will cost, because they
don't really know. Shopping on a cost/quality basis has always been a
logical impossibility.

How are you going to buy your next car? Are you going to buy a
Toyota or a Ford? A hybrid, a full-size pickup, or a fun little sports car?
New, used, restored antique? Online? At your local dealer? At a dealer

50 miles away that gives better deals? Through a broker? Through a big box store? Will you compare the cars and the deals online? In magazines and newspapers? By talking to friends?

Compare that with how you make healthcare decisions. In typical pre-reform private insurance, you might choose among two or three very similar healthcare plans that your employer offers, using information that is confusing and complicated, that is not independent, and that you do not trust for a minute. You choose your doctor by talking to friends; by luck; by referral from the doctor you had before; or by Ouija board, channeling, crystals, and chanting. Then you do whatever your doctor tells you to do. You have little information, and few real choices.

Weird, or what? It's even weirder when you compare that with the way things are done in other parts of healthcare, outside the insured, fee-for-service mainstream. If you haven't done it, it can be amazing to pretend that you are shopping for any of a number of non-insured, elective surgeries, such as nose jobs, breast reshapings, or laser eye corrections. Choices and information abound. What has happened in these parts of healthcare over the past 25 years? They have gotten better, with new techniques and technologies. They have gotten cheaper — many prices have actually fallen. And there are more choices, more types of surgeries to choose from, more practitioners, and more payment plans.

Having trouble picturing this kind of expanded, low-cost medical product line? Take a closer look at cosmetic medicine: Over the last few decades, the industry has gone from the classic surgical face lifts, nose jobs, and breast enhancement to include a wide array of cheaper, less comprehensive, and less invasive techniques, from liposuction to microdermabrasions, chemical peels, laser skin rejuvenation, injections of Botox, collagen, hyaluronic acid gel, and other volumizing injectables to smooth fine wrinkles, among a host of other products. If you want to medically improve your appearance, you can spend a week in Rio and tens of thousands of dollars, or you can spend less than a hundred and get something done literally on your lunch hour.

Are these industry segments suffering from offering more for less? Not a bit. They are thriving. In mainstream medicine, most of the things that we do either have or could have alternatives that cost less and are less invasive. As customers become more involved and are paying more of their own money, mainstream medicine will follow the path that cosmetic medicine has pioneered.

So imagine a healthcare future in which the customer is, in essence, paying with his or her own money, so cares deeply about price and quality. Imagine a future in which the customer has a buffet of choices to make not just among doctors and hospitals, but among specialists, imaging centers, clinics, specialty hospitals such as birthing centers, and cardiac catheterization and bypass graft centers. Imagine a future in which the customer knows what each one charges for each procedure, what its success and complication rates are, and how it is rated by various third parties. Imagine a future in which customers can feel they actually know what is necessary and what is not. Imagine a future in which customers have lots of help in making these choices, both from apps and from live humans who really know the field. There you have it: incentive ("skin in the game"), choices, and information — all you need to make a real market.

It's Time to Get the Data

In buying a hot dog, getting the car serviced, going out to dinner — any time we make a buy decision — we always ask the value question: "Do I really need it, how good is it, and how much does it cost?" We have never been able to ask this value question until now in healthcare. Medicine has been thought too complex to evaluate, and the ways in which we choose it and pay for it have obscured the relationship between payment and outcomes.

The new data-driven world changes that. And it is brand new: Two years ago, the healthcare transparency business was in its infancy. Now it is burgeoning. At The Change Project we are continually tracking these advances in real time across different states, markets, and market segments.

For more and more people and employers, it is now possible to discover just what it costs to deal with common medical conditions, what are the consensus parts of the process, and how good particular medical teams are at performing them. We are rapidly moving into an era in which healthcare customers (patients, referring physicians, health plans, employers, government regulators, voters) routinely demand such information and will shift their business to the organizations that can give them the best answers — whether another facility across town, a Wal-Mart nurse-in-a-box, a specialty center elsewhere in the country, or somewhere in South Asia. Those who thrive will be those who are better faster cheaper, and can show it. Those who cannot will have a hard time surviving at all.

What Do We Need?

We need real prices for the whole episode / procedure / surgery (no "surprises").

Quality information is just as important: Without it, people will take price as a marker for quality. Give them price information alone, and they will tend to pick the most expensive choice. It is strongly counter-intuitive that "the best healthcare in the world" (such as at Mayo or the Cleveland Clinic) can cost half as much as "the best healthcare in the world" (such as at Cedars-Sinai in Los Angeles or NYU Langone in New York). They need some direct marker for quality. (We'll go into more detail in the next chapter, "Lever 3: Results.")

Finally, we need the information presented in plain language, in an easy-to-navigate form. Impossible to do? Nonsense. Hipmunk and Kayak and Amazon do it all the time. Presenting real price and quality information in readable, navigable format has become a major skill in the new information economy. The reasons we are not getting it yet for all of healthcare have nothing to do with technical difficulty. (For an example of a healthcare decision-making algorithm presented with brilliant clarity, go to WiserTogether.com.)

Where Can We Get It?

The information is emerging in new ways all the time, but for many people, it can still be hard to find — and many people don't yet use the information that exists.

For most consumers, the best place to get the real 411 is their health plan or employer. According to the Catalyst for Payment Reform's 2013 survey, almost all (98 percent) of health plans provide their customers with some kind of cost calculator — but almost no one uses them (two percent).[80]

What? Why? Probably because most of these tools are hard to find, and hard to use, and because they didn't have the kinds of information that people really need, such as "Can I count on the quality of this service?" or "How much will this actually cost me, with my health plan, my deductible, my co-pays?" But more importantly, until recently most people haven't had skin in the game — and that's changing.

Private data companies are stepping into the breach. Companies like Castlight Health, whose map of ankle MRI prices we saw in the introduction (Castlighthealth.com); ClearCost Health (ClearCostHealth.com); Compass Professional Health Services (compassphs.com); and Healthcare Bluebook (HealthcareBluebook.com) are working with health plans to provide better, more targeted and customized information. Some of them incorporate that wonderfully clear, interactive, almost game-like WiserTogether decision-making algorithm directly into their site, so that healthcare shoppers can make a good decision about what type of treatment to pursue for their problem, then see where they can get it for the best price.

Some provide information directly to consumers as well, outside of the health plan websites. HealthcareBlueBook.com, for instance, mines databases for commercial pricing and provides it for free to consumers and employers. It builds custom websites for employers and health plans that pursue a transparency strategy — and even for providers willing to advertise their wares and true, bundled prices. Similarly, the Healthcare Cost Institute has launched Guroo, which culls data from private insurers to give averages of costs for common procedures and tests locally and regionally.[81]

HCI3 itself has developed a smartphone app called INQUIREhealthcare that searches for nearby practitioners who meet

---

80 Delbanco S, "Has Price Transparency's Time Finally Come?" The Institute for Healthcare Consumerism, April 14, 2014. Available at: http://www.theihcc.com/en/communities/tools_technology/has-price-transparency's-time-finally-come_htvs7lnc.html
81 Guroo: http://www.healthcostinstitute.org/about-guroo

national standards of quality.[82] Websites like NewChoiceHealth.com work like Kayak, Hipmunk, or Orbitz for travel, like Zillow for home prices: They crowd-source what used to be considered proprietary, trade-secret information. New Choice will even send quote requests to all local providers who do what you are looking for: Who wants to bid on this lady's new hip?

These tools are, in themselves, a growth industry. Some will be better than others. At The Change Project, Inc., we are tracking them and their results as they develop.

Shoppers alert! If you are shopping for a particular procedure or test and concerned about price and quality, chance are increasing that you can use one of these tools to spend less for high quality healthcare that is available to you with your health plan in your area.

The base level of the new transparency is coming from federal and state governments, though most government information is not as penetrable, useful, or certainly as customizable as we customers need. What the federal government pays for Medicare cases at every hospital has been available for decades — but only on paper, in a hard-to-use database. Now it is available (though still not for free) online at the Cost Report Data website and the American Hospital Directory.[83] On May 8, 2013, Health and Human Services Secretary Kathleen Sibelius released a huge database of what the federal government pays to every U.S. hospital for Medicare cases for the most common 100 inpatient services — and what the chargemaster rates at those same hospitals are.[84]

Some 40 states now have report cards of one kind or another giving prices and quality ratings for hospitals and healthcare institutions. But the Healthcare Incentives Improvement Institute (HCI3) gives only five

---

82 INQUIREhealth. Available for iPhone at: https://itunes.apple.com/us/app/inquire-healthcare/id648414515

83 Cost Report Data: http://www.costreportdata.com; American Hospital Directory: http://www.ahd.com

84 Rosenberg T, "Revealing a Healthcare Secret: The Price," *The New York Times,* July 31, 2013. Available at: http://opinionator.blogs.nytimes.com/2013/07/31/a-new-health-care-approach-dont-hide-the-price/

states a passing grade — Colorado, Virginia, Massachusetts, Vermont, and Maine.[85] Most states give average prices, ranges of prices, charge-master prices, or partial prices that do not include the many surprise charges that any hospital stay or procedure can quickly run up — and they are mum on quality. In other words these report cards cannot tell a consumer what something will really cost, and how good it is likely to be, let alone which provider is covered by his or her health plan, or what the co-pays and coinsurance are likely to come to. In some cases, like California's, "Its so-called public price transparency website is a quag-mire, with complex navigation that ultimately leads to an Excel file of hos-pital chargemaster data, a poor correlate to actual price information."[86] In other cases, like Minnesota's, the website exists, but is down, and has been down for many months for lack of good information.

Change is a-coming, though slowly. Colorado is building a website based on its all-payer claims database. Both Carolinas have passed legis-lation mandating cost websites. Washington State has at least passed leg-islation mandating that private insurers provide such cost information.[87]

Even now, though, with much more price information available, very few buyers are informed shoppers. The consumers are bad enough, but even most employer CEOs and CFOs still have no idea how much they are really paying or what they are really buying when they pay for their employees' healthcare. Most have no idea that prices vary so crazily, that no one really audits the bills, or that they could do anything about this mess. And those are the executives. We would expect that their very job description keeps them laser focused on keeping costs down. This at-titude, though, is changing quickly, as employers begin to realize how large an effect they can have on healthcare costs. Here at The Change Project, we are working with more and more employers and employer groups, helping them map out exactly these issues.

---

85 Healthcare Incentives Improvement Institute, Inc.: "Metrics For Transformation: Trans-parency." Available at: http://www.hci3.org/content/transparency-metrics-transformation; Full 2014 report available for download at: http://www.hci3.org/sites/default/files/files/Re-port_PriceTransLaws_2014.pdf

86 Delbanco S, "The Price Reform Landscape: Price Transparency," *Health Affairs Blog*, April 2, 2014. Available at: http://healthaffairs.org/blog/2014/04/02/the-payment-reform-land-scape-price-transparency/

87 Delbanco S, *ibid.*

Transparency Drives Change in the Industry

Moving toward setting real prices and publishing real outcomes will in time mean moving toward selling complete packages — an uncomplicated birth, a cholecystectomy from diagnosis to rehab, a complete knee replacement, a diabetes management program, soup to nuts, with one price tag and one set of outcome numbers. Call it "price, product, performance."

How do you compete on price, product, and performance? Not, clearly, with a loose-legged congeries of practitioners who do everything the way they want to, the way they learned years ago, the way that is comfortable for them as individuals. You do it with tight teams — medically integrated practice units, as Michael Porter and Elizabeth Olmsted Teisberg call them in *Redefining Healthcare*[88] — who work together on the same diagnosis over long periods of time, honing their processes to continually raise their quality and lower their costs.

When healthcare providers begin to compete at the level of the medical condition, on real prices and real results, suddenly the feedback loops become extremely compelling. Offering the highest possible quality at the lowest possible price will no longer be voluntary. Health plans, as well, will be forced to compete on the basis of real results, real transparency, and genuine customer service, at the lowest price, rather than through elaborate denial-of-coverage games and shifting cost and risk to the providers as they have been used to doing in the past.

This can be done. Before Charles Schwab changed the game, stockbrokers formed an insular, inefficient industry with high-priced services that were thought too complex to be left to the consumer. Before FedEx, every mail order ad said, "Allow four to six weeks for delivery." It is already happening in bits and parts all across healthcare. Years ago, I went to speak at the Cuyuna Regional Medical Center in Crosby, Minnesota, 90 miles north of the Twin Cities. The night before the talk, at a little dinner given by the client, I introduced myself to my seatmate, a doctor, and asked his specialty. He was an eye surgeon. I offered my condolences — a few years before, Medicare had drastically lowered the price

---

88 Porter M and Teisberg EO, *Redefining Healthcare: Creating Value-Based Competition on Results*, Cambridge, Massachusetts: Harvard Business School Press, 2006.

it would pay for cataract and glaucoma surgery, and many eye clinics had gone out of business or tried to shift entirely to the private market.

No, he said, he and his colleagues were doing just fine, thank you.

This sounded unusual, so I asked him to tell his story.

He had been working in the Twin Cities at one of the largest medical centers. The top two officers from Cuyuna came down and took him to lunch. They asked him, How's business? Not so good, he told them. Since the funding cuts, it's a struggle.

How many operations do you do a day?

Two or three.

If you sign up with us, we guarantee that you can at least double that.

So we signed with them and moved 90 miles north.

How many do you do a day now? I asked him.

A dozen, sometimes more. There's even time for golf.

Really? But you must be rushing the patients through. The quality must be down.

No, in fact, it's far better, he told me. He could show me the files — the infections, the do-overs, they were all way down. Patients love it, medical center loves it, docs love it.

Cuyuna had in fact done the opposite of what much of the market does. When rates dropped, it founded a new eye clinic with drastically re-engineered processes in which they could do the surgeries profitably, at higher quality, for the lower price, then set out to draw patients regionally instead of just locally.

This is a template for the future in much of healthcare: As the new transparency broadens in spread and detail, healthcare will be forced to emulate other industries in becoming better, faster, and cheaper.

Transparency within the industry

If a health system is going to be transparent to customers and provide the seamless patient experience that the "price, product, performance" rubric demands, it first has to build the ability to be transparent to itself and other healthcare providers. As they are building out new healthcare information systems, hospitals and health systems must make sure that their data are transparent and transportable.

Most data gathered by the most prominent commercial systems are not transportable and cannot be data mined. You cannot query the data with questions the system was not pre-designed to answer, because it is kept in a proprietary database rather than an n-dimensional queriable database — one whose parameters can be set up on the fly even after it is populated.

At least half the reason for digitizing healthcare is to mine the data for performance improvement — which few organizations in healthcare do as a serious, strategic practice. **You can't improve what you're doing if you don't know, in detail, what you're doing. To improve the process, you must expose yourself to the information.**

Rigorous cost accounting

Imagine going through every service, from performing a pregnancy ultrasound to excising a brain tumor, and just doing the arithmetic. Run down every step of every task, the labor cost of the person doing it, the actual cost of the supplies involved, then throw in something for overhead and for margin. Add it up to determine how much it costs you to install a hip or repair a hernia. That's time-driven activity-based costing or TDABC.

For the last few years Harvard's Michael Porter and Robert Kaplan have been running exactly such programs at MD Anderson, the Cleveland Clinic, the Mayo Clinic, Boston Children's, Brigham and Women's Hospital, and other top hospitals.

Rigorous, tough, time-consuming, expensive to do, yes, but combined with lean manufacturing techniques, such analysis can drive real costs down. Organizations find that they do many things that don't help, or that could be done by someone less highly trained and expensive. MD Anderson, for instance, was able to cut the staff in its pre-operative anesthesia center by 17 percent while seeing 19 percent more patients and dropping the internal cost by 46 percent with no loss of quality.[89] If this seems impractically difficult, it's still where we have to go. We simply

89 Beck M, "Searching for the True Cost of Healthcare," *The Wall Street Journal*, February 24, 2014. Available at: http://online.wsj.com/news/articles/SB1000142405270230488840457939122507671850?linkId=7535312

must know our real costs, how we can cut them, and which costs we can safely cut.

Standardized Information

Standard file formats that would allow one vendor's system to talk to another's already exist, developed by the industry. Any system that follows those standards and a few basic tests for reliability, security, privacy, and accountability should be allowed to enter the market. Not meeting such standards, which include complete data transparency with all other healthcare data systems, should disqualify the vendor from being considered by any healthcare provider — providers should simply exclude non-transparent IT systems from any bidding process for new or updated systems.

This is the way computers and music players and smartphones work now: Any player that can play an MP3 and any photo program that can read JPGs and TIFFs can enter the market and compete for customers. I can e-mail anyone with an e-mail address, no matter what kind of computer he or she uses. Properly coded web pages built to strict standards can be viewed on any computer, in fact any browser, or even on a cell phone, or a reader for the blind. The true barriers to data transparency across healthcare are commercial, not technical. They are there because the major IT vendors don't want to play nice with other vendors.

Getting a grip on processes is the only way that hospitals and health systems can substantially reduce the cost of doing business. The only way to reduce system cost is to think systemically and to teach and incentivize every manager to think systemically: align every job, every incentive, not to excellence on one narrow measure (such as reducing unit cost on materials), but to systemic excellence (such as reducing the costs of whole processes, including materials, labor, and resources).

Transparency, Consolidation, and Price

This leaves the only real issue in setting prices: a hospital's or health system's market indispensability. If a healthcare provider is unique in some important ways, or perceived to be so special that it would be hard to sell a health plan that left it out of the network, that hospital can resist attempts to bargain the contract prices down.

So consolidation has a profound effect on prices. If a significant part of the local hospital market can band together in a system that bargains as one, the system can push prices up. Economists call this "monopoly rents," the pricing advantage of a dominant or indispensable market position. Northwestern University's Leemore Dafny has demonstrated this firmly: **When nearby hospitals consolidate, they typically raise their prices by 40 percent or more.**[90]

But this works only when your customers have full coverage and no skin in the game, when they can be assumed to want the best with no reference to price, when they can't find out the real prices or the real alternatives, and when the end payers in the private market are willing to play along.

The End of Opaque Pricing

For most of healthcare, opaque pricing is becoming yesterday's toast. Bundling, transparency, patients with high-deductible plans, and activist employers are pulling the spokes out of this whole dynamic. Suddenly there are real shoppers out there, increasingly armed with real information, who won't set foot in your store if you have the highest prices and can't show them why they should pay more for the luxury model.

---

90 Porter O, "Healthcare's Overlooked Cost Factor," *The New York Times*, June 11, 2013. Available at:
http://www.nytimes.com/2013/06/12/business/examinations-of-health-costs-overlook-mergers.html

Special Focus: How Drug Prices
Distort The Healthcare Market

I T STARTED ON Skype. A pharmaceutical industry association dedicated to market intelligence had invited me to discuss the future
of global markets at its convention. To help me prepare, my hosts
agreed to put together a conference call with some of the top pharma
market intelligence people in the world. So there I am on Skype with
these six top experts and I decided to ask them the one thing that really
confused me the most. Could they explain the pricing of drugs to me?
Why are the prices of drugs so wildly different from each other, and the
prices in the United States so different and so much higher than prices
for the same drug elsewhere?

They would be happy to. In most countries, drug prices are negotiated with the government or the national health system.

What about in the United States?

Well, that's substantially different.

What followed was a long and confusing discussion of a massively
multi-layered system of distributors and specialized financiers, of pricing
formulas for government programs and military buyers and large medical systems and medical buying groups and on and on. In the end they
promised to send me a paper that would lay it all out.

They sent me the paper, a dense, 45-page .pdf. I read it carefully,
took notes, highlighted relevant sections, read the other papers it drew
on. I still didn't understand drug pricing.

Or let me be a little more accurate: After reading that paper I felt I did understand drug pricing in the United States, but the main thing that I understood about it is that it is a highly complex system that is intentionally designed to be opaque and as invulnerable as possible to bargaining or other real market forces.

The results can be unbelievably weird and arbitrary. It's easy to find billions of examples, and you probably have some from your own life. But let me just describe one extreme example: Getting stung by a scorpion is no picnic. Some varieties can be deadly to children. Luckily, there is an anti-venom available for it: Anascorp, manufactured for years by the Instituto Bioclon in Mexico, and approved for use in the United States by the Food and Drug Administration in August 2011. Picture getting stung while waiting in the pedestrian line in Nogales, Mexico, to cross the border into the United States, by a scorpion riding on your shoe. You stagger back into Mexico and head to the local clinic. Anascorp there will cost you $100 per vial, and you may need as many as six. So, maximum cost: U.S. $600.

Now change the picture slightly: Imagine that the scorpion rode your shoe into the United States, and stung you after you crossed the border into Nogales, Arizona: The very same Anascorp, manufactured by the same company, will cost you from $7,900 to $12,467 per vial, depending on which Arizona hospital you end up in.[91] So it could cost you — just for the drug, mind you — as much as U.S. $74,802, nearly 125 times as much as right across the border in Nogales, Mexico.

The federal government is the largest buyer of drugs in the world, by far. Picture the buying power in the hundreds of billions of dollars that the federal government spends on drugs through Medicare and Medicaid, in the military and veterans' health programs, through the Indian Health Service, and through the healthcare insurance programs for the approximately 2.7 million civilian federal employees. All together, the federal government spends more dollars and more percentage of GDP than countries in which all healthcare is government paid. It pays directly and indirectly for more than half of U.S. healthcare, including more than half of all the drugs.

---

91 Staton T, "Scorpion Antivenom's Price Stings AZ Patients," *FiercePharma.com*, November 15, 2011. Available at: http://www.fiercepharma.com/story/scorpion-antivenoms-price-stings-az-patients/2011-11-15

That's a lot of bargaining power — and it is not used at all to bring down prices. This powerful tool sits on the workbench unused. The federal government is forbidden by law to bargain with pharmaceutical companies over the price of drugs, much less to dictate prices. It is forced to buy drugs according to those complex formulas put together by committees filled with industry experts.

Pharmaceutical economics is a vast subject. Like some other subjects, we are not going to get into it deeply here, because it is largely out of our control as consumers and buyers of healthcare. It is worth noting as a vast pool of potential savings should Congress and the president find the political will to do something about it.

The practice of allowing the drug companies to charge U.S. customers prices many multiples of what they charge in other countries is based on a number of beliefs that have been constantly pushed by the industry as if they are facts. They include:[92]

- New drugs are important, even life-saving, so we need to get out of the drug companies' way and let them do their jobs.
- Any side effects or contraindications are caught by the extensive testing ordered by the FDA.
- U.S. prices are higher because it costs billions of dollars to develop any one new drug, and those overseas prices just can't make up that cost. So Americans just have to suck it up and pay for it.

These are myths, or at least are unsupported by real evidence. Very few new drugs are even improvements on what we had before. We have explored in the segment "Waste" how few new therapies of any kind are actually proven improvements. Even fewer are life-saving. Drug companies tend to like developing drugs that are good for their bottom line and good for their shareholders, especially drugs that will be prescribed to millions of consumers for life, like statins.

There is widespread withholding of negative data about new drugs in development, as illustrated most famously by the Vioxx fiasco. The

---

92 Many authors have gathered, commented on, and punctured these myths. One convenient place to begin exploring that literature is the website of Donald Light: http://www.pharmamyths.net

amount that drug companies spend actually researching and developing new drugs is entirely self-reported under conditions that strongly encourage them to exaggerate. There is little to no reason to believe they are as high as the drug companies claim. And finally: They clearly make a profit selling into other countries. The major drug companies are public companies. Their annual reports typically break out their sales and net income by region — and they do business in these regions voluntarily. Nothing is forcing them to sell their drugs in Canada or France or Japan. Yet they do, at significantly lower prices, and they report a profit.

What Consumers and Buyers of Healthcare Can Do about Drug Prices

Not a lot. But you can take advantage of the cheap generics drug buying programs of the major drugstore chains and big-box retailers. For many types of drugs, you can buy them online from pharmacies in other countries. (But stick to well-regulated countries like Canada. Buy from Fiji or India and you may well up with a useless counterfeit or even worse.)

Or, if you live near the Mexican border, have a passport, and need a lot of pharmaceuticals, it may be worth your time to drive south into Mexico and buy retail from a pharmacy. The Mexican pharmaceutical retail market is fairly well regulated and widely considered safe by Americans and Canadians who use it in Mexico. It is legal to buy personal-use quantities and bring them home (though not legal to buy Schedule One narcotics). Just show the Mexican pharmacist your prescription, or even just the label on the bottle you already have. Most pharmacists near the U.S. border speak English, are eager for tourist business, and are familiar with the sometimes different names of drugs as sold in the United States. (Note: Most Americans and Canadians who spend time south of the border feel that the best and safest practice is not to buy from Mexican pharmacies online or from the pharmacies in tourist areas, hotels, and airports. They feel safer buying from pharmacies in their local town, where Mexicans also shop, or in such major national big-box retailers as CostCo, Mega, or Soriana.)

Shoppers alert! It is legal and safe to buy personal-use quantities of most pharmaceuticals from Canadian or Mexican pharmacies.

As noted above, stick to some common sense guidelines about where to shop and you will be all right. And of course it is legal and safe to substitute generics for name brand (though ask your doctor — generics are not identical to the name brand) and certainly to take advantage of the cheap generics programs of the big box retailers.

Over the longer run: Lobby your Congressional representatives to allow the federal government to bargain on pharmaceutical prices, or dictate them much the way it dictates the price of services in the Medicare market.

They Roll Up Together

Okay, now we've got two: Shopping and Transparency. Remember, these changes are systemic. Each one augments and depends on the others. The real tipping point will arrive when a sufficient fraction of healthcare and healthcare's customers and payers are using all seven levers.

So: We've got people shopping, and they have the information they need to be smart, fierce shoppers. But what are they really shopping for? They are not shopping for processes or procedures. They are shopping for results: the fixed knee, the healthy birthed baby, the controlled diabetes. That's our next Lever: Results.

Transparency: The To-Do Lists

Purchasers (Employers, Pension Plans, and Other Purchasers of Healthcare):

- **Self-fund:** Self-fund, so that you are directly responsible for your employees' healthcare costs, and profit from lowering them.
- **Offer high-deductible plans with HSAs:** If you have a choice, offer your employees high-deductible health plans that are eligible for health savings accounts that you (and they) can put deductible pre-tax funds into. These are savings accounts, usually paired with a HDHP (high-deductible health plan), used to pay routine medical expenses. They are typically funded by the employer, or both employer and employee. The funding is considered a tax-deductible expense for both the employer and the employee. There are several different kinds, with slightly different names (see the Acronymicon appendix) which have somewhat different rules and are administered in somewhat different ways.
- **Offer plans with info:** Offer only health plans that offer real shopping information, whether from Castlight or their own proprietary database, that will tell your employees how much a given procedure, test, or visit will actually cost them, with their deductibles, co-pays, and co-insurance.
- **Lobby your state legislators:** Get them to mandate an all-payer, all-provider database of real costs. This will do more than any single action to drive down costs in your state.

111

- **Talk with your employees about it:** Have open group discussions with your employees about why you are doing this, and how they can help keep their own costs as low as possible. Encourage them to use Castlight or other shopping resources, such as NewChoiceHealth.com.
- **Be a fierce shopper:** Establish prices through your health plan or administrator by shopping vigorously for bundled big-ticket items and by paying directly for primary care either on-site or through direct-pay primary care doctors (as in the Shopping chapter). Form or join a healthcare business group to both gather information and bargain for better prices.
- **Get involved with us:** Email me (joe@thechangeproject.com) or find me on LinkedIn to see if we can help you.

Consumers:

- **Go high-deductible/HSA:** If you have a choice, go for a high-deductible health plan that is eligible for a health savings account that you (or you and your employer) can put deductible pre-tax funds into. These are savings accounts, usually paired with an HDHP (high-deductible health plan), used to pay routine medical expenses. They are typically funded by the employer, or both employer and employee. The funding is considered a tax-deductible expense for both the employer and the employee. There are several different kinds, with slightly different names (see the Acronymicon appendix) which have somewhat different rules and are administered in somewhat different ways.
- **Get a plan with the info:** Look for a health plan that offers real shopping information, whether from Castlight or their own proprietary database, that will tell you how much a given procedure, test, or visit will actually cost you, with your deductible, co-pay, and co-insurance.
- **Use other information resources:** Use other shopping resources, such as those listed in the Resources section.

- **Talk to a navigator:** Increasingly, health plans offer navigators who can help you find the right provider at the best price for what you want. Use them.
- **Shop carefully:** Never assume that the price offered for a particular procedure or test is fair or normal. Be willing to bargain and haggle, like Ahmed on the street with the rug merchants. If you are not good at that kind of thing, enlist a friend who is, or join a posse that can help you.
- **Get your drugs cheaper:** If you can, buy your drugs through the cheap generic drugs programs of the chain drugstores and big box retailers. Ask your doctor if a cheaper generic will do just as well. Order your drugs online from Canada. Or drive over the border into Mexico.
- **Lobby your state legislators:** Get them to mandate an all-payer, all-provider database of real costs. This will do more than any single action to drive down costs in your state.
- **Be honest with yourself:** Be transparent with yourself about your real health problems, especially your mental problems such as depression, anxiety, and addiction. You can't get past these problems, you can't get help to get past them, until you level with yourself, and with your posse.

Health Plans:

- **Facilitate self-funding:** Facilitate self-funding so that employers are directly responsible for their employees healthcare costs and profit from lowering them.
- **Reward smart shoppers:** Offer features similar to Blue Options and Hospital Choice Cost Sharing from Blue Cross Blue Shield of Massachusetts, which directly reward customers for choosing low-cost, high-quality providers.[93]
- **Offer real shopping information:** Offer your customers real shopping information, whether from Castlight or another vendor or

---

93 BCBSMA website: http://www.bluecrossma.com/plan-education/medical/blue-options/index.html

your own proprietary database, that will tell them how much a given procedure, test, or visit will actually cost them, with their deductibles, co-pays, and co-insurance.

- **Give your customers live help:** Offer navigators who can help your customers find the right provider at the best price for what you want.
- **Lobby your state legislators:** Get them to mandate an all-payer, all-provider database of real costs. This will do more than any single action to drive down costs in your state. It will help you in your efforts to drive down healthcare providers' prices, and so help you offer your members lower premiums and broader networks.

Entrepreneurs, Inventors, and Investors:

Look for new technologies and business models that:

- **Uncover and aggregate** real information that compares cost and quality for medical care of all types across all available providers.
- **Translate that information** into usable, real-time decision-making and shopping models that fit the needs of individual consumers as well as employers and other payers.
- **Enable healthcare institutions to be transparent** to themselves, especially by enabling deep, detailed, realistic, real-time cost analysis, as well as rapid process improvement.

Hospitals, Physician Groups, and Healthcare Institutions:

Make transparency run in all directions:

- **Costs:** Run TDABC (time-driven activity-based costing) programs continually to stay on top of your real costs.
- **Lean:** Run lean processes to drive down those real internal costs and drive out waste that you may no longer be paid for.
- **Scan:** Use the emerging transparency to be as aware as possible of your competition's actual costs and prices.

- **Know your customer:** Use predictive analytics to discover not only who your customers are but who your most likely future customers are.[94]
- **Run phantom financials:** Pretend those trying to push down your prices have already won. Run what-ifs on different revenue levels and compositions to guide your strategy. Don't fly blind by assuming that won't happen.
- **Look beyond the horizon:** Be aware that your competition is not just the institutions near you. Rather, it is any choice your potential customers may make instead of buying medical services from you — including doing nothing, using alternative and complementary medicine, or getting their medical services in another country.
- **Lobby your state legislators:** Get them to mandate an all-payer, all-provider database of real costs. If you want to compete on a strategy of transparency, it helps you greatly if your competitors have to release their real prices as well.

State Legislators and Policymakers:

- **Make it public:** Mandate a public website displaying cost information for all healthcare providers doing business in your state.
- **Make it real:** Mandate that the information be real prices paid, not largely irrelevant chargemaster rates.
- **Make it comprehensive:** Mandate that the information encompass all payers, public and private.
- **Build it into Medicaid:** Make sure that your Medicaid program makes it super easy for the poor population to find what they need to know to make good use of their Medicaid benefits — because having them well cared for will actually save the state more money than the hide-the-pea tactics many states employ.

---

94 Singer N, "When a Health Plan Knows How You Shop," *The New York Times*, June 28, 2014. Available at: http://www.nytimes.com/2014/06/29/technology/when-a-health-plan-knows-how-you-shop.html

Lever 3: Results

Problem

WHAT WE WANT from healthcare is a result: a cured infection, a birthed baby, a healed leg fracture. What we typically pay for is a process that may or may not bring us the result we want — yet it is hard to guarantee any given result in medicine.

Solution

Examine business models and revenue streams carefully to find ways to pay for better results in as much of healthcare as possible, and elsewhere for process markers that are strong stand-ins for the best results.

Is It Possible to Pay for Results?

One saying common across American culture, so common that we say it as a statement of fact, is "You get what you pay for."

Do you get what you pay for in healthcare? How would you know? How can we measure it? The traditional answer from healthcare providers has been that it's the wrong question, you can't really measure quality versus cost in healthcare, that it's just way too complicated with way with too many variables.

To people who pay for healthcare, especially employers, it has become ever clearer that they are not getting what they are paying for, simply because healthcare costs vary wildly more in the United States than in other countries, vast amounts of it are wasted, and they keep paying more for increasingly restricted services.

Increasingly, employers are refusing to buy the claim that there is no way to pay for results in healthcare. According to an Aon Hewitt survey, some 31 percent of employers said that they already base what they pay healthcare providers on specific performance targets, and another 44 percent are considering doing so in the next three to five years.[95]

Within the industry, there is a buzz phrase for the shift in economic underpinnings that it is going through. The phrase is "Volume to Value." In a fee-for-service system, healthcare providers (doctors and hospitals) make more fees for providing more services. That's the Volume part. We have been paying them to do more, not necessarily to give us more value. How do we measure and pay for Value instead? It's a real question, and not an easy one.

How Do You Measure Performance in Healthcare?

In most fields, we don't pay for process. We pay for the entire product, delivered. We don't pay the chef to put the steak on the grill, to season it, to plate it. We pay for the entire meal delivered to our table. If it never shows up, or if the steak is burnt to a crisp, we don't pay for it. In most fields we pay for an outcome.

That's a lot harder to do in medicine. Bodies are different, tumors can do unexpected things, you can do everything perfectly and still the patient dies. We can't pay only for successful outcomes and still ask doctors to struggle against the odds in desperate cases. And some hospitals actually do have sicker patients. Major teaching centers, cancer centers, and children's hospitals often constitute the end of the line — if they can't fix you here, there is no place they can send you that is better or has smarter doctors or fancier equipment. If we paid

---

95 Aon Hewitt, "Employers plan pay tactics to cut costs: Companies weigh performance pay, value-based pricing," June 10, 2013. Available at: http://www.healthcarefinancenews.com/news/employers-plan-pay-tactics-cut-costs

hospitals and doctors only for success, no one would want to take the tough cases.

Yet patients are already fairly good at choosing better, more effective, and more efficient hospitals, even without having hard numbers at their fingertips and despite the fact that healthcare organizations in the past have not really gotten rewarded for being better. Studies show, for instance, that even people in the throes of a heart attack will often direct that they be taken not to the nearest emergency department, but to one that might be farther away but has a better reputation.[96]

What happens if we enhance that tendency by giving people real information about healthcare quality: Who does it best? Who makes the fewest mistakes? Who has the lowest percentage of patients readmitted with problems?

The Goal: Get What We Pay For

The goal is to reshape healthcare so that we get what we pay for. In econ-speak, this is the "cost/benefit ratio": How much money we are paying, compared with how much value we are getting. There are two sides to any ratio. Enhancing the cost side of this one means shopping for better price and having the transparency we need so that we can see what we are getting and what we are paying for it. The other side of the ratio is the result: What, specifically, are we getting? How good is it? How do we know? Could we pay for things differently so that we pay for higher quality, or at least reward it in the marketplace by bringing more business to the higher quality producers?

When we work both sides of the cost/benefit ratio hard, we will get better healthcare for far, far less money. How do we work the benefit side? The same we do in any other industry: by bringing more business to the better providers — by paying for results.

---

96 Syverson C, "Market Forces Appear To Apply To Hospitals, Too," FiveThirtyEight, March 28, 2014.
Available at: http://fivethirtyeight.com/features/standard-market-forces-appear-to-apply-to-hospitals-too/
Chandra *et al.*, "Healthcare Exceptionalism? Productivity and Allocation in the U.S. Healthcare Sector," NBER Working Paper No. 19200, July 2013.

Paying for Results

We can pay for results in healthcare in three ways:

1. **Process:** In many of the most common subfields of medicine there are established procedures that constitute doing the right thing, processes that rarely vary. We can pay for those processes. This is called "pay for performance."
2. **Quality:** Besides using process measures of what clinicians should do, we can also measure the things they shouldn't do: the mistakes and the truly avoidable bad outcomes. The appropriate number for puerperal fever in a neonatal ICU is zero — it shouldn't happen. It doesn't matter if a hospital gets sicker patients; they still don't get a pass for hospital-acquired infections or amputating the wrong leg.
3. **Pay for improvement:** Though we can't pay only for success, there are specific ways in which primary care practices especially can get better at improving the health of their patients and keeping them from needing emergency services or surgery — and we can reward that through new payment methods.

Process

Pay for performance is the most common way of paying medical practitioners for doing processes right. For instance, many primary care practices are adopting a practice model called the "patient centered medical home" in which they accept responsibility for monitoring all of their patients, rather than simply waiting for them to show up. A patient-centered medical home (PCMH) will, for example, have a registry of all of its patients with diabetes, with a date when each one was last checked for A1c score, when his or her feet were checked by a podiatrist, and his or her eyes were last checked by an ophthalmologist. Under many contracts, a PCMH practice that keeps all these monitors properly and keeps patients up to date with their chronic conditions will receive a sizable pay for performance bonus.

The accountable care organizations established under the Affordable Care Act all incorporate some version of PCMHs enhanced with pay for performance (PFP) bonuses.

Quality

Is there one number that is a prime stand-in for quality? Many health-care industry figures argue that there is not, that it's just too complicated for any one number or set of numbers. If you just measure outcomes, they will argue that their patient population was sicker to start with, or they only get the really tough cases.

The Healthcare Incentives Improvement Institute (HCI3) uses and recommends the PROMETHEUS measures of potentially avoidable complications (PAC) .[97] Avoiding complications such as infections does seem like one major quality standard that sticks for all different types of patients, and does speak for a carefully run system.

Centers of Excellence: Lower cost is only half of the Centers of Excellence strategy that we mentioned in the "Lever 1: Shopping" chapter. Steering patients to quality is the other half. The strategy starts by assessing the available healthcare providers, using publicly available data to decide which providers in your area can claim to provide the highest quality in particular clinical areas. Only then does the health plan or employer enter negotiations for a bundled lower price. This steers more business to organizations that are more tightly run, and can accomplish both lower price and higher quality.

Pay for Improvement

In some parts of healthcare, we can directly measure and pay for im-provements in the patient's health. Here are a couple of examples:

Alaska Native Healthcare: In a 2008 paper describing their health system in *Family Practice Management*, Katherine Gottlieb, Ileen Sylvester, and Dr. Douglas Eby of the Alaska Native Healthcare system commented:

> There's a lot of talk in healthcare today about being "patient cen-tered." Unfortunately, what that usually means is that the patient is put in the middle and then all the "really smart, professional peo-ple" stand around and try to decide what's best for that person.[98]

97 Hibbard J *et al.*, "An Experiment Shows That A Well-Designed Report on Costs and Quality Can Help Consumers Choose High-Value Healthcare," *Health Affairs* 31, no. 3, 2012.
98 Gottlieb K *et al.*, "Transforming Your Practice: What Matters Most—When Customers

The Alaska Natives healthcare story is really quite different, unexpected, yet it illustrates one working model of much of what we are talking about here.

The healthcare of Native Alaskans for generations came under the Indian Health Service. In 1975, Congress recognized that it would be better if Native Americans could be in charge of their own healthcare, and set up a mechanism to hand over the management of healthcare to tribal governments that could take it on. In the 1980s, under the tribal authority of the Cook Inlet Region, Inc., the Southcentral Foundation began the process, contracting from the Indian Health Service for specific services. By 1999, they were ready for the new Alaska Native Health Corporation to take over all the health services for Native Alaskans in 150,000 square miles of Alaska from the Kenai Peninsula to the Bering Straits, and from the Aleutian Islands to Anchorage. With the Alaska Tribal Health Consortium, Southcentral owns and manages the Alaska Native Medical Center, which includes a 150-bed hospital in Anchorage, along with an array of clinics and other services.

Rather than simply duplicate the traditional, straight fee-for-service, doctor-centered care, Southcentral set out to build a service entirely on what the Native Alaskans saw as their tribal values. They asked the people they were serving: What would medical care look like if it started from the patient out — the patient, the family, the tribe — rather from the doctor and the payer?

The first instance is obvious to any outsider: When a Native Alaskan shows up at a Native Alaskan health facility, the people behind the counter look familiar, because most of them are Native Alaskans, as well. So are most of the clinicians and other people they might encounter in the exam room or lab.

But the differences are far more pervasive and subtle. Tribal culture tends to be more family- and group-oriented. So the exam rooms are large enough to include the family in the discussion, when the patient would like the support.

Similarly, the doctors have no private offices. There are private talking rooms available for confidential discussions, but the doctors' desks

Drive the System, It Changes Everything—for the Better," *Family Practice Management*, Vol. 15, No. 1, 2008, pp. 32–38. Available at: http://www.aafp.org/fpm/2008/0100/p32.html

are in group carrels especially designed as a base for the entire core clinical team: one or two primary care providers (doctors, nurse practitioners, or physician assistants), their medical assistants, the nurse case manager and the case management assistants, and the behavioral specialist.

This team together manages the health of a panel of patients that typically might number 1,400 or so. The patients can pick their own team to be attached to. But as much as possible, those patients see only that team and the team sees only the patients for whose health they are responsible.

And responsible they are, for the core of the system is this: The doctors and other clinicians are on salary. How much money they make does not depend on how many patients they see in a day, or how many procedures or tests they order and bill for. Their bonuses, salary increases, and promotion depend not on their own individual success, but on the team's success in caring for that panel of patients, measured by improvements in a number of measures of health.

So the service has exploded the fee-for-service business model at the primary level, and built teams that can make more money not by doing more procedures, but by improving the health and healthcare of a set group of patients.

How's that working for them? Tracking the data of their patients from the time of the tribal takeover to the present, the Southcentral Foundation reports that their population has shown a 50 percent drop in emergency and urgent care, a 53 percent drop in hospital admissions, a 65 percent drop in the use of specialists, a 70 percent drop in pediatric asthma admissions, and even a 36 percent drop in primary care visits, since many problems are now taken care of over the phone or through email.

At the same time, their quality scores (using the industry-standard Healthcare Effectiveness Data and Information Set tool) have risen into a consistent 75 to 90 percentile range. And satisfaction surveys of both staff and customers have risen from the 20 percent range to be consistently over 90 percent.

And the cost? Taking the period from 2004 to 2009, after the new system had become well established, their per capita spending on hospital costs rose only seven percent, over a period when nationally it rose some

44 percent; their per capita spending on primary care (a lot of it now done remotely and taking the place of hospitalizations) rose 30 percent, against a national background of 40 percent.[99]

Box Score — Results for Alaska Natives Healthcare:

- **Emergency and urgent care down 50 percent**
- **Hospital admissions down 53 percent**
- **Specialist use down 65 percent**
- **Pediatric asthma admissions down 70 percent**
- **In-person primary care visits down 36 percent**
- **Quality scores up; satisfaction scores over 90 percent**
- **Hospital costs up seven percent 2004–2009 (national 44 percent)**
- **Primary care costs up 30 percent 2004–2009 (national 40 percent)**

Alternative quality contracts (AQCs): Massachusetts passed its state version of healthcare reform in 2006. That got a lot more people covered by insurance, but it didn't do much to cut costs. Massachusetts is a major state, with world-class medical institutions and high costs. The largest commercial insurer, Blue Cross Blue Shield of Massachusetts (BCBSMA), decided to get down in the weeds to figure out the details of a plan that would really work, over time, to bring healthcare inflation down.

Here's how an alternative quality contract works:[100] First, it's based on primary care. Organizations that sign up for it have to have primary care docs caring for at least 5,000 patients. It's a five-year contract, so the organizations have time to adjust.

BCBSMA negotiates with each organization. The starting point is the total amount BCBSMA paid in the previous year for all services for the

99 "A Formula For Cutting Health Costs," Editorial, *The New York Times*, July 21, 2012. Available at: http://www.nytimes.com/2012/07/22/opinion/sunday/a-formula-for-cutting-health-costs.html

100 BlueCross/Blue Shield of Massachusetts website: http://www.bluecrossma.com

Chernew *et al.*, "Private-Payer Innovation In Massachusetts: The 'Alternative Quality Contract,'" *Health Affairs*, 30, no. 1 (January 20, 2011), pp. 51–61. Available at: http://content.healthaffairs.org/ content/30/1/51.full.html

Personal interviews by the author with BCBSMA executives.

patients for which the organization provided primary care. They told the providers something like this:

> "Here are these 10,000 patients that get their primary care from you. Last year, counting all their care, even surgery and complex care they received in other hospitals and systems, we paid out this amount. That is your starting budget for all of their care."

Each year a small increment is allowed to keep step with general inflation (not the much higher medical inflation), plus quality bonuses for meeting specific pay for performance targets. The healthcare providers who sign up are responsible for the total amount spent on their patients, even if it is spent somewhere else. For example, if the organization is an independent physicians organization (IPO) that owns no hospitals, and one of its patients ends up in the hospital, that cost comes out of the IPO's contract.

Throughout the year, the organization continues to bill BCBSMA as in a fee-for-service system. But at the end of the year they settle up: If the organization's billings came in under the budget, it gets the difference back from BCBSMA. If it came in over the budget, it has to pay BCBSMA the differences.

As the year goes on, BCBSMA uses sophisticated tracking databases to let the organizations know exactly how things are going for them. For instance, if one of their patients is admitted to another hospital or shows up in an ED, BCBS alerts them immediately. The alerts can get quite detailed.

For example, the drug costs for managing high blood pressure can vary all over the map among different doctors. The biggest difference is which class of drugs the doctors prescribe: angiotensin-converting enzyme (ACE) inhibitors or angiotensin II receptor blockers (ARBs). ARBs cost a lot more than ACE inhibitors. Medical evidence suggests that only 10 percent to 15 percent of patients actually need the expensive ARBs, but 30 percent of patients get them — a big unnecessary cost.

BCBSMA drills down into the claims data and gives provider groups physician-specific numbers on who is prescribing a lot more ARBs than seems called for. The provider groups can encourage those doctors to take a look at what they are prescribing, and have good conversations with their patients regarding the costs and benefits of each class of drugs. If the drugs cost less, patients are more likely to actually take them, keep their blood pressure down, and avoid heart attacks and strokes.[101]

So the doctors actually make more money if their patients stay healthier, stay out of the emergency department, and avoid unnecessary surgeries and procedures: From the customers' point of view, the better attention tends to just show up, without any announcement or fanfare or special sign-up procedure. Suddenly, rather than the patients begging for appointments, the doctor's office is calling them to check on their situation, eager to get them in to keep all the preventive scores up, because the doctor has new incentives. Some patients have called it "concierge care without the concierge fees."

> **Payers and purchasers alert: There are payment systems, such as the AQC, that in effect pay primary care physicians to take business away from hospitals, emergency departments, surgery centers, and specialists not by denying the patients access, but by giving them more attention, treating them better and earlier, keeping them healthier. If those who are making clinical decisions do better financially when the patient does better and the treatment costs less, we will see quick improvements in both cost and quality.[102]**

What Hospitals and Health Systems Can Do

If institutions are going to offer whole packages, be transparent about their outcomes, and improve all their processes, they need rational

---

101 Greene R, Beckman H, and Mahoney T, "Beyond the Efficiency Index: Finding a Better Way to Reduce Overuse and Increase Efficiency in Physician Care," *Health Affairs*, Vol. 27, No. 4, 2008, pp. w250–59.

102 Song *et al.*, "The 'Alternative Quality Contract,' Based On A Global Budget, Lowered Medical Spending And Improved Quality," *Health Affairs* 31, NO. 8 (2012): pp. 1885–1894, July 11, 2012. 10.1377/hlthaff.2012.0327 Available at: http://content.healthaffairs.org/content/31/8/1885.full.html

Burns J, "Leveraging Population Health Management to Financial Success," *Healthcare Finance News*, January 23, 2014. Available at: http://www.healthcarefinancenews.com/news/leveraging-population-health-management-financial-success

control of their processes. You can't do this with pickup teams of free-lancers and loading-dock relationships (deliver the product, get a re-ceipt, send an invoice, you're done) with other service providers. The Chicago Bulls don't work that way, Home Depot doesn't work that way, and neither, it is becoming clear, can a medical system.

If you are running a hospital or health system, you need to work strongly with the physicians. This means more than hiring them or buy-ing their practices. It means getting them on board with the new busi-ness models, which means finding not only where the costs are, but how those costs become profit across the organization. So primary care physi-cians who help the bottom line by keeping people out of the ED and the surgical suite should benefit from that and see it as part of the way they make their living. You have to solve the physicians' dilemma.

The Dilemma for Physicians

Money is the oxygen of any business. Organizations, and the careers of the individuals who make up those organizations, and even their actual life arcs, evolve to maximize the money flow. When the economics shift, not only do the sizes of the money flows change but their types do too. You get different customers and different payers. The items on the in-voice above the line that reads "Please remit" — what exactly they are paying for — shifts radically. When all these things shift at once, the organizations and the people who make them up face a stark multiple-choice question:

_____ Adapt
_____ Die

The Next Healthcare is based on just such an economic shift, the Volume to Value shift, the movement away from strict code-based fee-for-service toward risk contracting, shared savings, bundled offerings, hybrid insur-ance/practice models, the thousand flowers of new revenue streams. The success of all of these is cradled in significantly different models of medical practice and compensation — new ways of being a doctor, and new ways of getting paid for it. So the economic shifts offer considerable possibilities and opportunities for physicians, especially physicians in group practice. It is physicians that have the greatest possibilities of gaining market share by working together to sharply modify their practice patterns, work flows, patient flows, and the compensation models built on them.

Physicians, however, are risk averse — and highly resistant to any possibility of reduced income, or uncertainty of income. They have built their careers, their lives, and the lives of their families around certain income expectations. So it is difficult to get them to agree to move into new practice models and new compensation arrangements.

This is one major reason for the consolidation going on in the industry: Physician groups see this dilemma and many are essentially turning the problem over to a higher power.

There are some very successful existing models of physician groups working under different value-based compensation arrangements. But almost all of them are not only quite large, they are quite old, such as Mayo, Kaiser, Geisinger, and Cleveland Clinic. Doctors entering practice in these groups are entering a large organization with a long-established track record with these business models and compensation models. And they are self-selecting for a culture that is much more integrated, more minutely collaborative, team-built in its DNA. It's a very different thing for a doctor to feel forced into a radically different business and compensation model that depends for its success on a radically different practice style and even personality style.

Unfortunately, turning the problem over to a higher power by selling the group practice and becoming part of an integrated system does not solve the problem. It only delays it and puts the locus of power elsewhere. To the extent that these economic shifts and new revenue streams are neither temporary nor minor, physicians will have to adapt both their practice patterns and their compensation models. They can do it for themselves, with more control over the details, as part of an independent group. Or they can sell themselves to an integrated health system, then watch as their corporate parents come to the same realization: As the payers pay us differently, so we will have to get the physicians to practice differently, and we will pay them differently.

The core of the problem in making healthcare better and cheaper lies in the everyday practice of medicine, and how doctors can be led, paid, and helped to practice medicine differently, more efficiently, more effectively, for far more people at half the cost.

However, independent medical groups that have pioneered the shift to value-based payments seem at least to have not suffered. A Rand Corporation study of 34 medical groups across the country found that the results, for the doctors, ranged from neutral to positive. None of the 34 practices they studied suffered by adopting risk contracts and moving to value-based payment systems. They had done well by translating the risk into collaborative team-based preventative efforts and greater patient access.[103]

What Investors, Inventors, and Entrepreneurs Can Do

The most successful mold-breaking products for the Next Healthcare will have a focus different from that of traditional medical software and hardware.

Traditional medical products, from the electronic health record to billing and financial management, from heart monitors to joint implants, support classic medicine based on an episodic encounter between the single physician and the single patient, taking place in a dedicated medical environment. They deal with a narrow problem set: What test, drug, or procedure can you order that might fix the patient's presenting problem? **The Next Healthcare presents an altogether new and different problem: How do they get better health results across whole populations?** How can the managers of medical organizations or payers track the resulting juggling of revenue streams, as some unnecessary acute care drops out while fees for managing prevention and health maintenance come in their place? Software and hardware that helps them solve that problem will have a big market.

At the same time, products to link the individual patient with clinicians are also advancing rapidly, with completely different assumptions. The traditional feedback loop of medical information is fractured and episodic:

---

103 Rand Corporation, "Effects of Health Care Payment Models on Physician Practice in the United States," March 19, 2015. Available at: http://www.rand.org/pubs/research_reports/RR869.html

Patient has a complaint, makes an appointment to see the doctor. The doctor orders a test to confirm what the problem is. The results come back days or weeks later, and the doctor orders some procedure or pharmaceutical to solve the problem. Maybe months later, maybe with next year's physical, the doctor orders a re-test to see if the problem has been corrected. The patient's blood tests for high LDL cholesterol, physician writes a scrip for Lipitor, then orders a new blood test at their next meeting.

When medical organizations are paid on results, they will have to tighten that feedback loop, making it far easier and faster to track not just gross measures like weight and blood pressure, but the patient's actual biochemistry — in close to real time, close to continually, for almost no cost.

Take Elizabeth Holmes, like most people a little scared of needles, very concerned about how to make healthcare better and cheaper — and eager to do something about it. At 19, she dropped out of Stanford and used her tuition money to launch Theranos, a company built to research the problem of making blood tests easier, faster, and cheaper. Now that she is 30, Theranos is offering its breakthrough tests that can use a single drop of blood to search for the DNA marking dozens of conditions and pathogens — all in four hours, including follow-up tests if necessary. A fertility panel, usually costing $2,000 plus weeks of waiting? $35 and four hours. Cholesterol test? $2.99. Iron? $4.45.[104]

Or there is Scanadu, one of a number of companies running in a global competition to produce something like the handheld TriCorder that Bones used on *Star Trek* to run myriad diagnostics in the time it took him to wave it over the patient. "I'm a doctor, Jim, not a magician," he'd say, but it sure looked like magic. Other apps and dongles now coming available at consumer prices can scan your ear for infections, take your EKG, measure your blood oxygen level, or take a sonogram of your heart valves — and transmit the results to your doctor or nurse remotely.

---

104 Roper C, "This Woman Invented a Way to Run 30 Lab Tests on Only One Drop of Blood," *Wired*, February 24, 2014. Available at: http://www.wired.com/wiredscience/2014/02/elizabeth-holmes-theranos/?cid=18964974
Theranos, Inc.: http://www.theranos.com

And as boomers move into their Medicare years, increasingly with health plans that require co-pays and co-insurance for every test and doctor visit, these cheap reliable alternatives will become very popular very fast. We are only in the first years of this market. If this were personal computers, the year would be 1985.

Special Focus: Drop That Business Model!

A Game-Theory Analysis

IT'S TIME FOR hospitals and health systems to toss the whole business-as-usual model — for their own good and the good of their customers.

What has been emerging as the Default Model of healthcare — the "consumer-directed," insured, fee-for-service model in which health plans compete to lower premiums by bargaining providers into narrow networks — not only does not work for healthcare's customers, it cannot work. This is not because they are doing it wrong or being sloppy. By its very nature the Default Model must continually fail to bring healthcare's customers what they want and desperately need. Ultimately it cannot bring the healthcare providers what they want and need.

I know the players here. I know how this works. I have consulted with, worked with, or spoken before almost every major health plan in the United States, from the huge national for-profits to national, regional, and state Blue Cross/Blue Shields to Kaiser, as well as hundreds of hospitals, scores of major medical groups and group management associations, many state medical societies, almost all state hospital associations, hundreds of convocations of healthcare executives, scores of board meetings — the list is mind-bogglingly long and tedious. And I listen. In the pre-event interviews, on facility tours, in the group processes, over lunch, over drinks, in the Q&As, on the panels, I ask what their concerns are, what their strategies are, what the goals are, how they play the game. I've done this with stupefying persistence since Jimmy and Rosalind lived in the White House. I know the players and I can see where we are stuck.

So take a dive with me into the real-world, game-theory mechanics of the healthcare economy, and you will see they have to change. It's time to rebuild the fundamental business models of healthcare.

The Default Model Healthcare Game

It's a little easier to find our way around an economic model by picturing it as a game and asking: "What defines winning for each player? What does each player need to do to win?"

Health plans: For health plans, winning means surviving, succeeding, and growing as a business. But there are a couple of rule changes now. They used to be able to stay more profitable by pushing down their medical loss ratio (MLR — the percentage of premiums actually paid out for medical care), by "rescinding" the plans of people who cost too much, and refusing to cover anyone with pre-existing conditions. Now they have to take everybody, can't toss them out, and their MLR has to be at least 80 percent (or 85 percent for large customers). So their administrative expenses, advertising, executive salaries (and the profits and stock price of the for-profits) are all tied to a percentage of the actual costs of healthcare. Hmmm. When they are confronted with a way to make healthcare cost half as much, would they be interested? Would they make it a top priority? Not so much. They have little incentive to actually drop the real costs of healthcare.

On the other hand, the only way they can grow is by capturing more market share in a highly price-sensitive market. So they have an incentive to keep premiums low enough relative to each market to keep and even gain market share. And the market share rodeo is replayed each year.

Their way out of this dilemma? Put together narrow networks based on lower fee-for-service prices for each item. In order to do this, they must (it's not optional) re-negotiate every year with every provider — and often even during the year, and even over individual bills. So the health plans cannot promise to actually cover whom they say they are covering, or even the procedures they say they are covering, much less that they will cover them next year. Nor can they promise to the providers that they will actually pay what they say they will pay, nor that they will stick to that price next year.

This is not a result of playing the game badly, but of playing it well. It is built into the structure of the game.

Healthcare providers: Providers win by surviving, continuing to provide great service to their service populations — and expanding and changing enough to serve the newly insured. To win at this game, providers must play hard-to-get with the private payers. They must either opt out of these low-cost networks (which they can do if they are in some way indispensible in their market, or get their customers in some other way). Or, having agreed to accept the low fee-for-service reimbursement, they have to cut their internal costs so that they at least believe they are making money, then make it up on volume.

"Believe" is a key word here, because most healthcare providers do not do cost accounting deeply enough to know their total cost of ownership for their products. "Volume" includes not just more customers (greater market share), but performing more items from the approved list (more unnecessary tests and procedures), and performing more of the big-ticket items. In other words, they have to cut costs internally while doubling down on the waste and over-treatment that characterize the fee-for-service regime. So while agreeing to lower fee-for-service prices, the providers cannot truly promise lower actual costs.

Physicians who are not on staff are strongly tempted to game the system by bringing in higher-priced out-of-network colleagues as co-surgeons, or referring the patient to out-of-network colleagues, or performing other sleights of hand that hugely burdens the patient with unforeseen, uncovered costs.

Healthcare providers have little incentive to develop long-term relationships with patients and families or to prevent next year's diseases (by helping patients stop smoking, for instance) because they can't say for sure that they will be in the network next year. Given their deductibles and co-pays and co-insurance, actually using healthcare is still an expensive proposition for the consumer. So providers using the Default Model have little incentive to offer truly lower-cost healthcare (prevention; active relationships; medical management; real, no-horsefeathers, necessary, and helpful medical care).

The healthcare providers cannot promise lower costs, cannot even give real prices, and have no incentive for prevention, as long as they stay in the code-driven, fee-for-service game. Again, this does not come from playing the game badly, but from playing it well. The game is structured so that the provider cannot really win as long as the provider sticks to the Default Model game, because all payers (government and private) will continually seek lower fee-for-service prices. To bargain strongly, both sides must intentionally keep the relationship mercurial, must keep the networks always in flux. This puts the provider in a very narrow, unstable situation. The best the provider can hope for is a stalling, rear-guard action.

Yet still the healthcare providers are in turmoil about this. Not long ago I stood in front of a small room at an upscale restaurant along the San Francisco waterfront, speaking to a couple of dozen people, the board and top officers and affiliates of a hospital in a wealthy Bay Area suburb. I spoke about the need for radical business model shifts and diversification. Barely six feet in front of me, the CEO who had invited me became visibly more agitated as I proceeded, shifting his weight, drumming his fingers. He seemed barely able to contain himself.

Finally I decided to pull the cork: "Gee, John, you look like you're uncomfortable with these ideas. What do you think?"

He immediately came out with a full-throated defense of the Default Model and how well they were doing with it. But he got interrupted by (as it turned out) the physician managers of several affiliated medical groups and specialist organizations. These were the very people who were doing the best under the Default Model, and they were loudly debating John, telling him that the change is coming, they had to diversify, find different business models, and take on risk in different ways, because the big systems in the area are doing exactly that, and will steal their business if they don't compete strongly for it.

Not long after that I was speaking at a very different place, a medium-sized community hospital system out in the gritty industrialized agricultural heart of California's vast Central Valley. This time there were several hundred people in the new high-tech auditorium, and several hundred more connected by video from the system's other campus. After I gave my talk, we started a Q&A session, and the system's chief operating officer joined me on stage, partly to debate me about whether radical change is necessary. I expected that. What I did not expect was the wide array of people in both audiences, many of them heads of the system's divisions or affiliates, who jumped up to join in the debate and advocate stronger and faster moves toward more diverse revenue streams and new business models.

The debate is happening all across healthcare right now, and will continue to happen as this change moves forward. It is risky to move toward new business models, but many people across healthcare have come to feel that it is actually riskier not to move.

How to Win: Purchasers and Consumers

If you are older than about 45 you probably remember the classic 1983 film *War Games*, in which the artificial-intelligence computer in charge of strategic nuclear war (nicknamed Joshua) thinks it is playing a game called Global Thermonuclear War. The teenage computer geek David Lightman (played by a young Matthew Broderick) madly tries to get Joshua not to blow up the world. With the help of his co-conspirator Jennifer (Ally Sheedy), he challenges it to a game of tic-tac-toe. At the climax of the film they are sitting in NORAD headquarters, watching the computer play tic-tac-toe thousands of times at the same moment that it is moving through the steps of the game Global Thermonuclear War, counting down to a real world-destroying conflagration.

> Jennifer: What is it doing?
> David: It's learning.

Ultimately, from playing tic-tac-toe the computer comes to the realization that there are games that have no winner, that the only way to win the game is not to play it.

Purchasers: Employers and other large purchasers are beginning to see that this is true of the Default Model for producing lower-cost, high-quality, reliable access to healthcare: By its very nature it cannot give them truly lower costs, higher quality, or reliable access. The only way for purchasers to win is not to play the game. So, many of them are self-funding their healthcare and searching for ways to not play the fee-for-service, narrow-network Default Model game. These ways include bundled prices, reference prices, medical tourism contracts, Centers of Excellence contracts, on-site clinics, direct pay primary care, captive accountable care organizations — all of which in one way or another opt out of the fee-for-service Default Model and instead pay directly for the desired medical results at an agreed price without paying for wasteful unnecessary overtreatment.

Consumers: The Default Model makes the term "consumer-directed" laughable because it takes away the consumer's real choice. Consumers cannot choose based on price and quality; that choice is done for them. They can only go to the in-network physicians and institutions, and there are usually darn few in the network to choose from. The consumers have to take what they can get and be glad of it.

Individual consumers have few opportunities to participate in the strategies that the big purchasers (such as reference pricing and captive accountable care organizations). The closest they can come is combining really high-deductible catastrophic health plans with direct pay primary care or retail care.

Consumers do not trust the healthcare system and do not feel they have any real consumer power, because they are typically asking the system (the combine of payers and providers) the kind of questions buyers ask about any product (Does this work? How do I know? How much will it actually cost?), and getting no answers they can trust from anybody, much less anything like a warranty.

We will discuss these questions more in the chapter "Trust," but I will list them here. The eight major, life-changing questions healthcare consumers ask are:

- Am I actually covered for the institutions, facilities, and doctors that you tell me I am covered for?
- Will I be covered for them next year?
- Will my specialist, on whom I have relied for years, and who has taken my insurance for years, suddenly be out of the network?
- When I choose an institution and physicians who are in-network, will someone sneak in an out-of-network doc with a huge fee?

- Will my premiums go up unreasonably, at a time when I read that the real costs of healthcare are nearly flat?
- Will you come up with some fine-print reason that I am not covered for something I was told I am covered for?
- If I get surprised by huge medical bills caused by fraudulent inclusion of out-of-network docs, by balance bills, or by denial of coverage for something I was told was covered, will you help me? Or will you say it's not your problem?
- Can you guarantee through my arrangement with you that I will not be financially ruined?

The healthcare system, payers and providers playing the Default Model Game, are delivering an unreliable, unguaranteed, financially and medically dangerous product to their real customers — the large purchasers and the consumers of healthcare.

This is not stable.

How Healthcare Providers Can Win: Change the Game

How can hospitals and health networks win this game? Only by imitating Joshua: Find a different game to play. Stop thinking of payers as your customers. They are financial organizations that stand between you and your customers. If they are not helping you move beyond the Default Model, they do not truly have the best interests of either you or your customers at heart. I have never met a healthcare executive who would say, "I got into this business to make sure the insurance companies stay profitable."

The Default Model is the payers' game, designed to do just that. You don't have to play it any more. That's not your circus; that's not your monkey.

Getting out of the game is not easy. It must be done stepwise. But providers cannot wait for payers to do it for them. Providers must make it a corporate strategic goal. Getting there has three parallel pieces:

1. **Operations:** Bringing better health to a population, preventing disease, helping them manage chronic conditions so that they

do not become acute, requires drastically different operational capabilities, structures, and capital flows. It takes a significant amount of time to make this shift. So start now, developing your operations as if you are in the business environment, then go after the revenue flows to support them.

2. **Payers:** Negotiate with the payers for the revenue flows that will in one way or another pay you directly for the kind of close patient tracking and care that will make the population healthier. Accountable care organizations already do this, but their revenue flows amount to a few percentage points. You need substantial shifts in your revenue flows to support the new model.

3. **Purchasers:** Go to the large employers, pension plans, and other big purchasers of healthcare in your area and offer them bundled products of various types that meet their specific needs while paying you not for volume but for improving the health of their employees or members.

If you are a healthcare provider, you need to set a goal of getting out of the fee-for-service business as much as possible. Provide your large customers (employers, pension plans, and other large purchasers) the products and non-fee-for-service financial arrangements they are looking for, product line by product line, region by region, population by population. Then find or invent ways that individual consumers can take part in the same strategies as the large purchasers — even if this means inventing your own insurance mechanism tailored to the needs of your institution and its real customers.

Drive down internal costs and bid actual prices that you know you can support. Drive toward a future that is not supported by wasteful overtreatment in a fee-for-service world, but as much as possible by multiple revenue streams that pay you directly for real, necessary, helpful medical care supported by long-term, trusted relationships. That, after all, is really why we got into this business: to provide for the health and well-being and financial well-being of the millions of people who depend on us so heavily.

They Roll Up Together

Once again: These seven levers are systemic. They work together and feed back into each other. The tipping point shows up when they are all operating for at least some large portion of this massive sector.

If we imagine that people are acting like real shoppers, and they have the information, and they are shopping for real results, what's the biggest, best, cheapest result they could possibly have? It would be to not get sick in the first place. So that's Lever 4: Prevention.

Results: The To-Do Lists

**Purchasers (Employers, Pension Plans, and
Other Purchasers of Healthcare):**

- **Self-fund and reinsure:** Take control of your costs by taking control of your risk.
- **Redesign benefits programs:** Work with your insurance company or third-party administrator to design a benefits program that funnels employees only to institutions with proven best-in-category outcomes. Don't settle for less.
- **Reference pricing and Centers of Excellence:** When you work with the insurance company or third-party administrator that administers your self-funded plan to set bundled reference prices for big-ticket tests and procedures, make sure that only the most highly rated providers are on the list.
- **Medical tourism:** Be willing to guide and reward employees for taking their high-cost medical needs to the best provider with the best prices and quality scores, wherever they may be.

Consumers:

- **Track yourself:** If you are to take charge of your health, you first have to know how you're doing. No need to get all OCD about it, but you should track your basics, such as your weight and blood pressure, well enough to notice any changes. Pay attention to what you eat and drink, and when, and how that makes you feel. Women need to self-inspect for breast lumps. You are your own best laboratory. If you think it would be good to make a change in your diet or your exercise habits, establish a baseline first so that you can tell what difference the change makes.

- **Connect:** Work with a healthcare provider who will stay connected with you and help you track yourself. How constant should the contact be? That depends on who you are, at what stage of life you are now, whether you are going through changes, whether you have chronic conditions that need to be managed, and so on. But don't fool yourself. "I'm fine" is not a health program.

Entrepreneurs, Inventors, and Investors:

- **Focus on populations:** Software and hardware that help medical organizations better track, monitor, and improve the health of populations will find an enormous worldwide market in the coming years.
- **Focus on tracking results:** Dongles, apps, and gadgets that link the vulnerable patient into the medical establishment on a tight, continuing, inexpensive basis will be the core of tomorrow's healthcare.

Health Plans:

- **Measure results:** Stop treating all healthcare providers as equivalent. Go deep into serious big data analysis so that you can fairly rate healthcare providers on their actual quality, as well as their cost for entire cycles of care.
- **Pay for results:** Use bundled payments and other innovative payment methods to pay for entire cycles of care rather than for individual items.

- **Redesign benefits programs:** Use variable co-pays, reference pricing, and other incentives to funnel patients to the medical organizations with the best outcomes at the lowest cost.
- **Risk:** Design and use payment structures (similar to alternative quality contracts) that reward primary care providers when their patients require less acute and emergency care than they have historically. Base these payment structures on quality measures, excluding any primary care providers that get to low utilization simply by denying or discouraging care.
- **Harmonize performance measures:** Any incentives work best if they are clear, few, and not contradictory. Physicians typically may contract with many different payers. Payers are demanding measures of quality and performance that are typically all some-what different, and in some case contradictory. This mutes the ability of payers to pay for better results.

Hospitals, Physician Groups, and Healthcare Institutions:

- **Bank on results:** Get used to the idea. Then act on it. Set an over-all strategic goal that you will survive by being extremely good at what you do — not just for particular procedures but over entire cycles of care. Not "close enough" but best in class. And not just extremely good, but extremely lean and efficient. This is a pre-requisite for survival in the Next Healthcare.
- **Measure results:** Develop true, reliable measurements of your quality and cost. These will be different from the quality check-offs required by CMS or insurers. They will have to be much more fine-grained and realistic, because you are using them not just to show off, but to guide your improvement over time. If they are not realistic and high-resolution, they are useless to you.
- **Learn to manage the data about your results:** Clinicians and sys-tems typically have too much data, often with little notion how to draw from the data a clear, real-time picture of how they are doing as individual practitioners, or how that relates to the goals of the organization.

- **Improve your results:** Use teams and "lean manufacturing" techniques to drive down costs and improve your outcomes at the same time. Make improving the job a continuous part of the job.
- **Get paid for results:** Get out of the narrow-network, code-based fee-for-service Default Model as much as possible. Take on risk contracts in which you make more money or do better in other ways by bringing the best outcomes to patients over entire cycles of care, or over months and years in chronic cases. Don't be random. Look specifically for the contracts in areas in which your specific capacities and expertise can make the most difference in patients' lives — then search for ways to get paid for making that difference. Notice that it will not be uncommon that this will lead you to voluntarily seeking out and taking on what have been the "worst" patients, because those are the ones who have the greatest potential for improvement.

Federal and State Lawmakers and Policymakers

- **Mandate transparency of results:** Most state quality reporting projects mask the real results. Employers, other big purchasers, and consumers deserve to know the providers' batting averages and error rates, and it is increasingly possible to produce realistic, objective statistics. "It's hard" is not an excuse to not do it, nor is "the doctors and hospitals hate this."

Lever 4: Prevention

Problem

THE CHEAPEST WAY to deal with disease is not to get sick in the first place. A huge amount of healthcare costs go to dealing with preventable diseases — and comparatively little effort or expense goes to preventing them.

Solution

Invent new business models that put healthcare organizations at financial risk for the health of the populations they serve — so that they make more money if people are healthier.

Chronic Disease

Chronic disease is huge. In fact, it's most of healthcare. Chronic diseases cause 70 percent of all deaths in America. This statistic has held fairly steady over time: Just three of these diseases — heart disease, cancer, and stroke — cause half of all deaths.[105] Chronic diseases (and the acute episodes that spring from them) account for 75 percent to 85 percent of all medical costs in our system.[106]

105 Kung HC, Hoyert DL, Xu JQ, and Murphy SL, "Deaths: Final Data for 2005," *National Vital Statistics Reports*, Vol. 56, No. 10, 2008. Available at: http://www.cdc.gov/nchs/data/nvsr/nvsr56/nvsr56_10.pdf

106 Lynn J, Straube BM, Bell KM, Jencks SF, and Kambic RT, "Using Population Segmenta-

Most chronic disease is preventable. When it has not been prevented, most chronic disease is manageable and treatable. The opportunity to save money — and to prevent vast amounts of suffering and poverty — is larger in dealing with chronic disease than in anything else in healthcare. In fact, that opportunity is larger than anything else our nation could save in any field for anything.

Cost-cutter alert! If you have a concern about the federal deficit, about government overspending, or about waste in the economy in general, read that again: The largest cost-saving opportunity in our entire nation of any kind is not in cutting the military budget, or foreign aid, or food stamps. It is in preventing, managing, and treating chronic disease. Given that approximately half of our entire medical spend comes through the federal government, *optimally reducing the cost of chronic disease through prevention, management, and proper treatment would in fact reduce the federal budget deficit to zero.*

Buzzword

Prevention is the big buzzword in healthcare reform, and population health management is the big buzz phrase. And this makes sense. Prevention looks like a gold mine. After all, some 86 percent (that is, almost all) of U.S. full-time employees are either overweight or have a chronic health condition that significantly raises their healthcare costs, or both. Most of those conditions are preventable, and all of them are manageable for lower cost and better health.

So why isn't everybody having a raging success at prevention? It's not like they aren't trying. Some 92 percent of big employers (over 200 employees) offer wellness programs.[107] At the same time healthcare organizations across the country are trying various ways to move from Volume

tion to Provide Better Health Care for All: The 'Bridges to Health' Model," *The Milbank Quarterly*, Vol. 85, No. 2, 2007, pp. 185–208.

107 Mattke S, Schnyer C, Van Busum KR, "A Review of US Workplace Wellness Market," The RAND Corporation, 2012. Sponsored by the U.S. Department Of Labor. Available at: www.dol.gov/ebsa/pdf/workplacewellnessmarketreview2012.pdf

to Value, getting away from fee-for-service care by taking on risk for the health of whole populations, for instance getting paid a set fee per patient per month (PPPM), especially for primary care. **Put simply, they're making money by keeping patients healthy.** This puts them right into the business of population health management.

Over the years there have been many case studies[108] that show very high return on investment for employee wellness programs. But these were just case studies of successes, not rigorously controlled studies comparing similar groups and similar interventions across different companies. **The best-known metastudy[109] of well-constructed employee wellness programs from the last few decades showed an ROI of $6 for every $1 spent.** This included $3.27 in lower medical costs, plus $2.73 in lower absentee costs.

So why the long faces? Why are we not (or at least not yet) showing big drops in healthcare costs because of these wellness programs? Dig a bit deeper into a broader range of studies and you'll see that there are a number of reasons. For one thing, practically everyone has wellness programs but almost no one uses them. Typically only about 20 percent of the employees sign up.[110] They are commonly the healthiest 20 percent anyway, the employees who could least benefit from them. The incentives are low, often only a few hundred dollars a year, and often given only to people who succeed in changing some major health marker,

---

108 Ozminkowski RJ, Dunn RL, Goetzel RZ, Cantor RI, Murnane J, Harrison M, "A return on investment evaluation of the Citibank, N.A., health management program." *American Journal of Health Promotion,* 1999 September-October; 14(1), pp. 31—43.

Bly JL, Jones RC, Richardson JE "Impact of worksite health promotion on healthcare costs and utilization. Evaluation of Johnson & Johnson's Live for Life program," *Journal of the American Medical Association,* 1986, December 19;256(23), pp. 3235—40;

Fries JF, Harrington H, Edwards R, Kent LA, Richardson N, "Randomized controlled trial of cost reductions from a health education program: the California Public Employees' Retirement System (PERS) study," *American Journal of Health Promotion* 1994 January-February 8(3), pp. 216-23;.

Leigh JP, Richardson N, Beck R, Kerr C, Harrington H, Parcell CL, *et al.,* "Randomized controlled study of a retiree health promotion program. The Bank of America Study." *Archives of Internal Medicine,* 1992 Jun;152(6), pp. 1201-6.

109 Baicker K, Cutler D, and Song Z, "Workplace wellness programs can generate savings." *Health Affairs* 29(2): pp. 304–311. doi:10.1377/hlthaff.2009.0626. Available at: http://nrs.harvard.edu/urn-3:HUL.InstRepos:5345879

110 Mattke *et al., ibid.*

such as losing a significant amount of weight or quitting smoking. No wonder people don't sign up. Quitting smoking or losing weight is really hard. Seriously. You ever tried it? If the incentive is just money, that's not nearly enough money. **For people to change their lives in some significant way, you have to do more than wave a few dollars at them. You have to engage them, be their friend, really help them to do something they really want to do.**

This gives us a clue to what turns out to be the two deeper reasons, and the two ways we can differentiate wellness and prevention programs between those that work and those that don't.

Before we get to those, first note this: Under the ACA, the new rules say that you can't punish people for being obese or having high blood sugar by giving them higher premiums. You can differentiate the premiums, but only in a way that doesn't discriminate.

Programs That Work

There are two essential identifiers of wellness and prevention programs that actually work: engagement and disease management. That is, actually engaging with people (employees, local citizens, health plan members), as in forming trusted relationships. And actually engaging with their real disease states and helping them manage them.

In other words, wellness and prevention programs that actually work are not like an activities director on a cruise ship: "Hey, everyone! Time for yoga!" They are about actually getting involved.

Engagement: I'm going to let my friend Darrell Moon describe it. He is the CEO of a Utah company called Orriant that has some 11 years' experience building incentivized prevention programs that don't discriminate, actually help people get healthier, and drop costs significantly all at once:

> Here's how they work. Employees who chose to take responsibility for their health and join the wellness program pay a reduced contribution toward their premium, often less than half that paid by non-participants (but the reduction can't amount to more than 20 percent of the total premium, raised to 30 percent

under the new rules to encourage participation). Those with blood pressure or other readings outside accepted standards are then offered an alternative way to keep receiving the reduced premium. They can work with a health coach to at least try to reduce their health risks.

They don't have to lose weight, or even quit smoking, to enjoy the reduced premium. All they have to do is work with a personal health coach and *try* to get healthier, unless their doctors advise against it. The programs are completely voluntary, and even the most unhealthy can earn the same reward as the healthiest, so long as they work with a health coach. Even a person born with diabetes, for example, can still work with a coach to help manage the disease.

This is the key. Indeed, **it turns out that simply working with a personal health coach is the secret sauce of employee wellness** [emphasis mine]. A recent study[111] we conducted of four midsize employers with health-contingent wellness programs found that their total annual paid claims dropped to $2,269 per participant, as opposed to $6,187 for non-participants.

This despite the fact that 68 percent of all employees in the wellness programs started out with significant health risks and therefore had to work with a health coach. They initially had high rates of ill health, emergency room claims, pharmacy claims, and hospital claims, but all showed a sharp drop, versus a steady rise among non-participants.... The key is participation. Unless your employees actually participate, your company will continue to hemorrhage red ink from health claims and premium costs.[112]

Disease management: Here's why it is difficult to tease out real guidance from most of the studies of wellness and prevention programs.

---

111 Moon D, "Can CEOs Find Relief From Skyrocketing Health Costs?" ChiefExecutive.net, October 24, 2011. Available at: http://chiefexecutive.net/can-ceos-find-relief-from-skyrocketing-health-costs

112 Moon D, "New Obamacare Rules Offer Big Gains for Employers," Forbes.com, December 7, 2012. Available at: http://www.forbes.com/sites/forbesleadershipforum/2012/12/07/new-obamacare-rules-offer-big-gains-for-employers/

Those programs typically have many components, such as health risk assessments, on-site wellness events, and lifestyle coaching, and may include disease management and complex care management (helping people manage their care when they have multiple chronic problems).

So you get studies showing huge reductions in healthcare costs, and other studies that show great advances in the health and risk factors of employees, but no reductions in actual healthcare costs.[113] What's the difference?

Two studies[114] teased out what the difference is, and it is essentially this: The lifestyle management part of the program reduced people's risk factors some, reduced absenteeism some, and even reduced actual healthcare costs some, but no more than the costs of those lifestyle components. **The disease management parts of the program dropped healthcare costs significantly**. The largest and most thorough study, looking at PepsiCo's program over a seven-year period, showed that targeting people with the most chronic problems and helping them manage their diseases produced a reduction in actual healthcare costs (net of the costs of the program) that averaged $136 per member per month.

We will talk about this more in the next chapter, "Lever 5: Targeting," because it is about directing special care to those who need it most. There we will talk about, for instance, the Boeing program.

Cost-cutters alert!
Lifestyle wellness programs by themselves do not drop medical costs. Real disease management programs do.

Patient-centered medical homes: One of the simplest and most effective prevention strategies is making sure that all patients have a "medical

---

113 Mattke S, Liu H, Caloyeras JP, Huang CY, Van Busum KR, Khodyakov D, *et al.*, "Workplace Wellness Programs Study." Santa Monica (CA): RAND Corporation; 2013. (Pub. No. RR-254-DOL). Available at: http://www.rand.org/pubs/research_reports/RR254.html

114 Nyman JA, Abraham JM, Jeffery MM, Barleen NA. "The effectiveness of a health promotion program after 3 years: evidence from the University of Minnesota." *Med Care.* 2012; 50(9):772–8. Available at: http://www.ncbi.nlm.nih.gov/pubmed/22683588

Caloyeras *et al.* "Managing Manifest Diseases, But Not Health Risks, Saved PepsiCo Money Over Seven Years," *Health Affairs,* January 2014.

home," that is, a primary care physician's office that pays attention to them whether they show up sick or not. In a PCMH, the physician is paid a bit more per person per month to keep track of all patients and screen them appropriately. It's what we imagine in our fantasies of what the old-time family doctors did in the Norman Rockwell small-town world: They kept their eye on you and thought about your health. In modern terms, it means the doctor calling you instead of waiting until you manage to bull your way into his or her appointment sheet.

Employers are increasingly aware of the power of someone keeping a good medical eye on you. By 2013, only 14 percent of employers used models of care that including patient-centered medical homes; another 61 percent planned to do so within the next few years, according to an Aon Hewitt survey.[115]

Public health: Whatever role you play, you must seek partners in all of this. For healthcare organizations, payers and employers are the best possible partners, since they shoulder a lot of the cost burden of ill health. But federal, state, and local public health officials are equally important. In my years of talking to healthcare executives, I continue to be astonished at how many of them do not even know the names of local public health officials, much less collaborate with them on a regular basis.

Healthy Communities: At the furthest remove from the emergency department threshold is the Healthy Communities movement. There are local groups in most places across the country, supporting programs dealing with everything from effluents to traffic to education to AIDS awareness. The return on investment is always large because the investment is so small compared with the ED visits, surgeries, premature births, and NICU and ICU use that they eventually prevent.

Attention employers and payers! It's true: You can actually save money by improving the health of whole populations — but only if you pay attention to what actually works.

---

115 Aon Hewitt, "Employers plan pay tactics to cut costs: Companies weigh performance pay, value-based pricing," June 10, 2013. Available at: http://www.healthcarefinancenews.com/news/employers-plan-pay-tactics-cut-costs

Raise a Glass to Carlos

You drink beer? Next time you pop a cold one, raise a toast to Carlos Olivares.

Why? Beer is made from hops. That's about all I know about hops, except for one more thing: Three quarters of all the hops in the United States come from the thousand square miles of the Yakima Valley in eastern Washington state. You can't have beer without hops. You can't have hops without farmworkers to plant them, irrigate them, harvest them, and load them into trucks bound for the breweries. The growers know that you can't have farmworkers if somebody doesn't patch them up when they are injured and dose them when they are sick.

That's Carlos and the doctors and nurses he employs. The small, soft-spoken, energetic man from Bolivia has run the Yakima Valley Farm Workers Community Clinic for 25 years. He does things that are simple, basic, and smart, things that go right to the point, like this: He convinced local doctors to open after-hours clinics so that the farmworkers don't have to drive all the way to the hospital in Spokane and show up in the emergency room when all they have is the flu, or an infected cut. Farmworkers don't have much money, and most of them don't have health insurance, so doctors weren't interested in serving them better. The docs have practices to run, and bills to pay. So Carlos did the math, put together a PowerPoint, called a little meeting, and showed the doctors that they could actually make a good bit of money at it, all by saving money for the poor farmworkers, and making it easier for them to stay healthy at the same time.

The doctors who took part nearly doubled their income. The farmworkers were healthier. The agricultural giants who grow the hops got better, more productive workers — and they weren't even paying for health insurance for these employees. Would it be smart of the agribusiness companies to subsidize the clinics to keep the workers even healthier? Yes. But it was even smarter of Olivares to build a lean, smart, well-run clinic that could help the docs make a living doing what they do best — for the poor farmworkers.[116]

---

116 Author's interview of Carlos Olivares.

In the hop fields of the Yakima Valley or the barrios of Southern California or the baking suburbs of Phoenix, healthcare costs less when you do it right, when you do it smart, close to the customer, ethical, with heart and brain, not just by the book.

What Employers Can Do

Employers want to increase productivity and cut healthcare costs. Employees look askance at talk like that, because "productivity" is often code for "make the employees work harder and longer for less," and "cut healthcare costs" often codes for "cut benefits and get the employee to pay more for them." But good health is one point on which employers and employees want the same thing. A healthier workforce helps the bottom line by lowering healthcare costs, turnover, absenteeism, and presenteeism (people coming to work even though they are sick and infectious), and by raising productivity. It helps employees because, well, everybody wants to be healthy. Health is a value in itself.

Employers have traditionally thought of "health benefits" only as "paying for medical stuff." Expand that definition slightly to "paying for health" and the picture changes significantly. Done right, especially in a self-funded benefits program, prevention efforts bring a massive return on investment, as the costs of prevention are so much less than the pre-vented medical costs.

What Health Plans Can Do

We used to call them "medical plans," because that's what they did — they funded your medical needs. Now they usually call themselves "health plans," because that sounds better, more holistic. But for most, what they do has not changed a bit. They don't fund health; they fund sickness. And frankly, they have had little incentive to actually drive down health-care costs by helping people stay healthy, because their income was and is a percentage of the cost of their members' healthcare. Their only true interest in prevention has been as a tool of marketing, not in actually driving down costs.

This is one of the major reasons that health plans are among the least trusted institutions in society: They have shown vividly and with astonishing frequency that they are really not on your side at all. It's a struggle to think of any other sector in which companies that are so roundly distrusted can stay in business.

Now that's changing. As employers and consumers increasingly realize that there are ways to drive down the costs of healthcare, they will gravitate toward health plans that help them cut their actual costs. If health plans want market share, they will have to visibly and actively help consumers and employers use every tool available to cut costs and get better healthcare — and that includes, powerfully, the tools of prevention, the methods of staying healthy and catching health problems earlier.

Now that many of their worst practices have been outlawed, health plans have an opportunity to re-emerge as partners in health and in reducing the true costs of healthcare. Those that don't may well find themselves cut out of significant parts of the market.

What Entrepreneurs, Inventors, and Investors Can Do

Population health management is hard to do, and most people running healthcare organizations and health plans today have little experience with doing it. Experience with actually changing the health profile of large numbers of people lies largely in the Healthy Communities movement and in the field of public health, but that experience does not include sharing the clinical information of individual patients, tying together multiple clinicians who may not be in the same organization, or balancing risk and rewards across networks.

Technologies to seamlessly and fully manage this complexity do not exist yet. Many companies have suites that they claim can do it all, but none have shown that they really are comprehensive. Most are based on their EHR (electronic health records) system. Bur EHRs are the wrong architecture. They are all about record keeping, which is not the same goal as easing engagement between clinicians, between parts of the organization, and between the clinicians and the patients.

At the same time, healthcare organizations have mostly blown their wad on building electronic health record systems. The smaller ones especially have neither the capital nor the stomach for buying even larger and more expensive software systems — and at the same time they often lack the deep understanding of what they need it for.

What we will see increasingly is healthcare organizations cobbling together software suites to match their particular situation out of modular parts. This is why we see more than half of U.S. healthcare organizations declaring that they will invest in population health management software in 2015[117] — but exactly what they mean by that can be highly varied.

In a highly useful report,[118] Chilmark Research has outlined five capabilities that such software must have for comprehensive population health management:

- **Analytics:** Population health management needs sophisticated data crunching and tracking. There is no standard package that brings together the myriad pieces that would support wise decisions. These would include geodata, public health data, patient tracking statistics, revenue flows, identification of risk levels, performance management, and analysis of gaps in care and quality.
- **Health information exchange:** Shares clinical data among everybody serving the population (whose organizations may not have compatible EHRs).
- **EHR:** The core patient record system, made capable of sharing data through the information exchange.
- **Care management:** Balancing the resources available across the community, and insuring seamless continuity of care as the patient moves from one provider to another as needed.
- **Patient engagement:** Mobile apps and web services to help connect the patients and their caregivers and families to the system,

117 Page T, "peer60 Report Projects 2015 Healthcare Technology Spending," press release, March 3, 2015. Available at: http://www.prweb.com/releases/2015/03/prweb12555374.htm

118 Chilmark Research, "Inside Peek at Forthcoming PHM Report," March 11, 2015. Available at: http://www.chilmarkresearch.com/2015/03/11/inside-peak-to-forthcoming-phm-report/

and to help them work with the system to manage their own health.

Let's expand a bit on that last piece.

Personal health apps: The easy, no-brainer end of tech in prevention are devices like Fitbit and apps like Couch to 5k, which help people track their own diet and fitness regimes. These are great. There are thousands of them available. I use some of them, and you probably do, too. But they will not change healthcare. Why? Because you and I are not the people who need the most help in shifting their behavior to become healthier. Personal health apps are used by people who already worry whether they should go gluten free, who read the ingredients on packaged food, and who know seven different kinds of yoga. They make staying fit more convenient for the fitness-conscious. They do not connect the disconnected.

Connect consumers to their families and their posses: There are apps and devices that help connect families over health matters, and help family caregivers monitor and work with their parents, their children, or the friends in their health posse. These are more valuable, because they begin to mimic the way we really take care of our health, in the context of trusted relationships of family and friends.

Connect consumers and caregivers to the health system: Imagine software that has your whole medical situation tracked on it. It has the goals for your current situation that you have worked out with your doctor or health coach, whether it is just losing some weight, or controlling your diabetes, or avoiding a stroke. Imagine it built into a smartphone with its sensors, or into wearables (a belt, a Fitbit-style bracelet, a smart watch, smart glasses, a patch). As you work out, or just go through your day, the data it generates not only displays to you when you want it, it uploads it to your file in the cloud. You can share any part of it that you want to with your doctor or health coach. Analytics can determine if some key factors (heart rate, blood sugar level) go outside pre-set boundaries, and alert your healthcare provider to call you and see what's going on — or send the emergency medical technicians (EMTs). And it goes both ways: If you see something that you have a question about, tap here and you can talk directly to a live nurse at your healthcare provider.

"Patient engagement" has been a buzz phrase in healthcare for years: How do you get patients engaged in their medical care and in taking better care of themselves? In the Next Healthcare, providers will live or die based on their ability to engage the patient. It's not easy. The spread of smart tech, and people's eagerness to engage with it in every imaginable way, is a true opportunity to work with patients in whatever medium they might prefer.

What Healthcare Organizations Can Do

In the Next Healthcare, medical providers of all kinds need to become world class in tracking, characterizing, and understanding their customers and potential customers. This is miles beyond marketing research. It's population health management on steroids. The skill set is in its infancy, but it includes:

- tracking on individual and aggregate levels
- mining and understanding the now very deep literature on prevention, incentivized wellness, and healthy communities
- geographic information systems to geocode the data onto neighborhoods, workplaces, churches, and other community connections
- predictive modeling to suggest which interventions will have the best effect
- and tracking the return on investment of particular interventions

The skill set will have to include the ability to create targeted, flexible responses, to mass-customize interventions and resources to individuals and to micro-populations (such as the residents of a particular convalescent home, or employees on a particular site, or all of your customers who have a particular condition).[119]

119 Dimitropoulos L, "Health IT Research Priorities to Support the Health Care Delivery System of the Future," Agency for Healthcare Research and Quality, AHRQ Publications No. 14-0072-EF, October 19, 2014. Available at: http://healthit.ahrq.gov/sites/default/files/docs/citation/health-it-research-priorities-to-support-health-care-delivery-system-of-future.pdf

All of this is new, and there will be an extraordinary premium on getting it right. Some healthcare providers and some health plans are forging ahead. The insurance division of UPMC (University of Pittsburgh Medical Center), for instance, has recently started combining traditional healthcare information about its members (such as patient claims, admissions, prescriptions, and census data) with deep shopping information such as members' marital status, number of cars, education levels, household incomes, and number of children at home. It gets such information through marketing companies such as Axciom, which in turn gets it from both public and private sources.

We worry about our privacy and feel exposed when Facebook, Google, and online marketers gather information about us. But here the intent is quite different: not to sell us more stuff but to help us be healthier, and so cost the system less. Pamela Peele, the chief analytics officer for the UPMC insurance services division, told *The New York Times'* Natasha Singer that such information would be used, on one hand, to improve the predictive modeling of what clinical resources UPMC would need; and on the other hand to track down high-risk members who aren't getting proper care and assign them personal care coordinators. Similarly, the healthcare analysis company Predilytics, working with an East Coast hospital, discovered that people who had trouble getting an appointment with their primary care provider, or people who did not own a car, were more likely to end up in the emergency department. This makes intuitive sense, but it is more than statistical data: Such programs can actually identify individuals who might need a little extra help. [120]

Small and Rural Hospitals

Managing the health of populations takes scale and capital. For a lot of small and rural hospitals, this seems out of reach. It can feel like they are doomed to stay in the reimbursed fee-for-service "sickness care" Default Model, and get less and less income for doing it.

---

120 Singer N, "When a Health Plan Knows How You Shop," *The New York Times,* June 28, 2014. Available at: http://www.nytimes.com/2014/06/29/technology/when-a-health-plan-knows-how-you-shop.html

I see organizations in this trap all across the country. Just in the last few years I have seen it in my work with the Iowa Medical Society; with the Free Clinics of America; with healthcare financial managers in Alabama; with the Duke Endowment's Conference on Small and Rural Hospitals; with VHA Georgia; the University of Missouri; and hospitals and systems in Canton and Licking, Ohio; Duluth, Minnesota; Cap Girardeau, Missouri; Lancaster, Pennsylvania; and Yakima Valley, Washington; among others.

The most promising way out of the trap is partnership, both with other larger healthcare organizations and networks, and with other community interests, such as local "community building" organizations, churches, and employers.

The Health Research & Educational Trust and Hospitals in Pursuit of Excellence, two projects of the American Hospital Association, released a report in 2013 that amounted to a detailed how-to guide: "The Role of Small and Rural Hospitals and Care Systems in Effective Population Health Partnerships." The guide includes checklists for everything your need to do to partner for population health.[121]

Attention rural healthcare leaders! Here is a very helpful resource: "The Role of Small and Rural Hospitals and Care Systems in Effective Population Health Partnerships," from the Health Research & Educational Trust and Hospitals in Pursuit of Excellence, American Hospital Association

Special Focus: Behavioral Health

If you are looking for savings, this is where the money is. If you are looking for better, earlier, more effective healthcare, that's where the big opportunities are. Behavioral health has to form a big piece of any strategy for building better and cheaper healthcare.

---

121 American Hospital Association, "The Role of Small and Rural Hospitals and Care Systems in Effective Population Health Partnerships," Health Research & Educational Trust and Hospitals in Pursuit of Excellence, June 2013. Available at: http://www.hpoe.org/resources/hpoehretaha-guides/1385

The problem: Some 70 to 80 percent of healthcare costs are associated with behavioral problems, including addictions, accidents and violence fueled by addictions, and domestic violence, as well as the more chronic vectors such as smoking, poor diet, and lack of exercise. A study of "super users" who show up in emergency departments more than 10 times in one year showed that 79 percent have behavioral health issues, and 45 percent have substance abuse issues.[122] How we think and feel has enormous impact on our overall health.

Yet in healthcare we tend to shove behavioral health to the side. Over the last 30 years, as healthcare costs have climbed year after year, the amount of our national economy devoted to behavioral health care started small and has gotten smaller.

Some of the reasons are good news, such as the introduction of more effective short-term behavioral therapies, and better anti-depressants and anti-psychotics. Other reasons are more brutal realities, including shredded state budgets, Medicaid cutbacks, and more people who simply don't seek care because it is not available or they can't afford it. As access to actual treatment has dropped, the main thing we now do with mentally ill people is arrest them when they act out, and then treat them cruelly in jail and prison. The majority of people in U.S. prisons and jails have some kind of mental problem serious enough to call for treatment, and few of them receive it.[123]

At the same time, medical doctors tend to feel that there is not much to be done, and it's not their department anyway. They are here to heal the liver disease, not to discover the roots of alcohol overuse; to set the broken bones, not to inquire into the domestic violence or reckless inattention that broke them. Healthcare executives have tended to see mental health care as a tar pit, a hopeless and everlasting money drain

---

122 Raths D, "States Use Big Data to Target Hospital Super-Users," GovTech, April 3 2014. Available at: http://www.govtech.com/health/States-Turn-to-GIS-Analytics-to-Target-Hospital-Super-Users.html

123 Williams T, "Mentally Ill Inmates Are Routinely Physically Abused, Study Says," *New York Times*, May 12, 2015. Available at: http://www.nytimes.com/2015/05/12/us/mentally-ill-prison-inmates-are-routinely-physically-abused-study-says.html

Human Rights Watch report: "Callous and Cruel: Use of Force against Inmates with Mental Disabilities in US Jails and Prisons," May 12, 2015. Available at: http://www.hrw.org/reports/2015/05/12/callous-and-cruel

from which they can never extract enough reimbursement. But the tables have turned. Behavioral health care is now where big savings and improvements in outcome can be found.

What's happening now: Several pieces of legislation, including the ACA, have mandated "parity," which means that mental health care must be covered to a level at least 80 percent of what physical health care is. [124] Healthcare insurers and providers have been slow to respond, but for the first time in decades more money is flowing into mental health care. Yet still healthcare organizations tend to see behavioral health as something at which they are not competent and that has the potential to drain them of their resources. So they often subcontract the services to a behavioral health "carveout," an independent company that specializes in delivering care and managing symptoms. Large institutions and networks often relegate it to a separate department with its own separate records and billing.

They are missing a huge opportunity.

The big opportunity in mental health

If you are at risk for the health of a population, if your bottom line gets better when the people you serve get better, the big opportunity is to seek out people with mental and behavioral problems and help them, and to incorporate that help directly into your workflow.

Why?

Level one: Improving physical medicine. When you do treat the mental and physical problems at the same time, your patients have shorter lengths of stay, fewer re-admits, lower infection and re-infection rates, all down the line. It's a big lever. [125]

---

124 Humphreys K, "We just had the best two months in the history of U.S. mental-health policy," *Scope Blog,* January 21, 2014. Available at: http://scopeblog.stanford.edu/2014/01/21/we-just-had-the-best-two-months-in-the-history-of-u-s-mental-health-policy/

125 Trendwatch, American Hospital Association: "Bringing Behavioral Health into the Care Continuum: Opportunities to Improve Quality, Costs and Outcomes," January 2012. Available at: http://www.aha.org/research/reports/tw/12jan-tw-behavhealth.pdf

Level two: Driving down costs. Seeking out people with mental and behavioral problems, and providing care that is truly and easily available and affordable for them, can play a big part in keeping them out of your emergency department in the first place.

But simply having mental health services is not enough. If you build it they will not come. The new image of patients as consumers, as involved shoppers, doesn't work so well with people who have behavioral problems. Think about the hoops patients have to jump through in order to use your services. They have to:

1) understand that they have a problem (many feel that it's everyone else that has a problem),
2) identify the problem as a mental health problem,
3) be willing to ask for help,
4) know that there are people who could help them,
5) be able to locate those people in the massive scary bureaucratic dogpile that is healthcare,
6) realize that they are covered for the care in a way that they can afford, and
7) bootstrap themselves past their depression or anxiety (or other symptom) enough to pick up the phone and make an appointment,
8) then actually keep the appointment, go somewhere unfamiliar and institutional,
9) have the right insurance card, and go through the proper paperwork.

That's a lot to ask of someone whose executive functions are already impaired or who have tried before and failed to get the help they needed. If you are really going to work with people effectively enough to change the cost profile of the population you serve, you can't wait for them. You have to use every opportunity to find them. Remember, it's taken a long time to disillusion your customers, it's going to take some effort to recruit them. You have to show up in their lives somehow and let them know that you can help them.

Level three: Merging physical medicine and mental healthcare. At the core, the problem is that even when your patients show up on your doorstep, they have to decide ahead of time which doorstep: Is this a mental or physical problem? Where do I ask for help? What kind of help do I need? Where will they believe me?

They have to self-diagnose and they have to make a strategic decision, based on how they're feeling and based on the politics of healthcare. Stigma deforms the simplest of choices about behavioral health complaints, and huge costs threaten when most medical problems loom. Most patients (most of us humans) don't really know, can't really know what's going to be best for them, because the causes of mental difficulties are too numerous and too varied to identify easily. So far, a simple "I feel terrible" has not been on the menu of choices; historically, it's been a crapshoot what kind of care such a patient will get, partly because it has depended so much on which door they chose to enter and which practitioner of which specialty they say it to.

Yet "I feel terrible" is actually the right answer for many potential behavioral health patients, and certainly for the majority of patients who spend the most healthcare resources, who need the most help. Discovering the nature of the problem requires more open-mindedness on the part of clinicians and patients than it ever has before. Why?

We are learning vastly more these days about the intimate entanglement of the mind and body. Separating the two makes it impossible to get a real, full diagnosis and a real, full treatment plan for mind or body, as though we could separate them.

Besides the huge impact of mindset on patients' ability to care for themselves (control their blood sugar, control their addictions), consider such emerging facts as:

- The makeup of your gut biome (the bacteria in your intestines) can actually change your thinking.[126]
- Your mind is constantly influencing your digestion patterns and vice versa.

---

126 Multiple studies cited in Nett A. "Heal Your Gut, Heal Your Brain," California Center for Functional Medicine, April 28, 2015. Available at http://chriskresser.com/heal-your-gut-heal-your-brain/

- Medical conditions create cognitive problems, such as the "pump head" cognitive deficit after stopped-heart surgery
- Brain inflammation causes physical illness

This is a very small part of what we are learning. An emerging field of research and evidence, the field of functional medicine, is starting to unravel these complex mind-body interactions. Recognizing this new opportunity, the Cleveland Clinic has just opened a Department of Functional Medicine, a pioneering step in bringing functional medicine into mainstream medicine. This is one of many important steps in giving the patient one door, one easy door, to walk through, instead of a maze of hallways and color coded tiles on floor.

What we need to learn
Giving the patient one door is just the half of it.

In the past, when we sent the patient off to the Psych Department to manage their symptoms, we lost our ability to learn enough about what was causing the symptoms, making it impossible to intervene in an efficient, successful, and cost-effective way. By giving the patient one door to enter, we're not just making it easier for the patient, we are setting the stage to learn from an integrated discovery process.

When treatment teams combine behavioral and medical care, the questions get much more interesting. As teams track each patient's process from beginning to end, team members train each other to be curious about what is actually going on, and to pick up on data each of them might miss, had they been working on their own. What a patient might report to her internist as a simple failure to miss the bus, can take on much more significance if someone else notices increasing mental difficulties due to a subtle overdose on a psych medication. Catching these stray bits of information becomes much more likely, less a matter of chance, if behavioral health and medical are asking the questions.

Which comes to a key point often missed in conversations about the role of behavioral health in the Next Healthcare. A true continuity of care is the single biggest opportunity for Big Data to do its magic. If we ask the right questions and keep track of what we're seeing in a queriable database, we will be able to learn much more than ever about the complexities of mind/body issues and how to intervene quickly and effectively.

What healthcare can do

As healthcare organizations increasingly move to payment models that reward them for taking better care of their patients and saving money at the same time, getting mental health right is a high-leverage strategy. Here are specific parts of that strategy:

- Demand that health plans, employers, and other purchasers truly cover behavioral health according to the parity laws.
- Base your primary care on comprehensive care teams working across the continuum of care.
- Find or fund behavior-change programs that help people especially with the most common and damaging behavior problems, such as addictions.
- Incorporate behavioral healthcare directly into the normal clinical workflow.
- Do this without regard to whether the patient is covered for mental health care, regardless of what you can directly bill for, because it lowers your cost structure to do it for everyone.
- Go deeper by funding and implementing a capacity for functional medicine within your system.
- Get Big Data working for you. Set up your record keeping to track what you actually learn from each of these contacts, behaviorally and medically. You will probably find patterns in usage and diagnosis that will tell you a lot about how behavioral intervention can help you lower costs on the medical side, and how recidivism — for both medical and behavioral health issues — can be reduced more quickly as you discover more about the medical conditions contributing to mental illness.

You can see these dynamics in action in many examples in this book. It's why the Vermont Blueprint integrates behavioral health directly into the care team, as does the Atlantic City Special Care Unit (both discussed in "Lever 5: Targeting"), and Mayo Clinic in Rochester, Minnesota, for the 140,000 patients in its primary care program.[127]

People in need of behavioral healthcare mostly show up in your system in two ways: through the Emergency Department and through your primary care network. Some systems across the country have put a mental health office in the ED, with mental health triage taking place before the ED doc even gets to the patient in most cases. They often have quiet rooms where such patients can wait so that the stress, noise and overstimulus of the ED does not exacerbate the crisis they are already in. The results of these measures can be dramatic. St. Anthony's in Oklahoma City, for instance, found that besides getting better, faster care to those patients who need it, this program cut the wait time for all patients nearly in half. And even while the ED has seen more volume, admissions from the ED to the hospital have dropped 12 to 20 percent.[128]

The American Hospital Association published four case studies illustrating these initiatives in spring of 2015 in an excellent article by Geri Aston.[129] For instance, Montefiore Health System in New York is rolling out a program of installing social workers and psychiatrists in all 23 of its primary care sites. Patients at every visit (or at least once a year) take a quick two-question screen for depression. If they score positive for depression on that, they answer another nine questions. If that comes up positive, they talk to the social worker, usually right in the same visit. The social worker talks to the patient, does a full evaluation, and consults with the psychiatrist to see if the patient needs to be referred on. The social workers can often do basic therapy themselves centered around life skills and problem solving. The primary care physician can handle prescriptions for common problems, and the psychiatrist sees those in need of deeper help.

---

127 Trendwatch, American Hospital Association: "Bringing Behavioral Health into the Care Continuum: Opportunities to Improve Quality, Costs and Outcomes," January 2012. Available at: http://www.aha.org/research/reports/tw/12jan-tw-behavhealth.pdf

128 *Ibid.*

129 Aston G. "Four Ways Hospitals are Improving Behavioral Health Care," *Hospitals and Health Networks,* American Hospital Association, May 2015. Available at: http://www.hhnmag.com/display/HHN-news-article.dhtml?dcrPath=/templatedata/HF_Common/NewsArticle/data/HHN/Magazine/2015/May/cov-behavioral-health

Atlantic Health System in New Jersey has built out a continuum of behavioral help across multiple departments, embedding psychologists not only in primary care but in such areas as diabetes, pain management, oncology, cardiology, and bariatrics. Lori Ann Rizzuto, Atlantic's director of behavioral and integrative health services told Aston that normalizing it removes the stigma associated with mental health care and improves patient compliance with treatment. In diabetes care, for instance, "You have the nutritionist, the diabetes educator and the psychologist. It doesn't seem to be odd in any way because they're part of the team."

After a state mental hospital shuttered in 2010, 11 hospitals and seven community mental health clinics in the St. Louis area developed the Hospital-Community Linkages project. The network was built to fill in the holes in behavioral care, especially for the uninsured and people on Medicaid who don't already have a provider and who have a serious mental problem. On the ED side, the network formed a Behavioral Health Response 24/7 outreach team. The results in a few years have been quite favorable: Among the target population, a 47 percent reduction in ED visits and a 57 percent drop in inpatient days. For the Medicaid patients, the drop in annual costs for all healthcare averaged $5,450 each.

Functional medicine: We can no longer afford to wait until the onset of disease before we treat it. And we don't have to. Now, earlier signs can lead us to earlier diagnosis and treatment, especially now that we're discovering so much more about the mind/body interaction. The emerging trend is investigating the complex interactions of mind and body, and studying the dynamics of the body as a whole, for example, through the gut/brain axis, the microbiome, hormonal balance, and metabolic issues, like the role of diet and exercise. Functional medicine is an integrative field of research helping inform evidence-based practice, seeking out ways to reestablish balance in the body before full-blown disease process sets in. Practitioners include doctors of medicine, of naturopathy, acupuncture, and chiropractic, all of whom are medically trained and who are getting past the guild battles and sharing notes. (see "Lever 1: Shopping" for a full discussion of Functional Medicine.)

What employers can do

Behavioral health is a big problem on the job. A 2011 study of 2,000 employees in the UK showed that fully a quarter of them reported a mental health problem on the job. Another study estimated that in the United States alone, employees lost some 200 million work days, at a cost to employers of some $31 billion, due to depression alone.[130] The overall costs of poor mental health are estimated at about eight percent of the economy in all of the most-developed countries.[131]

Employers need to deal with this. Here's what you can do: Work with healthcare organizations that operate on the model above, with behavioral health integrated into comprehensive healthcare teams. Tell your health plan or design your self-funded plan to fully fund and include behavioral health.

What consumers can do

Be honest with yourself, as difficult as that is. Take a look at what's getting in your way, at what may be preventing you from feeling good and being fully engaged in your life and with the people around you. You may have gotten so used to being stressed out or overworked that you no longer believe you can do anything about the health problems that are causing or being caused by that stress.

It may be time to revisit your options because the treatment of addictions and mental illness has evolved in recent years. There is new research, new drugs, and new forms of psychotherapy that are more efficient and more effective.

The causes of our health problems are starting to look much more interesting than most of us have grown up believing. The new research on the microbiome alone may lead to breakthroughs in how we think about and treat illness of all kinds. Do not assume you know what's

---

130 "Should You Tell Your Boss About A Mental Illness?" *Scientific American Mind,* August 2014. Available at: http://www.scientificamerican.com/article/should-you-tell-your-boss-about-a-mental-illness/

131 Else L, "Know This: Better Psychotherapy Transforms Lives," *New Scientist,* July 15, 2014. Available at: http://www.newscientist.com/article/mg22329770.200-know-this-the-latest-psychotherapy-transforms-lives.html

causing what ails you. And don't assume the first doctor you talk to does either.

Talk with a physician or psychotherapist who can help you restabilize your life. Keep in mind for the longer haul that much of what we're learning has not yet filtered into your local medical or behavioral practice. By educating yourself and pushing for answers, you raise the standard for yourself and for your practitioners and you'll find better care, if necessary. That will be a lot easier to do, once you're getting more help and as transparency increases (For more information, see the Resources section in the back of this book.)

If you think you have no addictions (no obsessions, no trances, no part of your life that you do mindlessly, by rote, that you feel you have no control over, and that interferes with your life) you may be kidding yourself. We get addicted to a lot more than drugs and alcohol. We get addicted to food, sex, work, to the Internet, to gaming, to complaining and self-pity, to our own voices, to being right, all kinds of things. Every addiction remains out of your power as long as you try to hide it from yourself.

Think about the costs to you of the time, the relationships, and the opportunities that are just slipping away because you're feeling overwhelmed, and then get the help you need. Don't give up. Instead, connect with others doing the same thing.

Special Focus: Violence

THIS IS A big one. We can't talk seriously about creating a healthier America without talking about violence. I'll let American Hospital Association researcher Julia Resnick summarize the size of the problem:

Every year, about 56,000 violent deaths occur in the United States, 17,000 of which are homicides.[132] Homicide is the leading cause of death for African-Americans, Asians and Pacific Islanders, and for American Indians and Alaska Natives between the ages of 10 and 24; it is the second-leading cause of death for Hispanics of the same age. More than three women a day are murdered by their husbands or boyfriends in the United States. About 15.5 million children live in families in which partner violence occurred at least once in the past year, and 7 million children live in families in which severe partner violence occurred. Episodes of violence take a toll on our health care system, costing the United States $107 billion in medical care and lost productivity.[133]

---

132 Statistics from the Centers for Disease Control. Available at: http://www.cdc.gov/violenceprevention

133 Resnick J "Breaking the Cycle of Violence," *Hospitals & Health Networks Magazine,* December 19, 2014. Available at: http://www.hhnmag.com/display/HHN-news-article. dhtml?dcrPath=/templatedata/HF_Common/NewsArticle/data/HHN/Daily/2014/Dec/behavioralhealth-violence-resnick

Violence is the poster boy for problems that we in the healthcare world label "beyond my pay grade." How do you fix, or even affect, what is clearly a social problem?

You can't, at least not by yourself.

What you can do — what any of us and any organization can do — is gather and lead community efforts to address the problem, to help break the cycle of violence. Resnick addresses what hospitals can do:

> Some hospitals are reaching outside their walls to address violence in their communities. Organizations such as the National Network of Hospital-based Violence Intervention Programs (http://nnhvip. org/) provide resources and guidance for hospitals engaging in violence prevention. Last year, Community Connections,[134] an initiative of the AHA, highlighted hospitals' outstanding work to reduce violence in their communities. Other examples include:
>
> - **Children's Hospital of Philadelphia Violence Prevention Initiative:** This is a hospital-wide effort to interrupt the cycle of violence by addressing bullying, assault re-injury, and domestic violence. CHOP translates prevention research into policy, community engagement, and violence prevention and treatment interventions.
> - **San Francisco Wraparound Project:** Based on the public health model for injury prevention, San Francisco General Hospital and Trauma Center serves as a vital point of entry, provides mentorship, and links clients to essential risk-reduction resources to reduce violent injury recidivism (repeat behaviors) and criminal recidivism for young people representing the most vulnerable populations in San Francisco. The Wraparound Project operates on the belief that when a trauma occurs, it provides a "teachable moment," and an individual is more likely to change his or her life direction to secure better health and welfare for the future. Case managers work with victims of violence to establish trust and provide mentoring. Then, they shepherd clients to

---

134 Community Connections: http://www.ahacommunityconnections.com

risk-reduction resources based on a needs assessment and provide long-term follow-up from six months to one year.[135]

Violence is also clearly tied to substance abuse and behavioral health problems. It is a further reason healthcare providers need to get much deeper into weaving behavioral health directly into the patient experience, particularly in primary and emergency care. They need, as well, to practice "trauma-informed care," which considers the physical trauma an opportunity to help patients and their families not only heal the physical wounds, but find a way as well to deal with the post-traumatic stress, anxiety, depression, and substance abuse which accompanies and follows it.

They Roll Up Together
You know the drill by now: These seven levers are systemic. They support each other. Any one by itself will be ineffective in changing healthcare deeply.

So if people are acting like real shoppers, have the information, are shopping for real results, and we are helping most of them prevent and manage their preventable diseases and chronic conditions, where can we make the biggest impact? By targeting the few who really need most help — and cost the most money. That's Lever 5: Targeting.

---

135 Resnick, *op. cit.*

Prevention: The To-Do Lists

Purchasers (Employers, Pension Plans, and Other Purchasers of Healthcare):

- **Make health a thing:** Make healthy living a thing in the workplace. Make the health of your employees a group project. Talk about health. Encourage a culture of wellness around the workplace. Help your employees form groups for sports, for healthy eating and cooking, for hiking, cycling, rowing, dancing, and other activities. For morale, make all this as inclusive as possible. No shame, no blame. Everybody can do something fun, even if it's a short walk at lunch time.

- **Give health a spot:** There are likely some not-too-expensive ways that you can modify your facilities to help make health a thing at work and make it easier for employees to stay fit. For instance: Showers for people who cycle to work. A gym (if you are a large employer) or memberships in a nearby gym. If you have a cafeteria, does it offer healthy choices? How about your vending machines?

- **Your own doc:** Build an on-site clinic, or give your employees membership with a nearby direct-pay primary doc. It will help your people stay in tight communication with their primary care.

- **Target:** (See next chapter.) Find or create a program that offers extra attention to the five percent of your employees who use the most resources because of multiple chronic conditions.

- **Incentivized wellness:** The right kind of wellness/prevention program with the right incentives can drop your costs significantly.
- **Mental health:** Build in a strong mental/behavioral health and addiction component. This not only saves you money, it helps build better employees by helping them deal with stress, isolation, and depression; find better motivation; participate better in their medical treatment; and prevent their problems at home from becoming problems at work. Don't worry, there are ways of doing this that preserve privacy and make utilization feel safer.
- **Health plan with an alternative payment structure** such as the alternative quality contract (AQC) for primary care, which gives physicians direct incentives to work with your employees to prevent chronic disease, will help hold costs in line and drop them over time.
- **Healthy Communities:** Get involved in local "Healthy Communities" efforts. Health is social. The data show clearly that how healthy you are has a lot to do with the healthy habits of the people you hang out with. Helping your whole community have a healthier culture helps make your employees healthier, while lowering your healthcare costs.

Consumers:

- **Get a partner, get a posse:** It's hard to get healthier, and stay healthy, alone. Find someone to do it with — your partner, a friend, someone you can really trust. As the boomer generation gets older, we are increasingly hearing of groups of older friends forming health circles who not only help each other stay healthy, but will actually go along on medical appointments to take notes and to advocate.
- **Help others:** True fact: The most direct path to health and happiness is to help other people. Seriously. Put poor kids through school. Become someone's Big Brother or Big Sister. Build a community garden. Start a festival. Look in on a neighbor. You're busy, you've got troubles of your own. But nothing will

contribute more to your health and happiness than being a great neighbor and helpful friend. Love somebody.

- **Change your habits:** One at a time, one day at a time. Try this rule of thumb: If you do anything for 21 days in a row, it's a habit and you can do it forever.
- **Exercise:** Getting off your ass is the miracle drug. Doesn't have to be two hours at the gym every day, or even 40 minutes three times a week. You can do seven minutes a day — just seven minutes of vigorous exercise. It's not about sweating off the calories — honestly, the math doesn't work out. It's about changing your body's metabolism so that it builds muscle instead of storing fat, creates new brain cells, re-balances your hormones, all that good stuff. Stay active. Walk, cycle, row a boat somewhere, go for a hike, toss a ball with your kids, get away from your screens. Look at the sky every chance you get, and then make more chances. Go up on tall places and breathe. Walk by the water. Everything is better by the water. Dance. Dance even if no one else is. Sing. If you think you can't sing, drive around in the car and sing along to your favorite songs at the top of your lungs like my wife does. Get your body going!
- **Stay mentally fit:** On airlines, the cabin attendant will tell you that if the oxygen masks drop from the ceiling, put yours on first before helping anyone else, because you will be no good to them if you have fainted. Your mental health is job one, because you cannot help your kids, your spouse, or your co-workers if you are depressed, stressed, crabby, or addicted. And your brain can't do your body much good in that condition either. Under the new parity laws, increasingly health plans and employers offer some access to counseling and psychiatry, and every community has some resources, from community mental health to AA, to harm reduction, to volunteer peer counseling. Something will be right for you. Something will help. These things can be stubborn. Don't give up. Reach out. Don't cave.
- **Meditate:** Meditation is very simple. It's not some magic state, some special transport. You want the simplest version? Get as bored as you can possibly get for a while. Seriously. Try being

empty-headed for a few minutes. You know what? It is amazingly relaxing. Just sit down and shut up. Sit some place quiet, where you won't be disturbed. Doesn't matter how you sit, you can even stand or walk, but be calm and keep your spine straight. Listen to your breath or stare at a candle or watch the waves on the beach. You will immediately, instantly, pop up with a thought, a worry, and anxiety. That's fine. Just don't obsess. Say, "Oh, hello, worry." Or, "Oh, yeah, there's that anxiety." Then set it aside and go back to your breath or the candle or whatever. Hard? No. Impossible. It's just a training. Wait, wait, this is supposed to be about health, isn't it? Yes, it's about health. Try it. First time, just 30 seconds. Ramp it up. A minute, five, 20. Try it for three weeks and see what it does to your mental health. If you need to know more, one good non-sectarian place to start would be the University of California at Los Angeles School of Medicine's Mindful Awareness Research Center.[136] Along with its research on the benefits of meditation, it provides a number of free, recorded, guided meditations you can listen to. If you are Catholic, yes, saying the Rosary is the same thing. If you are Muslim, kneel and pray. If you are Sufi, dance. Get out of yourself for a while every day. Touch bottom.

- **DIY:** Don't ignore your health until you're sick and then go to the doctor. It's your body. Nurture it and protect it. Don't limit yourself to the orthodox Western medical world. Maybe you need acupuncture, or chiropractic. Maybe you need to change your diet in a thoughtful way. Maybe you need to train your body with yoga. The point is: You are your own doctor and your own laboratory. Try something, then observe closely what difference it makes with your weight, your blood pressure, your mood, whatever you want to change. If you want to search online for more information, you may be interested in the "the measured self" or "the quantified self." You'll find a world of people like you learning from their own experience and tracking the data. But you don't have to track a lot to improve a lot.

---

136 http://marc.ucla.edu

Health Plans:

- **Incentivized wellness plans:** Plans that reduce an employee's premium contribution if they simply work with a personal health coach and try to reduce their health risks show significant cost savings. If you are not offering such programs, you may increasingly find employers routing around you, because they see you as part of the problem, not part of the solution.

- **Alternative quality contracts:** AQCs and similar alternative ways of paying for primary care directly incentivize primary docs not for denying treatment, but for giving such good, connected, customer-friendly treatment that their patients actually don't need the emergency department or the surgical suite as much.

- **On-site clinics:** Employers' on-site clinics — full HIPAA-compliant medical homes with no co-pay right at the factory or in the office building — are increasingly popular, and usually seen as part of a self-funded plan. But there is no reason that health plans cannot build them into their corporate offerings as a way to reduce costs while increasing employee health and productivity.

- **Targeting programs:** (See following chapter.) Offering saturation services to the top one percent or five percent of health resource users has been shown to significantly improve their health and cut costs.

- **Health coaches:** Prevention is about getting people to change their lives — their habits, their diet, their attitude toward safety. People don't change their lives because an authority figure (or their health insurer) tells them to. They will work with a trusted well-informed professional who gets to know them and regularly spends some time with them. Many of these programs depend on contact with just such a health coach. Funding such health coaches through primary care services cuts costs and improves members' lives at the same time.

- **Behavioral health:** Health plans have tended to be careful and small about behavioral health coverage and efforts, focusing on how to keep costs for those efforts down. This attitude ignores the enormous impact that mental health has on physical health.

It ignores how great a percentage of hospitalizations, untreated chronic disease, accidents, and ED admissions have their roots in depression, anxiety, substance abuse, and many other disorders. Any program that is serious about reducing healthcare costs by reducing morbidity will focus much more strongly on aggressively helping members improve their mental health and control their addictions. This is the front line of prevention.

- **Functional medicine, and alternative and complementary therapies:** Health plans traditionally have defined their mission with an extreme narrowness: financing the use of strictly mainstream allopathic medicine for paying members who are sick. When the landscape of healthcare changes and health plans increasingly are making their living by providing the most efficient health and healthcare to whole populations, that definition must broaden. Many new and specific therapies outside those narrow boundaries actually work, have research to back them up, and almost invariably cost far less than surgery and hospitalization. A health plan that is serious about driving down healthcare costs for the populations they serve will get serious about financially supporting functional medicine and those alternative and complementary therapies which have proven their utility. The prime doorway into the capabilities of functional medicine would be The Institute for Functional Medicine.[137]

- **Apps:** Software cannot substitute for a relationship with a real trusted human health coach, but it can be part of the relationship, keeping the connection alive, giving members access to information, and helping them track their health and the health of their families.

- **Big data to understand the needs of populations:** In the Next Healthcare, health plans find themselves in the business of population health management — because they can no longer cherry-pick their markets, but have to take all comers. If they are going to do something about the health of any population they serve, they have to learn what that population's health profile and special problems are. Today we have new access to vast amounts of

---

137 https://www.functionalmedicine.org

data that help do exactly that. If you use this data only for marketing, you are actually missing a huge market opportunity. See the Resources appendix for some important ways to explore big data for your populations.

- **Healthy Communities:** Healthy Communities efforts cost next to nothing compared with the medical costs of a community. Many chronic health problems live in the community's social and economic structure. Shift a community toward a culture of health, and you drive down its costs and the suffering of the people in the community at the same time that you help give a different answer to your members' persistent question: Whose side are you on? Again, the Resources appendix has several places to get started on building a healthier community.

Entrepreneurs, Inventors, Investors:

The inventor/investor community can play a powerful part in prevention. There are already a lot of products on the market that help, but none of them can be thought of as dominating or saturating the space, or even their part of it. This is the land of vast opportunities. We have some resources to explore in the Resources appendix. But these are some categories to think about:

- **Apps and dongles** help consumers track their own health, diet, and exercise goals. There are obviously lots of these already, but the space is far from saturated.
- **Posses:** Apps, websites, and other technologies that help people form health posses of family, friends, and neighbors, then help them coordinate their mutual help
- **Healthy communities:** Apps, websites, databases, and meeting and decision software that help communities organize around health and healthcare
- **Population health:** "Big data" analysis, geodata apps, and other tech that help healthcare organizations determine the most cost-effective interventions they can make in the health of the communities they serve

- **Crowdsourcing solutions:** Apps, websites, databases, and meeting and decision software that help communities of interest organize around particular health problems
- **Mental health support:** Apps, websites, and other forms that help consumers wrestling with addiction and mental health problems
- **Healthcare navigation apps:**
  - Apps, websites, and other forms that help consumers find the best and least expensive healthcare in their area for their particular problem
  - Consumer medical decision support software to help people consider what their next step should be in dealing with their problem
  - Health insurance and financing software to help people compare all their options

Hospitals, Physician Groups, and Healthcare Institutions:

- **Population health management:** Investigate the special health needs of your population, asking particularly: What turns into medical costs? What would it take to reduce those costs? Develop preventive programs with others in the community. Don't assume that you can't make a difference. The Healthy Communities movement and the American Hospital Association's (AHA's) own Association for Community Health Improvement share many success stories of reducing teen pregnancy, drunk driving, addictions, and other risky behaviors in communities.
- **Primary care:** Build your patient centered medical home network explicitly as a trusted pathway for population health management.
- **Wellness:** Work with employers in your area to set up incentivized wellness plans tied to their health insurance.
- **Behavioral health:** Integrate behavioral health specialists directly into your comprehensive care teams and workflow, as well as into your emergency departments. Invest heavily in mental health and addiction outreach programs and community-based

programs, designed especially to reach those with the least contact with the traditional healthcare structure and the least ability to pay. Given the high contribution of addiction, substance abuse, and mental health problems to accidents, child neglect, domestic violence, violent crime, and poor self-care, you should view behavioral health as the front line for the general health of the populations you serve.

- **On-site clinics:** Get into the on-site clinic business, building and staffing full medical homes at employer work sites, billed on a cost-plus basis with no hospital premium added in. To the extent that you are at risk for the health of these employees, it's a better business proposition to take care of them where they are, at their convenience. Convenience is clinical. Convenience is preventative.

- **Healthy Communities:** Champion Healthy Communities initiatives in your regions. Don't brand them. It's not a marketing move, it's a serious move to improve the health of your region. Partner with employers, civic organizations, neighborhood groups, churches, and regional not-for-profits, and allow them to share ownership, or they won't play.

- **Alternative quality contracts:** Take on risk contracts at the primary level à la AQCs. If your primary groups are successful, they will undermine your acute fee-for-service lines by keeping people too healthy to be in the hospital. But you will also undermine the acute business of your direct regional rivals. And you need to get good at this, because this is the shape of the economic landscape we are headed into. This is the scoreboard of the Next Healthcare.

Federal, State, and Local Legislators and Policymakers:

- **Expand and re-shape Medicaid:** Expanding Medicaid can provide a strong economic basis for prevention programs in poor communities. Medicaid has almost universally been used only to pay for medical care for people who are already sick, usually waiting until they show up in the middle of a health crisis — and controlling costs by cutting people out of the program, throttling access, and reducing reimbursements. A more muddle-headed approach could not be designed if you tried, whether your goal is cutting costs or helping poor people. It is far more cost effective to channel Medicaid funds to nurse visiting programs, parish nursing programs, and others who know how to work with the local population on their health.

- **Support Healthy Communities efforts:** Such efforts exist across the country and around the world. They can be highly cost effective in meeting specific health goals, and they rarely get any government support. They could use not only cash but often local changes in policy to promote public safety, clean environment, and other determinants of health.

Lever 5: Targeting

Problem

HALF THE COSTS are used by five percent of the people.

Solution

Target the people who need the most help. Put healthcare organizations at risk for their costs, so that they make more money if these folks are healthier and will find ways to help them, in order to bring the costs down dramatically.

Half the Costs?

You read that right. Over any period of time, take any group of people (New Jersey steamfitters, the entire Nevada population, everybody you went to high school with), add up all the healthcare resources they used over that period of time, all the money spent on them, and you will find that the costs break down very unequally.

Let's make this a little easier to visualize. Let's imagine that we have 100 people in a gymnasium, and we have 100 bags of gold to distribute. I have given you the job of distributing the bags, because they're heavy and I'm lazy. I've got a hammock set up in one corner, and somehow I have scored a nice margarita (on the rocks, with salt).[138] I'm going to give you precise instructions about how to distribute the money. Got it? Okay.

First, pick 50 people at random and herd them into one corner. Once you've got them there, carry three bags of gold over there for them. That's right, half the people get three percent of the gold.

Now pick another 30 people at random, herd them into another corner, then carry 17 bags of gold over into their corner.

Right, 80 percent of the people now have 20 percent of the gold — the 17 bags plus the three bags.

Pick out 15 more people and give them their own spot in the gymnasium. Now carry 30 bags of gold over to them. Yeah, that's a lot. But just wait. You now have 95 percent of the people in these groups, but you have set out only 50 of your 100 bags of gold.

You have only five people left. Stack 30 more bags of gold over on the other side of the gym. Pick four of your remaining five people, and lead them over to that stack of gold.

What do you have left? You have one guy, and 20 bags of gold. You can stack them right here, at the head of the room. Now the gym floor looks like this:

People and money

Each human = one percent of the people.
Each money bag = one percent of healthcare cost and resources

---

138 Don't use margarita mixes. They are way too sweet. You want the right mix of sweet and tart. So a couple of big fat limes, or up to four smaller ones. Salt the rim. A jigger of a decent "silver" or "blanco" tequila, the youngest kind, no need to get fancy in a mixed drink. Half a jigger of some orange liqueur like triple sec or, if you want to get fancy, Cointreau or Grand Marnier. Half a jigger or less of Damiana (remember, though, that some guests do not like Damiana). A slice of fresh orange squeezed into the drink. A dab of agave syrup, stirred in. Fill with ice. Are you the same person who read the footnote about marijuana in the shopping chapter?

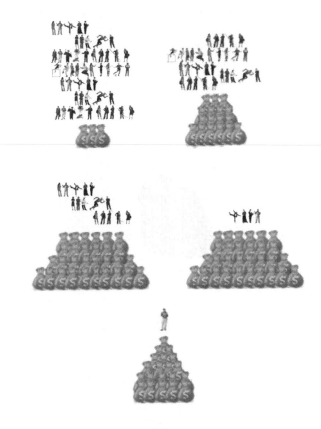

Whoa! Who is that guy toward this end of the gym with the 20 bags all to himself, and why does he cost so much? Who are those four people with the 30 bags between them?

Second thought, almost as obvious: You seriously want to cut costs in healthcare? Those people in the first two groups are not a problem. The people in the last three groups are spending most of the money. If we could move more of them more quickly out of that high-spending category, and prevent others from moving into that category, we've solved a lot of the problem.[139]

---

139 Stanton M, "The High Concentration of U.S. Health Care Expenditures," *Research In Action*, Issue 19. Agency for Healthcare Research and Quality, June 2006. Available at: http://archive.ahrq.gov/research/findings/factsheets/costs/expriach/

So who are those people in the one percent and the five percent categories and why do they cost so much? Good question. How they got into those categories gives us a clue to how to drive down those costs. There seem to be several different types of people and cases in the "high use" categories:

1. People with serious disease (such as pancreatic cancer or acute cardiomyopathy)
2. People with serious trauma (car accidents, violence...)
3. People having major preventive/ameliorative work done (new hips, knees, for instance)
4. People who keep reappearing in the emergency department and the surgical suite because they have multiple chronic conditions that are not receiving proper care and attention

These are obviously not hard and fast categories, but they give us a way to think about these really expensive cases in several ways: Are they preventable? Are they necessary? Are there less expensive ways to treat them?

Type 1, the people with serious diseases, are just going to be expensive. And actually that's fine. We might say that's what we have built this enormous complex of medical research and treatment for: to take care of you when you are really sick with something that is hard to treat.

Type 2, the serious trauma, is also going to be expensive. But can we prevent some of it? Think how much of this trauma has "alcohol involved," as the police reports put it, or some other substance overuse, how much domestic violence and street violence is grounded in mental health problems — and then review what we have been saying about the need to put mental health at the forefront of population health efforts. Much of this trauma is preventable through vigorous behavioral health efforts.

Type 3, getting work done like new hips and knees and complex spinal fusion? A lot of this type of work shows up in our lists of wasteful procedures that we spend hundreds of billions of dollars on every year.

Type 4, people with unattended chronic disease — most of their acute problems are definitely preventable, and their conditions are both preventable and manageable so that they never reach an acute phase.

Vigorous population health management pushed through real outreach programs and medical homes for all would virtually remove this category from the "high-spending" column.

In other words, if we got serious about it, we could prevent most of the need for most of the spending on those folks in the top five percent and top one percent categories — by keeping them healthier, helping them sooner, taking care of them in their homes, helping them improve their lives. Here is where we see that better healthcare for everyone (not just for those with the best coverage) is way cheaper for the whole society.

You see what I did there? We flip this problem into an opportunity, a big one.

> **Attention cost cutters! Attention entrepreneurs! By far the biggest opportunity for making a pile in the Next Healthcare is the same as the biggest opportunity for saving a pile:**
>
> - **Find the one percent, find the five percent.**
> - **Help them.**
> - **Be at risk for their costs (so that you do better if they use less of the truly expensive acute healthcare resources).**
> - **Put a crew on it.**
> - **Lower the costs dramatically.**

Aggressive and Personal

If you want to try this, you have to get aggressive and you have to get personal. People don't automatically take care of themselves. Your opinion doesn't count. Your opinion about whether they should take better care of themselves, or whether they have or can get the information they need, or whether their motivation is sufficient or where they could get more — just doesn't matter. Neither does mine.

What matters is whether someone who seems to be on their side, and seems to care about them, and has the requisite "expert" letters after their name (MD, DO, RN, PA, NP…) comes after them strongly and gently and persistently to help them. That's why the next chapter of this handbook is all about the biggest hidden and underappreciated lever in healthcare, trust.

Didn't Healthcare Reform Take Care of This?

No. Many people still don't have coverage, many still won't next year and the year after that ad nauseum, including millions with incomes under 138 percent of federal poverty level in states that chose not to expand Medicaid coverage.[140] Many more will be poorly covered, including some whose coverage does not include any hospitalization. Many will have such high deductibles and co-pays that they will act as if they have no coverage. Many will be unaware of what preventive parts of their care are covered without deductible or co-payment, or will be afraid that if they go in for the free part, they will end up paying for something anyway. So they will not take care of themselves, and will stay away from those who could help them.

Those who stay away from the system will be those who need it the most. They still will burden the local hospital's bottom line not only by showing up in the emergency department and surgical suites without the ability to pay, but in other ways if the hospital is in a risk relationship with the population — and more and more hospitals are. This means that the hospital or its system will have a tactical need to find ways to provide these folks care — early, attentive, preventive care — as close as possible to where they are. This may mean building free clinics in certain parts of town, or supporting nurse visiting programs that actively seek them out at home and help them.

In a fee-for-service system, patients who continue to incur high costs over time are not a business problem; in fact, if they have some kind of insurance, such patients could be thought of as your best customers. If they have no insurance, or if you are at risk for the costs and outcomes of a population (as in a capitated contract, a Medicaid risk contract, or a "mini-cap" per patient per month payment for diabetes care or back care, for instance), the situation flips completely: Those

---

140 A map of the states, as of this writing, that have not accepted federal Medicaid expansion money, with the population affected: "24 States Are Refusing to Expand Medicaid. Here's What That Means for Their Residents," http://www.whitehouse.gov/share/medicaid-map.

high costs become your costs, and the high-cost patients are a distinct business problem.

Numerous programs using long-term trusted relationships with real health professionals working in teams have proven the cost effectiveness of such targeted care, including the Boeing Intensive Outpatient Care Program, the Camden Coalition of Healthcare Providers, and the Atlantic City Special Care Center.[141] The Boeing program was a precursor to its present ACO pioneering program, mentioned earlier.

The consistent results across similar programs showed a 20 percent to 25 percent drop in costs for the targeted populations, including the cost of the more intensive care program. Since they generate 50 percent of the total costs, dropping costs for the high-cost target populations by 20 percent to 25 percent should result in overall drops of 10 percent to 12.5 percent for the whole population.

Let me teach a technical economic term, in case you don't know it. The term is "bupkis." It's from Yiddish and means "nothing, an inconsiderable sum." Or, as one healthcare CFO put it to me, "lost in the noise." That's what it costs to reach out to people with some smart prevention, or to treat them in a clinic, compared with treating them when they are hauled in to the ED comatose with something that could have been prevented or caught in an earlier stage. That's the relative cost. Crumbs. Footnotes. Bupkis.

What Can Health Systems, Hospitals, and Group Practices Do?

If you put your system at risk for the costs of populations in the post-ACA era but you don't do anything to give special help to the high-cost parts of those populations, good luck with that. As your fee-for-service reimbursements fall you're going to have a rough time staying within spitting

---

141 Smerd J, "Boeing Pilot Program Focuses on Medical Home: Initial Results Show Program Saved 20% in Healthcare Costs," BusinessInsurance.com, August 8, 2010. Available at: http://www.businessinsurance.com/article/20100808/ISSUE01/308089981

Camden Coalition of Healthcare Providers. Available at: http://www.camdenhealth.org

The Camden group and the Atlantic City group are also featured in Gawande A, "The Hot Spotters," *The New Yorker*, January 24, 2011. Available at: http://www.newyorker.com/reporting/2011/01/24/110124fa_fact_gawande

distance of a black bottom line. You need to give special help even and especially to the uninsured, because their costs will likely end up on your system's books anyway.

Find and go after that five percent, that one percent who are costing the most money. Some of the cost will be recoverable, some will not, but go after them anyway, because the costs spiral out of control once they cross your threshold. Find this semi-permanent five percent, one percent, and give them special attention. How much? More than seems reasonable. That is the only way to drive their costs down dramatically.

Many people, clinicians and citizens, will tell you that those folks are untreatable, because they are addicts, or you can't affect their behavior, and this and that. True of some, but it's a numbers game. When the Camden Coalition of Healthcare Providers began targeting the worst, most complex, most expensive cases, they were able to reduce hospitalization of those they took on by 56 percent.[142] Any way you add it up, that's a huge saving.

You can target in a number of ways.

Clinics: Forward-base clinics in the parts of town from which you get the most costly cases. Make them free or sliding-scale. You can find ways to help the Federally Qualified Health Centers that may already exist in those parts of town. You can subsidize independent free clinics that already exist — anything that will help the people who need help the most and have the least access to it. Some systems, like Spectrum Health in southwest Michigan, are setting up special clinics to go after and treat anyone who has shown up in their ED 10 times in one year.[143] Maryland's Anne Arundel Health System established a patient-centered medical home in an underserved area of Annapolis that had a large volume of 911 calls, a lot of emergency department runs and hospital admissions.[144]

---

142 Gawande, *ibid.*

143 Spectrum Health: http://www.spectrumhealth.org/body.cfm?id=677&action=detail&ref=704

144 Raths D, "States Use Big Data to Target Hospital Super-Users," GovTech, April 3, 2014. Available at: http://www.govtech.com/health/States-Turn-to-GIS-Analytics-to-Target-Hospital-Super-Users.html

Big data: You can use big data from geographic information systems such as Stratasan GIS; Explorys Population Explorer; the Healthy Communities Institute; and the free, open-source Community Commons[145] to hotspot your community, that is, find the sources of the most costly cases. Or you can do a first pass on it the way the Camden Coalition of Healthcare Providers started out, just by talking to the cops and EMTs that come into your ED, and to the emergency docs.[146] You can establish a crack Camden-style team to go after the 0.1 percent most expensive individuals.

Maryland got a jump on the problem through its statewide health information exchange, CRISP (Chesapeake Regional Information System for our Patients). As CRISP's director Scott Afzal explained to GovTech.com's reporter David Raths, hospitals are penalized for Medicare or Medicaid re-admissions no matter where those re-admissions occur. Until this changed, they had no way of knowing when a patient was re-admitted elsewhere in the state.[147]

Outreach: A well-designed, vigorous medical-home outreach program, staffed with real humans in the community, run out of clinics and primary care offices in the community, will do the same thing without the market segmentation. If you call everybody, you are going to spend the most time with those who need the most help. It's highly efficient. The Vermont Blueprint, for instance, added a five-person outreach team to major primary care medical groups. The cost of each team was approximately $350,000 per year, and those five people could serve 20,000 people since, of course, most people most of the time don't need help. So the cost averaged out to $17 per patient per year or, to use the technical term, bupkis. Peanuts. Lost in the noise. For that $17 they were able to drive down the overall costs for the whole population it served by 12 percent.

The Vermont Blueprint did not specifically target the top five percent, but if you call up everybody, who do you spend most of your time

---

145 Stratasan GIS: http://www.stratasan.com/healthcare-mapping-stratasan/
Explorys Population Explorer : https://www.explorys.com/
Healthy Communities Institute: http://www.healthycommunitiesinstitute.com;
Community Commons: http://www.communitycommons.org.
146 Camden Coalition of Healthcare Providers: http://www.camdenhealth.org.
147 Raths, *op. cit.*

with? Another Vermont program, the Vermont Chronic Care Initiative, did target the top five percent of Medicaid recipients, with similar strong, immediate, measurable results.[148]

The ACA put some money behind the idea. The Comprehensive Primary Care initiative is doling out some extra federal money to 500 practices in certain regions of the country, not as compensation to the doctors but to pay them to build more infrastructure in the style of the Vermont Blueprint. If the outreach results in savings, the docs will share in those savings.[149]

When hospitals get vigorous with this kind of outreach through their own clinics, some doctors will complain that the hospitals are stealing their business. By definition, if these people are showing up in the hospital emergency department with untreated chronic disease, either they are not those doctors' customers, or those docs are not doing their job. Steal away.

This is perhaps the most counter-intuitive idea in this whole handbook: Helping people more saves money. This is true, though, simply because acute care is very expensive. If we help people earlier, if we help them prevent acute episodes of their chronic conditions, if we help lower the level of violence, addiction, and substance abuse, the costs of healthcare drop by themselves. If we stop waiting passively for people to cross our threshold when they are really sick or suffering major trauma, if we instead begin aggressively exporting health, care, and attention to those who need it the most, we will do more than create a healthier, happier nation. We will also save vast sums. How much? **The techniques we are talking about here could give us all the healthcare we need for half or less than we currently pay. Just think of that. One side effect: The national deficit would disappear. By doing these seven things.**

---

148 Bielaszka-DuVernay C, "Vermont's Blueprint For Medical Homes, Community Health Teams, And Better Health At Lower Cost," *Health Affairs* March 2011, available at: http://content.healthaffairs.org/content/30/3/383.full.html
http://medicaid.gov/Federal-Policy-Guidance/Downloads/CIB-07-24-2013.pdf

149 Hirt T, "A Little Known But Potentially Fantastic Provision of the Affordable Care Act," *Daily Kos*, October 27, 2013. Available at: http://www.dailykos.com/story/2013/10/27/1250950/-A-little-known-but-potentially-fantastic-provision-of-the-Affordable-Care-Act
"Comprehensive Primary Care Initiative." Available at: http://innovation.cms.gov/initiatives/comprehensive-primary-care-initiative/

Special Focus: End The Drug War

ADDICTIONS ARE A public health problem. But the main tool we have chosen to struggle with this problem — criminalizing it and waging a hundred-year "War on Drugs" — only makes the problem of addictions worse, and is itself a far worse public health problem. The War on Drugs is worse than a failure. It is a public health disaster.

Think about these public health problems:

- a flood of addictive drugs completely outside of legal regulation and control
- overdoses and disease from impure drugs and dirty needles
- crime, violence, and prostitution from the need of addicts to pay exorbitant gang prices for their drugs
- violence of the drug gangs themselves
- addicts flooding the ED to get access to prescription painkillers such as oxycontin
- encouraging addiction to more damaging but more available drugs such as methamphetamines
- the spread of HIV and hepatitis C through sharing contaminated needles
- addicts avoiding healthcare all together, because their most obvious presenting problem makes them a criminal
- large portions especially of the poorest parts of the population put beyond any hope of involvement in real population health management because the criminalization of drugs effectively puts whole families and neighborhoods outside the law.

If you are a first responder, if you are in the emergency department business, you know what I am talking about. You recognize these people. They are often among your most common repeat customers — and that is why treating them differently is an important part of lowering health-care costs by providing better care.

It is important to recognize that these huge public health problems do not result from the addictions themselves. They are not caused by drugs. They are caused by the criminalization of the use of the drugs.

Alcoholism is a serious public health problem. Some 2,200 Americans die directly from alcohol overdose every year.[150] Much more importantly, read the police reports to see what high percentage of the reports on accidents, domestic violence and other assaults contain the words "Alcohol was involved." A century ago we tried to solve this problem in the U.S. by outlawing the substance. Didn't work. All it did was make criminals out of ordinary Americans and give a powerful business model to criminal gangs.

We outlawed recreational drugs at about the same time, driven not by any real research but largely by the rather spectacular racism of the first drug czar, Henry Anslinger (advocated in words so vile and racist I won't even quote them here).[151]

That hasn't worked at all, but instead of walking that decision back we have just doubled down on it, digging a deeper hole, putting more of our population in prison than any other society on the planet,[152] militarizing our police — while utterly failing to reduce the original problem that some people can become addicted to recreational drugs.

There is a growing movement around the country to legalize marijuana, and around the world to completely abandon the War on Drugs. As of this writing, 23 states have legalized marijuana at least for medical

---

150 Centers for Disease Control and Prevention, Morbidity and Mortality Weekly Report (MMWR), "Vital Signs: Alcohol Poisoning Deaths — United States, 2010–2012," January 9, 2015. Available at: http://www.cdc.gov/mmwr/preview/mmwrhtml/mm6353a2.htm

151 Quotes can be found in Sullum J, "Marijuana Prohibition Is Unscientific, Unconstitutional And Unjust," Forbes, May 14, 2015. Available at: http://www.forbes.com/sites/jacobsullum/2015/05/14/marijuana-prohibition-is-unscientific-unconstitutional-and-unjust/
Also in Caulkins JP et al., Marijuana Legalization: What Everyone Needs To Know, Oxford University Press, 2013

152 Population Reference Bureau, "U.S. Has World's Highest Incarceration Rate," August 2012. Available at: http://www.prb.org/Publications/Articles/2012/us-incarceration.aspx

use. Even the Texas Legislature, not famous for social radicalism, is moving forward a bill to decriminalize personal recreational possession.[153] Bipartisan groups including even conservative Congressmen have begun to speak out for decriminalizing marijuana to reduce tensions in our inner cities.[154] Polls show that a majority of the American public are ready to end the War on Drugs even against "hard drugs" such as cocaine and heroin.[155]

There are excellent, proven models for doing this in a number of places around the world, most notably Portugal and Switzerland. If you are, for instance, a heroin addict in these countries, you have a medical problem which you deal with by getting a prescription for your drug. Portugal strongly connects the prescription to social help, such as finding the addicts jobs and paying half their salary for the first year, or giving them microloans to start their own businesses. Portugal's addiction problem was severe. In 2000, one percent of the whole population were heroin addicts. Today, their heroin addiction rate is down by half, overdoses have dropped precipitously as has the spread of HIV — at a cost well below what the country used to spend on the War on Drugs. Switzerland, a quite conservative country, legalized heroin use 20 years ago, and has reaffirmed that stance twice in referenda that returned large majorities. Why? To clean up street crime, property crime, prostitution, HIV, and other public health and safety problems. It has worked exactly as planned. One fascinating detail: You have to go to a clinic to get your shot every day, but there is no requirement that you ever get off of the drug. There is no time limit. Nonetheless, no one who started in

153 Rosenthal B, "Panel votes to decriminalize small amount of pot," *Houston Chronicle*, May 4, 2015. Available at: http://www.chron.com/news/houston-texas/houston/article/Texas-committee-votes-to-decriminalize-marijuana-6242127.php.

154 Ferner M, "Legislators Say Marijuana Reform Could Ease Tensions In Baltimore And Beyond," *Huffington Post*, April 29, 2014. Available at: http://www.huffingtonpost.com/2015/04/29/marijuana-reform-baltimore_n_7171982.html

155 Drug Policy Alliance press release, "New Pew Poll Confirms Americans Ready to End War on Drugs, April 2, 2014. Available at: http://www.drugpolicy.org/news/2014/04/new-pew-poll-confirms-americans-ready-end-war-drugs
Rasmussen Reports, "7% Think U.S. Is Winning War on Drugs — Americans overwhelmingly believe the war on drugs is a failure, but there's little support for spending more on it to win," November 13, 2012. Available at: http://www.rasmussenreports.com/public_content/lifestyle/general_lifestyle/november_2012/7_think_u_s_is_winning_war_on_drugs

the clinics all those years ago still comes in. People tend to voluntarily titrate their dose, trade it in for methadone, then wean themselves off of methadone. They do not stay addicts forever.[156]

Looking forward, using legal and police means to prevent the spread of heroin use will become even harder, for a technical reason: Pharmaceutical scientists have engineered a strain of yeast to directly produce morphine and heroin in a process that involves zero Afghan warlords and in its basics is as easy as brewing beer in your basement.[157] The best prediction: this strain of yeast will escape the lab, and we will see homemade heroin within the coming decade. It's time to get out in front of it with legalization, coupled with regulation and real treatment for addiction.

At the same time, there are a number of true therapeutic uses not only for marijuana and cannabinoid extracts, but for a number of psychoactive drugs. We are foregoing the extensive research that would build out this part of our pharmaceutical armamentarium.

For the health of our communities, we have to get to a place where we can legalize, regulate and treat recreational drugs that are now illegal.

They Roll Up Together

To bring us back on track once more: These seven levers are systemic. They all contribute a part to the multifactorial equation that is change in the complex adaptive system of healthcare.

So people are shopping, they have the information they need, they are shopping for real results, we are helping most of them prevent and manage their preventable diseases and chronic conditions, and we are targeting the few who really need the most help. Okay, what makes all this work? Trusted relationships. That's Lever 6: Trust.

---

156 Hari J, *Chasing the Scream: The First and Last Days of the War on Drugs,* 2015.
"A War Well Lost : Sam Harris and Johann Hari discuss the 'war on drugs,'" SamHarris.com, April 7 2015. Available at: http://www.samharris.org/blog/item/a-war-well-lost

157 DeLoach WC *et al,* "An enzyme-coupled biosensor enables (S)-reticuline production in yeast from glucose," *Nature,* May 18, 2015. Available at http://www.nature.com/nchembio/journal/vaop/ncurrent/full/nchembio.1816.html

Targeting: The To-Do List

**Purchasers (Employers, Pension Plans, and
Other Purchasers of Healthcare):**

- **Investigate costs:** Use the big data abilities of your third-party administrator or insurer to verify that a small percentage of your employees drive a big percentage of your healthcare costs.
- **Investigate causes:** Without violating anyone's privacy, through your payment mechanism, you can find out whether these high-cost users have the kinds of multiple chronic conditions (including mental health and addiction problems) that could be improved with some help.
- **Investigate solutions:** Look into the kinds of intensive outpatient health management programs that have proven records in lowering costs by helping the most expensive employees stay healthier.
- **Apply vigorously:** Hire consultants who can help you implement these programs.
- **Join other employers:** If you are a small or medium-sized employer, look for an employers' coalition in your area that can collectively institute such programs — or start a coalition yourself.
- **Work with the union:** If your work force is unionized, work with the union to institute such targeted programs. Though they treat some employees differently from others based on their health status and their willingness to work with someone on

their health, such programs really are in everyone's interests — the high-cost employees, the low-cost employees, the employer, and the union.

Consumers:

- **Target yourself:** If you are having repeated medical crises that put you in the emergency department, you are what people in the business call a "frequent flier." If no one from the healthcare provider or your insurer is working with you, you need to get help managing your health. You need help from a case manager or health coach, a professional who will actively work with you over time to keep your problems from becoming crises.
- **Find help:** This will take some research. If you're sick, this is particularly difficult. So get help to find help. First, enlist the help of those who love you. If you are being cared for by someone in your family, do this together with them. Ask others in your family to help, or guide you to a support group, a social worker, a mental health practitioner, a local clinic, advisors at the local senior center, ask the health posse we talked about in the Prevention chapter. Once you have folks helping you suss this out, here are some places to call and ask if they know how you could get a real case manager to work with you:
- **Doctor:** If you have a primary care physician, call his or her office first.
- **Social workers:** They are often trained to help people gather and coordinate resources. If you are a senior citizen, look for a social worker specializing in geriatric social work.
- **Insurance company:** If you have insurance, look at the health plan's website. These days, a lot of them have some very useful resources, including programs to help high resource users.
- **Employer:** If you get your health plan through your employer, talk to someone in human resources who manages the health benefits. They may well know of a program to help people like you.

- **Online patient communities:** These online groups have turned out to be a more powerful source of information than any others, especially for people with specific chronic conditions. A list to start from is in the Resources appendix.
- **Pharmacist:** Your local pharmacist, whether independent or at a big chain store, is an often underrated and overlooked fount of information about programs available in your area to help you guide your health. Just go ask.
- **Hospital discharge department:** The discharge department of the hospital you keep ending up in should have a good idea what sort of help is available.
- **Federally Qualified Health Center:** There are over 1,200 FQHCs across the United States that are specifically designed to help people who have difficulty finding help elsewhere because they are poor or have no insurance coverage. The ones I have visited have been well run and highly professional. If you aren't poor, don't worry; they will be happy to take your credit card or your insurance, for prices that are often far less than other primary or urgent care outlets near you. Because of whom they serve, they are particularly good at knowing what resources there are in the community to help you manage your health. The federal Health Resources and Services Administration describes their mission this way:

HRSA health centers care for you, even if you have no health insurance. You pay what you can afford, based on your income. Health centers provide

- checkups when you're well
- treatment when you're sick
- complete care when you're pregnant
- immunizations and checkups for your children
- dental care and prescription drugs for your family
- mental health and substance abuse care if you need it[158]

---

158 bit.ly/FindFQHC

To find one, put terms like "federally qualified health clinic" or "community clinic" in your browser, along with the name of your town. Or go to: bit.ly/FindFQHC.

Health Plans:

- **Find the one percent. Find the five percent:** Use your mountains of data to identify chronic high resource users among your members, the top one percent and five percent in any area. The first, simple pass is to identify any of your members who has been to an emergency department or been admitted to a hospital 10 times or more in any 12-month period.
- **Offer them special help:** Offer special help to these folks. It will be different help for different people, such as a diabetes clinic for one person, and well-child intensive outpatient care for a young mother whose kids have chronic problems. You will be most successful if the actual care does not carry your brand. People do not generally respond positively to an approach that says, "I'm from your insurance company and I'm here to help." They are more likely to respond to an approach that says, "We see you have been having a lot of problems. We can put you in touch with a medical group in your area that might really help you, and we will pay for it. Would you like their phone number?"
- **Work with employers:** Work with employers to create intensive outpatient care programs for their most resource-consuming employees.
- **Work with health systems, physician groups, and clinics:** Work with medical providers to create the focused clinical teams that can provide these intensive outpatient care programs. Create new non-fee-for-service revenue streams for these programs, paying especially for improvements in measurable health status.
- **Fund targeted teams:** Work with other commercial payers, and state and local governments, to create funding pools to support

clinics and clinical teams to target those who need the most help, regardless of their insurance status. Over time, it will save money for all payers.

Entrepreneurs, Inventors, and Investors:

New technologies make mass targeting possible. Of the technologies we have been discussing, several categories are especially relevant:

- **Big data:** Without searchable medical records, health information exchanges (HIEs), and geodata systems, it would be much more difficult to locate the people most in need of help, and to maintain a consistent picture of them as they change location and slip in and out of the system.
- **Personal medical apps and dongles:** Once lines of trust are established, personal medical apps and dongles can maintain a much more constant and helpful connection with the high-use patient than simple relying on traditional appointments. This is especially true for this target population because, for reasons of poverty, addiction, and disability, transportation is often as significant a barrier to proper care as finances are.

Hospitals, Physician Groups, and Health Systems:

- **Find the one percent. Find the five percent:** Use your mountains of data to identify chronic high-resource users among your customers, the top one percent and five percent in any area. The first, simple pass is to identify anyone who has been to any of your emergency departments or been admitted to one of your hospitals 10 times or more in any 12-month period. The second simple pass is to ask the ED docs and primary care docs in your area to refer their worst repeat customers. Work with community aid workers, churches, and other community contacts to identify people in serious need who have not yet even shown up in the healthcare system.

- **Create special clinics:** Create special clinics built on clinical teams dedicated to these repeat customers. Work with the repeat customers regardless of their insurance status to lower the frequency with which their chronic conditions become a crisis. Create teams that have the manpower and tools to be very active in seeking out and helping people, doing whatever it takes, including home visits, translation help, even special mobile health vans. The return on investment is large.
- **Work with employers:** Create special intensive outpatient care programs with major employers in your area.
- **Create separate revenue streams:** Take these clinics and programs out of the usual fee-for-service revenue streams. Work with payers and employers to create separate revenue streams based on per-client per-month payments. Pay salaries to the clinicians on the team, along with bonuses based on reductions in ED visits and hospitalizations, and improvements in the measurable health status of the patients.
- **Put yourself in the addiction treatment business:** Connect this capacity directly into your comprehensive care teams' workflow.

Federal, State, and Local Legislators and Policymakers:

- **Expand and reshape Medicaid:** Specifically, use some part of Medicaid money to fund local and regional teams of clinicians to find and help the people who need it the most, whatever their insurance position. These are the people who are most burdening your local hospitals, emergency services, and first responders. No town would think of being without a working ambulance corps and emergency department. The flip side of that is: Don't wait until they show up or have to be picked up by the EMTs. It's much cheaper — as well as more humane — to find and help them earlier.
- **End the War on Drugs:** There is, of course, strong competition and uncertainty over jurisdictional issues. But even state and local governments can do much to decriminalize at least the medical

uses of marijuana, or the recreational uses as well. And they can lobby for a complete end to the militarization of the response to drug addiction, the so-called "War on Drugs." At the same time, state and local governments can beef up addiction treatment, especially though Medicaid.

Lever 6: Trust

Problem

EFFICIENT, EFFECTIVE MEDICAL care and prevention strongly depend on trust. Yet healthcare has offered less and less opportunity to build trusted relationships, especially with the patients who need care the most.

Solution

Turn that around: Use the trusted, personal relationship as the "mass-customized" backbone of the Next Healthcare.

Can't Give It Away without Trust

In the 1990s, in the wake of the failed Clinton healthcare reform effort, insurance companies began pushing "managed care," which would do everything the insurance companies had told the American people that the Clinton reforms would do, such as take away people's choice, come between them and their doctor, allow faceless and untrained bureaucrats to dictate their care, all that.

The fad began (as a lot of fads do) on the coasts, but all across America healthcare providers panicked, as they came to believe that managed care would mean that they would be at risk financially for the health of populations, especially of poor people who had not been insured up until then, and who were quite a lot sicker than their preferred patient population, the well off and well insured.

Leland Kaiser, the dean of healthcare consultants, a wise and compassionate man, deeply intelligent in how healthcare really worked and how much better it could work if it ever connected its heart with its brain and both with its wallet, was advising his clients to wade in ahead of the fad and figure out what would work to treat these populations in their market, to treat them efficiently and effectively and with dignity.

One of his clients was Memorial Hospital in South Bend, Indiana. Consulting with them at a board retreat, he rented a bus and took the whole board and the top execs on a tour of the poorer side of town, stopping to see a few highlights and talk to a few people. It wasn't the side of town most of them frequented. He told them they should learn about this side of town by giving free healthcare to 400 disadvantaged families for at least a year.

They took him up on the idea, and they learned a lot. But they learned the biggest lesson before the first client stepped into the first exam room.

This is how it went down: Back at his home in Colorado, Kaiser (no relation to Henry Kaiser, founder of the Kaiser health system) got a call from the CEO, who was frustrated and baffled. He and his team had worked through setting up a special health insurance plan, had printed out the forms, even printed the temporary ID cards, then set off on a weekend to walk the streets. It shouldn't be hard to give away something so valuable.

"Nobody signed up! We worked all weekend and nobody was willing to take what we are trying to give away for free!"

"Well, wait," said Kaiser. "Who went? Who knocked on the doors?"

"We did. My team and I."

"Bunch of white guys in suits from the big downtown medical center? Come to give away something very expensive for free? Right. Why would they believe you?" It was true. They were mostly white, mostly male, and they were definitely from a far different class than the people they most needed to reach, the black and Hispanic mothers and grandmothers who tended to be the managers of health and healthcare for their families.

Kaiser arranged a second try. He got the hospital execs to pull together a meeting with pastors from the black and Hispanic churches in town that served the poorer populations. When Kaiser and the hospital execs explained what they were trying to do, the pastors were delighted. "Sure, we'll go door to door with you. We'll make it part of the service on Sunday. No problem." With the pastors standing with them on the doorsteps and on the church dais, the hospital execs signed up 400 families in one weekend.[159] In the process, they learned an important lesson about trust.

The Memphis Experience

In working the "healthy communities" beat, you learn that lesson over and over again: You can't help people if they don't trust you. Your opinion of how genuine your intentions are, and how valuable the help is, and how they should live their lives if they would just pay attention and give it the focus that they should — that just doesn't matter. If you don't get their trust, not just their willingness to sit still and listen as if they are taking it in but their actual trust, you're just flapping your gums at a high rate of speed. All your efforts are useless without trust.

The Memphis experience sits as a kind of bookend to the South Bend experience, if only because Memphis' Methodist LeBonheur Healthcare understood this from the start. Memphis could fairly be described as the sickest city in America. It is certainly the poorest, according to Census data.[160] It's heavy on the black and poor population, heavy on the uninsured (and as of this writing the governor and the legislature were still tiptoeing around looking for some way that they could accept the federal money expanding Medicaid). Infant mortality for black people in Memphis is three times what it is for white people, as is the likelihood of a black person with diabetes to end up with a limb amputated because of complications. All that one can read about the health disparities between black and white, rich and poor, educated and less educated, apply strongly to Memphis, with high rates of high blood pressure, diabetes, cancer, and other major diseases among the poor and black.

---

159 As told to the author by Leland Kaiser.

160 Charlier T, "Census calls Memphis poorest in nation," *Memphis Commercial Appeal*, September 23, 2011. Available at: http://www.commercialappeal.com/news/2011/sep/23/census-calls-city-poorest-in-nation/

People who work that beat will tell you these high rates of disease are not just because many of them are uninsured, or if insured don't want to pay the co-pay or co-insurance to actually see a doctor. It is also because they tend to be private about health difficulties. They don't want some stranger, even a doctor or a nurse, to be "all up in their business." Many of them, as well, are deeply distrustful of the system. Segregation of the healthcare system is still within living memory. So is the ill-famed Tuskegee experiment, in which poor black men with syphilis were purposely denied treatment for decades so that medical researchers could watch the progression of the disease as they sickened, suffered, and died.

Memphis' poor black community, however, has one powerful asset: its network of churches.

When Methodist LeBonheur set out to try something different for the health of the city's poorer citizens, it turned to the churches. In 2005 it hired Gary Gunderson, a scholar of the interaction of faith and health. In what became the Congregational Health Network, Gunderson and Methodist employed trained navigators and enlisted volunteer liaisons in the churches to bring health information to people, get them to sign up for screenings, and help them learn about things like high blood pressure. They would work as well in the hospitals, visiting their members who were sick, and consulting with them on their release about whether they understood their medications, and whether they had someone at home who would help care for them.

In a helpful article exploring the Memphis model, *Salon* editor Alex Halperin wrote:

> Preventing and treating chronic disease for low-income patients is one of the most vexing and expensive public health problems in this country. Factors like poor diet and education, distrust of authorities and lack of access to primary care contribute to high rates of conditions that, once they arise, require decades of care.

Halperin sampled a conversation between a navigator and a volunteer that outlines that gap they are trying to cross with trust:

"People don't want you to know they've got high blood pressure," [registered nurse Carole] Dickens said. "It's already a silent killer. By the time they go and get the test to even identify, they're at stage four."

"A lot of people think that when God heals he don't send a doctor," [liaison Dorothy] Seawood, whose pure white outfit indicated her status as church missionary, said. "He does it that way sometimes, with the laying on of hands or by your faith. But God also has doctors out there. He's also got nurses out there. He's also got medication out there. I thank God for all of it. Some people think it ain't God."

"A whole lot of it is misinterpretation of scripture," Dickens said.

"They don't want anybody to know that they're taking pills," as if, she added, "that's a signal that 'I'm not trusting God.'"

"I can't understand," Seawood said. "When you say we have food to give away, there'll be a line down the street."

"That's right."

"For a medical exam ..."

"You can't get them there."

"You can't get them there."

The economic case for Methodist LeBonheur was straightforward: It was the top provider of uncompensated indigent care in the area. It could treat these folks expensively in its emergency department and surgical suites, or it could treat them much less expensively, and even prevent their disease — if it could find them first. And if the people would trust the medical system.

Gunderson collaborated with a dozen local pastors, who together crafted and signed a covenant setting out their intentions to collaborate for the health of their people. Since then, some 500 clergy have signed the covenant.

Halperin shows the results of the covenant and the Congregational Health Network:

The data is impressive. Methodist says that CHN members, many of whom are living with chronic diseases, are staying in the hospital for less time since they enrolled and the cost of caring for the same patients has fallen since they joined the network. A study of CHN patients showed that after discharge, a group of them stayed out of the hospital for a median of 426 days compared with 306 days for patients not in the network, an improvement of almost 40 percent — hospital administrators are watching readmissions data closely because the Affordable Care Act penalizes hospitals when patients are readmitted within 30 days. Over a three year period, CHN members also had a significantly lower mortality rate. Methodist says **CHN costs it about $1 million per year to run, not including outside grants, and saves the hospital $4 million in annual costs.** [emphasis added][161]

Can this be replicated without using church networks? Does it work as well using paid liaisons instead of volunteers? Many organizations across the country, such as Henry Ford in Detroit and Wake Forest in North Carolina, are trying variations on the theme — finding and enlisting the paths of trust into the populations that they most want to help.

The Efficiency Engine

Trust is the least understood business efficiency engine. Outreach that changes people's lives, gets them compliant with medication, gets them to eat differently or find a way to kick the addiction does not come from cold calling by unqualified strangers reading scripts. It must be built on trusted relationships, a nurse or doctor who lives in your community and knows you, calling up or coming to see you. Expensive? Highly efficient, because it works.

In the computer security world, a computer that accepts data from another directly, without any firewall or other barrier, is said to "trust" its source. Similarly, in human connections we accept information that we act on only from sources we trust.[162] The more important to us, and the

---

161 Halperin A, "It Really Does Take A Village: How Memphis Is Fixing Healthcare," *Salon*, September 3 2013. Available at: http://www.salon.com/2013/09/03/it_really_does_take_a_village_how_memphis_is_fixing_healthcare/
162 Brown and Duguid, *The Social Life of Information*, 2002.

more intimate the information and required action is, the more deeply trusted the source must be. Our health, our bodies, is about as important to us and as intimate as you can get.

Some studies have concluded that disease management programs simply do not work. But in most of these programs "disease management" meant having nurses or less qualified personnel in call centers attempt to change people's behavior over the phone. Do you change the way you live because a stranger calls you up on the phone and tells you to? Do you trust someone who represents the insurance company?

The best studies, clinical experience, and the record of such programs as Nurse Family Partnerships and the Iowa Chronic Care Consortium show that people trust someone:

- Who they believe is on their side
- Who knows them and has a relationship with them, or at least lives in their community
- With the credentials (such as an RN, an NP, or an MD after their name) to know what they are talking about

The Iowa Chronic Care Consortium, for instance, managed to lower diabetes events in the rural counties it covers by six percent. Part of their successful formula was to reduce the number of patients managed by each care coordinator to only 250, half as many as in other programs, and to use diabetes education programs that already existed in the patients' own communities.[163]

Nurse Family Partnerships have existed in a number of places across the country for decades, usually funded by state and local governments. Nurses in NFPs aggressively seek out young pregnant women in the community for special help and fundamental education.

How fundamental? One article about a similar program was headlined, "Don't put Mountain Dew in a baby bottle."[164] Seriously, that was

---

163 Lewis A, "Stop the Presses: A Disease Management Program Worked," *The Healthcare Blog*, July 30, 2013. Available at: http://thehealthcareblog.com/blog/2013/07/30/stop-the-press-es-a-disease-management-program-worked/

164 Browning F, "Don't put Mountain Dew in a baby bottle," *Salon*, August 10, 2012. Available at: http://www.salon.com/2012/08/10/dont_put_mountain_dew_in_a_baby_bottle/

a prime instruction that many of these young mothers had never heard. A recent long-term study showed that, over time, such programs reduce abuse, neglect, poisonings, and accidents by half — problems that would end up in the hospital emergency department as expensive cases. Counting those results as well as drops in arrests and other problems with both the children (up to age 18) and the mothers, the programs actually save governments considerable money. **In fact, the return on investment (ROI) is 570 percent — every dollar a state or local government invests returns nearly $6 in savings.**[165]

Despite this high ROI, Nurse Family Partnerships have continually struggled to find funding. In the Next Healthcare, in which health systems are often at risk for the health of populations, a smart health system would make a business out of it, finding a way to recoup some of that ROI.

Over time, the effort to short-circuit such trusted relationships has proven both expensive and fruitless. Real change in patient behavior happens only in the context of trusted relationships. The Next Healthcare is not a simulation, it's the real thing. It's what you would want if someone were helping you.

What Can Hospitals and Health Systems Do?
Build trust-based disease management programs and visiting nurse programs.

Study highly successful community-based programs such as the Nurse Family Partnerships, the Alaska Native Healthcare System, the federally qualified Adelante Clinic in Mesa, Arizona, and the Yakima Valley Farmworkers Cooperative's chain of low-cost clinics in Washington and Oregon. The Alaska Native Health System assigns patients to small teams

---

165 Bornstein D, "The Power of Nursing," *The New York Times*, May 16, 2012. Available at: http://opinionator.blogs.nytimes.com/2012/05/16/the-power-of-nursing
"Evidence Summary for the Nurse-Family Partnership," Top Tier Evidence Initiative of the Coalition for Evidence-Based Policy, January 2014. Available at: http://toptierevidence.org/wp-content/uploads/2014/01/NFP-updated-summary-for-release-January-2014.pdf
Olds *et al.*,. "Effect of Home Visiting by Nurses on Maternal and Child Mortality: Results of a 2-Decade Follow-up of a Randomized Clinical Trial," *JAMA Pediatrics*, July 7, 2014. Available at: http://archpedi.jamanetwork.com/article.aspx?articleid=1886653

of doctors and other healthcare workers, and evaluates the team according to how well those patients do. This automatically encourages the team to develop strong, trusted relationships with their panel of patients.[166]

Offer insurance yourself or in alliance with a not-for-profit cooperative (like Molino in many states) that is tailored to the low-income population, tied to the low-cost clinics, and shaped to finance the trust-based health management programs.

When you assume financial risk for the health of a population, everything headed your way is not a revenue stream, it's a cost. There is no doubt that everything coming your way will be easier and cheaper to deal with if you can get to it sooner. You must become your customer's friend, using real people (not just robo-nags and websites) and working through naturally trusted pathways in customers' schools, workplaces, churches, bars, police athletic leagues, and local hangouts.

What Can Health Plans Do?

Trust is the top strategic vulnerability — and the top strategic opportunity — for health plans. Most executives who run health plans are in deep denial about how little their customers trust them, and how huge a strategic problem this is.

What is the number one consumer need in healthcare? A partner they can trust.

What is the number one strategic problem for health insurers? For most, it is that your customers do not trust you. You can read it in scores of polls stretching decades. In a typical recent one, only seven percent of Americans say that they would believe something their health insurer told them, only six percent if it was an HMO or other managed care insurer.[167]

---

166 "A Formula For Cutting Health Costs," Editorial, *The New York Times,* July 21, 2012. Available at: http://www.nytimes.com/2012/07/22/opinion/sunday/a-formula-for-cutting-health-costs.html

167 Harris poll, "Americans Less Likely to Say 18 of 19 Industries are Honest and Trustworthy This Year," December 12, 2013. Available at: http://www.harrisinteractive.com/NewsRoom/HarrisPolls/tabid/447/ctl/ReadCustom%20Default/mid/1508/ArticleId/1349/Default.aspx

Their distrust is profound and it is based on experience — their own and that of their families, friends, and coworkers.

The lack of trust is a problem for health insurers in two ways:

1) Consumers don't want to be your customer. If they can find an alternative they trust more, they'll go for it.
2) None of the other strategies we have discussed here (such as prevention, targeting, disease management) work if they don't trust you.

Gaining the customers' trust marks the number one strategic opportunity in the health plan market. Any major insurer that could establish its brand in the public mind as being fundamentally trustworthy would gain enormous market share.

What is the consumer experience that causes this lack of trust? Rescission (finding ways to dump customers when their cases become too expensive) and denial of coverage for pre-existing conditions are both now illegal, but they are still powerful in the public's mind.

Under today's conditions, consumers have major questions to which the insurers have no reliable answers, such as:

- **Do you actually cover the places you say you cover?** (It is a common experience in the wake of the ACA to find profound gaps between the institutions and physicians that insurers put on their "covered" list and what those institutions and physicians say when you actually go there for services.)
- **Will you cover them next year?** (If you are renegotiating your "narrow networks" every year, you can't guarantee that.)
- **Will my specialist,** whom I have relied on for years, and whom you have covered for years, **suddenly be out of your network?** (Again, no guarantee.)
- When I choose to have an operation in an in-network institution, with physicians who are in-network, **will someone sneak in an out-of-network doc with a huge fee?** (Yes, this happens. In fact, it happens as a normal, planned business method worked out

by some physician groups, and propagated by consultants who teach them how to make more money — at the expense of the patients. Is this the insurer's fault? No. Does it damage the customer's trust in the insurance company? Absolutely.)

- Will you raise my premiums unreasonably?
- **Will you be raising my premiums forever?** Or at some point in all this talk of more affordable healthcare, will the amount I pay in premiums and out of pocket actually begin to drop?
- Will you find some fine print reason not to cover something you said you would? (Yes, health plans still do this all the time.)
- **If I have a problem,** if I get surprised by huge medical bills by fraudulent inclusion of out-of-network docs or by illegal balance bills, **will you go to bat for me?** Or will you make it my problem? Will you become a consumer advocate and use your huge financial and legal power to sue the providers and make them stop these fraudulent practices?
- **Can you guarantee** through my arrangement with you that I will not be bankrupted by disease?

Most health plans (and most healthcare organizations) have no solid answer to any of these questions, let alone to all of them. In other words, health plans' biggest strategic problem is that they cannot guarantee that the product they sell will actually work for its intended use: paying people's medical bills and sparing them financial disaster springing from health problems. Any company that sold cars or shirts or shaving cream or janitorial services with such a random chance that the product would actually deliver on its promises would fail so hard and so fast that there would be nothing left to remember it by but a smoking hole in the marketplace floor.

The customers' distrust is profound partly because these medical financial disasters hit people at the moments they are most vulnerable and frightened, battling serious disease. The amounts involved can be so large that denying a claim or dropping coverage on a specialist can change customers' lives, moving them into bankruptcy and permanent poverty, or forcing them to choose between their cancer drugs and a roof over their children's heads.

At the same time, this lack of trust is the most difficult strategic problem for insurance companies to deal with because it is structural. It is built into the company's legacy cultures, and their business models, which are largely built on:

- Narrow networks
- Micro-management of coverage
- Risk mitigation as an adversarial relationship with their customers

Large purchasers also don't trust the health plans (especially the for-profits) for purely financial reasons. They are not stupid, and can read the industry trends as well as anyone. They see lower Medicare costs per capita, flattened medical prices, and struggling medical providers. And they see health plans continuing to demand higher premiums. When they look at the health plans themselves, they see opaque bookkeeping. They see contracts and fee schedules considered "trade secrets." They see the health plans laboring under constricted MLRs (medical loss ratios) which allow them only 15 percent or 20 percent of the premium dollar for administration, marketing, executive salaries and bonuses, and everything else that is not medical. They see that the plans' traditional avenues of risk mitigation, such as rescission and medical underwriting, are now illegal.

As the CEO of one Fortune 500 company put it to me, "What's going on here? It's a chaotic market for them these days. It should be survival of the fittest time for them. We should be seeing consolidation, we should be seeing some bankruptcies. But all the big health plans seem to be doing okay. Their earnings are up, stocks doing fine, their forward-looking statements are optimistic. What's the deal?"

Purchasers are developing a deep distrust of health plans as reliable partners. They don't trust the numbers you give them.

In all systems, incentives work. For-profit insurance companies' profit, market cap, and stock price are tied to a percentage of the actual cost of healthcare. They have an incentive to keep their premiums low enough to be competitive in each market place. At the same time, though, they have no true incentives to drive the cost of healthcare down, but rather to keep it high so that the premiums can keep rising.

Increasingly, customers understand that. Both consumers and big purchasers of healthcare can see that there is no reason to believe that the health plan is really on their side in this battle.

Trust will remain a strategic problem for health plans unless and until some of them start doing something really different and new, paying for healthcare in ways that guarantee financial safety to their customers while actually driving down the real costs of healthcare. The company that figures this out will become the Apple or the Toyota of the health insurance industry. Those that don't will go the way of Univac.

So what could health plans do differently? Glad you asked.

Pioneer new business models: Abandon code-driven, fee-for-service payments as fast as you can. Try out different business models based on the strategies we are discussing here, so that you don't pay for waste or fraud, but give your customers what they need when they need it with speed and assurance.

The "narrow discount network, code-driven, fee-for service" Default Model used in much of healthcare now traps you into paying for wasteful services, because the provider assumes no risk for the appropriateness or effectiveness of the service. Yay, you got a discount price for a back fusion surgery for simple back pain, or a "full metal jacket" put into a heart patient. Oh, wait, too bad those actually didn't need to be done at all. These are medical decisions, yes, that health plans should not be making. But put the provider at some risk for the most cost-effective way to solve the medical problem (instead of just paying them for whatever they choose to do about it) and these wasteful practices will waste away, because they will no longer be a profit center for the providers.

The Default Model puts you in the position of constantly saying "no" to your customers, restricting their choices and punishing them severely for being treated by an out-of-network provider. Other business strategies (such as we have discussed earlier) leave the choice to consumers and make them your active partner in keeping costs down while getting the best and most appropriate medical care.

The Default Model also puts you in the position of trying to micromanage the medical process as the only way of controlling costs. Other business models leave the medical decision making to the doctors, while giving them no incentive to do anything more than is necessary and appropriate.

Drop adversarial risk mitigation: "Gotcha" is not the game you want to be playing with your customers. ("Oh, yes, a heart attack certainly qualifies as an emergency. That dying-and-being-jump-started-back-to-life thing is quite an experience, huh? And the EMTs took you to the nearest emergency department, as they should. And yes, you were unconscious, in fact technically dead, when they found you, so you could not have told them to go anyplace else. And then you were in a coma for 10 days. Unfortunately, there was an in-network hospital three blocks away, and according to our rules you could have gone there. So, bingo! Cough up $500,000. Now.")[168]

Treating your customers as adversaries (or worse, as criminals) is not the golden road to greater market share. It is an open invitation to any market-disrupting upstarts that decide to play on the up-and-up with their customers, that treat the agreement as it can be understood by the customer in plain language as a contract — and honor their contracts.

Give guarantees: When I buy healthcare insurance, what I want (and what I think I am buying) is actually pretty simple: I want to not be bankrupted by medical bills. Yes, there are now caps on out-of-pocket expenses, and health plans cannot put yearly or lifetime caps on what they pay. But due to balance billing and complex network rules and "gotcha" risk mitigation, people are still getting plowed under by medical bills.[169] Your product is paying my medical bills. Put a guarantee on that and I'm your customer forever.

Become a consumer champion: Some healthcare providers are using the trickiness of the network boundaries and balance billing rules consistently in a blatant pattern to go after your customers with crippling

---

168 Channel 3000 news report, "Woman taken to 'wrong' hospital faces bankruptcy," November 14, 2010. Available at: http://www.channel3000.com/news/woman-taken-to-wrong-hospital-faces-bankruptcy/29648000

169 Associated Press-NORC Center for Public Affairs Research, "1 in 8 privately insured adults under age 65—more than 16 million people—face major financial hardship as a result of medical bills," October 13, 2014. Available at: http://www.norc.org/NewsEventsPublications/PressReleases/Pages/national-survey-privately-insured-in-america-opinions-on-health-care-costs-and-coverage.aspx

medical bills. Along the way, they are eroding your relationship with your customers. You could regain your customers' trust by coming out swinging against such fraudulent behavior, using your legal war chest to file civil suits and criminal complaints, and your lobbying war chests to get state and federal laws changed to protect your customers from such shenanigans.

Go transparent: Health plans consider contracts and fee schedules to be trade secrets. Your contracts with hospitals, for instance, even forbid the hospitals from sharing information with each other about what they are paid. In many markets, physicians actually cannot find out the fee schedule that they are signing on for. And then the health plans turn to their customers and say, "Sorry, but you have to pay more this year. That's just the way the numbers worked out." Your shock and pearl-clutching when your customers and state regulators don't believe you is a transparent act that no one believes.

This is compounded when a company comes out with an average 29 percent increase in one year (as one company did recently), the regulators push back, and the company comes back a month later and says, "Okay, how about 10 percent?" And in the following year the company does just fine and makes a decent profit, leaving the customers and regulators scratching their heads and asking, "What was that other 19 percent? Were they just making stuff up? Are they just making stuff up now?"

When no one believes you, you would be better off dropping the charade. Sure, actuarial calculations are an arcane form of voodoo whose secret bone-shakings cannot be penetrated by normal humans. Nonetheless, the more forthcoming you can be, the closer you will be to gaining the trust of your customers.

None of this is easy. It goes to the very heart of your business model, your profit structure, and your corporate culture. It is very hard. But it is possible, and because it is possible someone is going to do it — and leave other health plans gasping in their wake.

Trust Is Required

Information includes not only data but attitudes, judgments, and perceptions. Information is less like water and more like electricity: It flows where the connections are strong. The name of a strong connection is trust. Whom do you trust? Who trusts whom in your organization?

Our existing industry and our organizations are built on distrust — between departments, between sites, between professions, between the suits and the stethoscopes. Perhaps the most bizarre manifestation of the communications breakdown in healthcare is the simple fact that, in most clinical environments, when multiple doctors are involved with the same patient, they do not actually talk to each other. The nephrologist, the pulmonologist, and the cardiologist write notes in the chart — often contradictory notes — but rarely actually confer, rarely have to deal with their divergent opinions and conflicting plans, rarely have to root out the way that their different lenses on the same problem might add up to a deeper insight than any one of them could have had.

Trust is the requisite lubricant of change. If you don't trust the riggers and your fellow acrobats, you are not going to step out on that high wire. For your organization to change and adapt, it needs trusted pathways of communication, trusted communities of practice that cut across the usual organizational fault lines.

They Roll Up Together
One more time, we rehearse the mantra: These seven levers are systemic. Together they are vastly more powerful than any one of them alone.

So people are shopping, they have the information they need, they are shopping for real results, we are helping most of them prevent and manage their preventable diseases and chronic conditions, we are targeting the few who really need most help, and we are doing all this through trusted relationships. What's the big tool set we need to deploy to make all this seamless, continuous, and way cheaper? We need Lever 7: Tech.

Trust: The To-Do List

Purchasers (Employers, Pension Plans, and Other Purchasers of Healthcare):

- **Shop for trust in healthcare relationships:** In shopping for healthcare, look for situations that use the trusted relationship with a clinician as the foundation of improved health. Disbelieve claims of achieving lower costs by not bothering with a trusted relationship with a skilled, accredited clinician. The costs may seem lower up front, but they produce no "health efficiency," the money saved by improving the patient's health over time.
- **Shop for trust in healthcare financing:** Do your best business intelligence on the insurers in the regions where you have employees. Do not do business with any whose numbers you doubt. Self-insure and re-insure if you can, using third-party administrators. This gives you direct access to the actuarial analytics you need to have trusted numbers.

Consumers:

- **Shop for trust:** In shopping for healthcare, look for situations that use the trusted relationship with a clinician as the foundation of improved health. Insist on a close communicative relationship with a skilled primary care provider, whether that is a doctor, a nurse, or a nurse practitioner. If you can't find one, keep looking.

- **Do your part:** Communicate with your primary care clinician, and take what he or she says seriously. In any visit, bring in all your questions. Write them down so that you won't forget, then write down the answers. Or audiorecord the conversation with permission.
- **Bring help:** It is easy to get a little "white coat anxiety" in a doctor visit. Bring someone along specifically to observe, write down the doctor's judgments and recommendations, and make sure nothing gets left out. Older people who do not have a spouse are now starting to form small groups called "health posses," all pledged to help each other look after their health.

Health Plans:

- **Pioneer new business models:** Abandon code-driven fee-for-service payments in favor of different business models based on the strategies we are discussing here.
- **Drop adversarial risk mitigation:** Stop playing "Gotcha" with your customers.
- **Give guarantees:** Your product consists of paying my medical bills. Put a true guarantee on that and I'll be your customer forever.
- **Become a consumer champion:** Use your legal and lobbying war chests to protect your customers from the shenanigans of health-care providers.
- **Go transparent:** The more forthcoming you can be, the closer you will be to gaining the trust of your customers.

Entrepreneurs, Inventors, and Investors

Examine the trust effect: Look at your ideas and investments and ask whether they support a trusted relationship with clinicians, or attempt to supplant it. Because of the clinical efficiency of the trusted relationship, this is one important way to judge whether the idea will be successful. If you're someone who tends to rely on yourself and not trusted partners, then get a truster to look at your work and tell you if you if it fosters trust in a clinical relationship. Don't fool yourselves; there is no getting around the need for this kind of human connection, but many ways to help strengthen it.

Hospitals, Physician Groups, and Healthcare Institutions

- **Make trust a system design imperative:** System design must conserve and nurture trust — between doctors and patients, between members of clinical teams, between different departments. It's hard to do, and easy to wreck. Hospital systems that buy physician primary practices, then move the physicians across town and assign them new patients (no kidding, you would be amazed) are throwing away the trusted bonds with the patients — and any trust that the doctors had in the executives of the system. Systems that routinely rotate clinicians through different jobs, and that do not allow teams to form and to work out their own assignments, are trashing the trust that could help their system work better, faster, and cheaper.
- **Reward teams on results:** Design pay-for-performance or other extra pay schemes to reward whole teams for working together productively, rather than rewarding an individual star performer.
- **Fire assholes:** Door, ass, bang. Fire them, or if they are not on the payroll, deny them admitting privileges. All the time, even these days, we continue to hear of physicians who yell at staff, throw things, make imperious demands ... These are rare people. Most doctors are not like this at all. Is it always doctors? Pretty much, yes. Almost anyone else would get fired for acting that badly. But in a fee-for-service system, doctors are seen as the rainmakers who bring big profitable cases to the hospital, so the ones with interpersonal issues are tolerated. Smart healthcare leaders will see that they destroy teamwork and trust. They are a huge drag on the efficiency and effectiveness of the team. Get them out

— and then solidify it in policy: People can play nice or they don't get to play at all. Young doctors coming out of medical school are better trained to expect and thrive on real teamwork, and healthcare managers have sometimes been slow to capitalize on this fact.

- **Invest in tech that nurtures trusted communication:** Too much of the tech that we have invested in actually reduces communication among teams and puts up barriers between clinicians and their customers (patients and family caregivers). Get fierce about finding the tech that helps actual communication, which is far more than the flow of data.

Federal, State, and Local Legislators and Policymakers

- **Make trust a system design imperative:** All health legislation and payment programs have systemic effects, most of them unintended. If a payment system, for instance, incentivizes numbers of patient contacts, but has no way to measure the depth or steadiness of the contact over time, then it is in fact disincentiving trust. Most policies tend in that direction, thoughtlessly encouraging healthcare professionals to weaken the bonds with their patients.

Lever 7: Tech

Problem

NEW TECHNOLOGIES — both personal and at the enterprise level — show huge potential to both reduce costs and improve quality. Yet so far these new technologies have done little of either.

Solution

Re-imagine and re-engineer these new technologies as the backbone of the Next Healthcare.

Healthcare Leaders: Why You Should Ditch Your IT System

So you spent millions to billions of dollars on information systems over the past few years, right?

How's that working for you?

For a large percentage of you, whether or not you admit it, not so well. What you bought needs some serious tweaks, re-engineering, re-thinking, re-vamping.

For an even larger percentage, maybe most of you, the best advice is: Junk it. Throw it out and start over.

Poorly designed and poorly implemented information systems are worse than useless, worse than a waste of those millions and billions of dollars. As we go through rapid, serious changes in healthcare, poor information systems will strangle your every strategy, hobble your clinicians, kill patients, and actually threaten the viability of your organization.

A lot of healthcare leaders dismiss the complaints about the new systems as the carping of stubborn technophobic doctors and nurses who should just get with the program. If you are tempted to do that, you need to take a step back. You need to get real. The complaints and concerns are too widespread, too deep, and indeed too frightening for that kind of blithe denial. And they are not just coming from disgruntled docs.

Dr. Clem McDonald of the National Institutes of Health, a true pioneer in pushing for electronic health records (EHRs) over the last 35 years, has called the current implementations a "disappointment," even a "tragedy." He is far from alone in this assessment.[170]

In the rush to digitize and automate, we've made a botch of it across much of healthcare. What was supposed to be a new fast track of efficiency and effectiveness has become a hemorrhage of money, efficiency, personnel, and the most important of all management tools: trust. You must deal with this, you must deal with it fast, you must deal with it effectively. The future of your organization is on the line.

Questions to Ask

Ask these questions about your electronic health record (EHR). Don't just ask your IT people, and certainly don't ask your vendor. Ask the users.

Does it slow clinicians' workflow?

- Is it transaction based, rather than patient based? If a patient, for instance, is admitted from the emergency department, is the ED information in a different record? If the patient is coding and your intensivist wants to know what the blood pressure variation was in the ED, does she have to close one record and go hunting for the other one?

---

170 Wall JK "The tragedy of electronic medical records," *Indianapolis Business Journal*, October 23, 2014. Available at: http://www.ibj.com/blogs/12-the-dose/post/50131-the-tragedy-of-electronic-medical-records

A *Medical Economics* survey published last February showed that over 70 percent of physicians would not buy their current information system, if they had the chance to make that choice again, because they hate the way it works. Nearly 70 percent have seen no improvement in care coordination with the hospitals. And 45 percent believe it has actually hurt patient care.[171]

Were clinicians involved in its design?

- Did anybody ask them what they needed in the major tool that runs their entire work life?

In the most notorious face-plant IT system failure, Cedars Sinai of Los Angeles outright junked a brand-new $34 million system after a physician rebellion in 2003. Cedars officials later acknowledged the system's many problems. Most of the problems seem to be rooted in the fact that Cedars designed it in-house, but consulted only a tiny fraction of the hospital's doctors in the design. They also did not beta-test it department by department before rolling it out to everyone in a "big bang" delivery.[172]

In a recent *Black Book* survey,[173] 98 percent of 13,650 registered nurses polled said nurses in their facility were never asked to help design the system; it was just imposed on them. As a result, 85 percent say the system is flawed and gets in their way, 94 percent feel that it has not improved communication among the care team, and 90 percent feel that it has damaged communication with the patient.

Do you worry about recruiting and retaining skilled, experienced nurses? In the same survey, 79 percent of RNs put the reputation of the information system among the top three reasons they would choose to work at — or avoid — a particular institution.

171 Verdon D, "Physician outcry on EHR functionality, cost will shake the health information technology sector," *Medical Economics*, February 10, 2014. Available at: http://medicaleconomics.modernmedicine.com/medical-economics/news/physician-outcry-ehr-functionality-cost-will-shake-health-information-technol

172 Connolly C, "Cedars-Sinai Doctors Cling to Pen and Paper," *Washington Post*, March 21, 2005. Available at: http://www.washingtonpost.com/wp-dyn/articles/A52384-2005Mar20.html

173 Miliard M, "Nurses not happy with hospital EHRs," *Healthcare IT News*, October 20, 2014. Available at: http://www.healthcareitnews.com/news/nurses-not-happy-hospital-ehrs

Does it require more work, rather than less, from your clinicians?

- Does it allow billing codes to be derived directly from the medical record, or does it make coding a separate activity — which often means a "coding assistant" hired just for that?
- Does it ask your clinicians to do more documentation?

The best estimate is that, on average, documentation demands have doubled in the last decade — and much more of those demands fall on clinicians rather than on transcriptionists and assistants.

A study by Woolhandler and Himmelstein in the *International Journal of Health Services*[174] reported: "Although proponents of electronic health records have long promised a reduction in doctors' paperwork, we found the reverse is true. Doctors with fully electronic health records spent more time on administration than those using all paper records."

Similarly, Dr. McDonald has just released a survey[175] that estimates these new systems add a full 48 minutes of work to each doctor's day — at a time when physician services are becoming a more and more scarce and precious commodity.

Does it hide critical information?

- Does it, like most EHRs, have a "flat" structure, in which the salient data is mixed in with tons of data that is not important for the clinical moment? While your clinician, in his head, is rapidly structuring the diagnostic information and going through his decision tree, is the information presented in a way that helps him, or in a way that fights him every step of the way?

---

174 Woolhandler S and Himmelstein D, "Administrative Work Consumes One-Sixth of U.S. Physicians' Working Hours and Lowers Their Career Satisfaction," *International Journal of Health Services*, Volume 44, Number 4, 2014. Available at: http://www.pnhp.org/news/2014/october/administrative-work-consumes-one-sixth-of-us-physicians'-time-and-erodes-their-mor

175 McDonald C. *et al.* "Use of Internists' Free Time by Ambulatory Care Electronic Medical Record Systems," *JAMA Internal Medicine*, Intern Med. November 2014. Available at: http://archinte.jamanetwork.com/article.aspx?articleid=1901114

- Is there a way for a clinician to flag, on the presenting page, in neon lights, an unusual but highly important piece of information — for instance, a patient's recent travel history from West Africa and his exposure to Ebola?
- Is it easy to get lost in the system, entering data in the wrong patient record or putting information in the wrong field?
- Do your clinicians feel that the software increases or decreases the possibility of "never events" and medical misadventure? Does it increase or decrease the clinician's and the system's exposure to malpractice suits?

The user interface is an art, and it is a big deal in medical information. Bad user interface kills patients and lands you in court. CRICO, the patient safety and medical malpractice company for the Harvard medical community, recently released a study[176] that identified 147 cases, costing more than $61 million, related to EHR mistakes — incompatible information systems, faulty routing on test results, faulty data entry, and mistakes in "copy and paste." That's one year, one medical community, one insurer.

How opaque is it for the user?

- Does it maintain different records for the same patient even within your system?
- Can other providers read the records from your system?
- Can your partners in any accountable care organization (ACO) read each other's patient records? Can they use the system to actually coordinate care? Or do they have use work-arounds — faxes and Post-It notes?

In the Black Book survey, 67 percent of the nurses said they have to use work-arounds to make up for the flaws in the system.

---

176 Ruder DB, "Malpractice Claims Analysis Confirms Risks in EHRs," *Patient Safety & Quality Healthcare,* January/February 2014. Available at: http://www.cci.drexel.edu/faculty/ssilverstein/PSQH_MalpractClaimsAnalyConfirRisksEHR.pdf

Is it secure?

- Can it be hacked? How easily? How do you know?

A survey by the Identity Theft Resource Center showed that medical records were the leading route for identity theft, accounting for 43 percent of all cases.[177] **According to the Medical Identity Fraud Alliance, the number of patients experiencing a theft jumped 22 percent just between 2013 and 2014, to over 2 million patients. Over 65 percent were out of pocket more than $13,000 to resolve the theft and regain their identity. Most of them never heard about it from their insurer or their healthcare provider; they had to find it out on their own. Only 10 percent felt the matter was ever fully resolved. And they do blame their healthcare provider: 79 percent say they expect their healthcare provider to protect their data and identity, and blame it when it doesn't happen.[178]**

Medical identity theft does more than damage your reputation, bother your customers and cost them money. When the thief is actually stealing healthcare by posing as someone else, it can lead to harming patients when new false information is added to their medical records.

Is it impermeable to data-mining?

- Are the vast amounts of data about your system available to you to help you analyze, for instance, where the outliers in expense are, or how much a given procedure actually costs?
- Can the software help you characterize all inputs and costs for any given procedure or class of procedures to assist activity-based cost accounting and lean efforts?

---

177 Ollove M, "The Rise Of Medical Identity Theft In Healthcare," *Kaiser Health News*, February 7, 2014. Available at: http://kaiserhealthnews.org/news/rise-of-indentity-theft/

178 Patterson A, "New Research Reveals More Than Two Million Victims of Medical Identity Theft Affected in 2014," medidfraud.org, February 23, 2015. Available at: http://medidfraud.org/new-medical-identity-fraud-alliance-research-reveals-more-than-two-million-victims-affected-by-medical-identity-theft-in-2014/

Interoperability

I've done this: In the course of speaking worldwide about healthcare, I have walked into businesses in Munich, Dubai, Beijing, Sydney, Tahiti, Cabo San Lucas, Amsterdam, London, Barcelona, Jerusalem, Toronto, Paris, and many other places, pulled out a credit card and paid for a meal, a shirt, a souvenir ... and the system has recognized me out of all the billions of people on the earth, and billed me correctly, in my own currency. How many times has that system gotten the amount wrong by an order of magnitude, or billed somebody else? As far as I can remember, never. Have there been security problems? A few, but the credit card companies have always made it good and sent me a new card instantly.

I have also done this, repeatedly: I have staggered or been carried into a healthcare facility that is not my own, but right here in the United States, and been handed a long form to fill out, starting from scratch. Fifty years after we began using computers in business, 35 years after the financial world hooked up digitally, 25 years after the Internet exploded into our lives, there is still no universal health identifier that I could give the ED docs so they can download everything about me. And if they had the identifier, the files they could access would likely look like impenetrable nonsense their computer system could not unscramble.

Through what lens does this even begin to make sense? Who designed these systems? Why?

In the Next Healthcare, which is built on population health management and seamless, ubiquitous care coordination, this astonishing question set moves to the fore.

Lack of interoperability is not just an inconvenience; it maims and kills patients. According to one study, "Up to 18 percent of the patient safety errors generally and as many as 70 percent of adverse drug events could be eliminated if the right information about the right patient is available at the right time."[179]

Care coordination is the whole idea behind accountable care organizations. Can ACOs actually coordinate care? In September 2014,

---

179 Kaelber DC and Bates DW, "Health Information Exchange and Patient Safety," *Journal of Biomedical Informatics*, December 1, 2007, Volume 40, Issue 6, Supplement, pp. S40–S45. Available at: http://www.j-biomed-inform.com/article/S1532-0464(07)00090-1/abstract

Premier's eHealth Initiative published a survey[180] of 62 ACOs. How many of them reported difficulty getting data from external organizations? Every single one. How many reported difficulty integrating data from different sources within the ACO? 88 percent. How about difficulty going beyond data to actual interoperability across all operating elements of the ACO? 95 percent. This is a huge roadblock in the way of any real, serious care coordination.

According to eHealth Initiative's CEO, Jennifer Covich Bordenick, "The cost of interoperability can be prohibitive for many organizations."

Why? Let's be clear about this: Interoperability and the secure, reliable, accountable exchange of data is not some kind of wild, impossible fantasy that vendors are struggling to make real. It is in fact the norm in electronic communication today. It's why you can put apps from thousands of different vendors on your iPhone or Android tablet and they can all work.

Some advocates of existing EHRs wave that all-defeating flag of the 21st century, security, along with its friends, privacy and accountability. They will tell you that the data have to be compartmentalized and hard to access to keep them safe from misuse.

This is so much hogwash and cornfeathers, limp excuses for not doing the job right.

You want to make a transparent EHR that is compliant with HIPAA (the Health Insurance Portability and Accountability Act of 1996, which has privacy provisions)? That is no larger a problem between institutions and data sets than it is within one. This is a bogus issue, a non-starter. It is absolutely possible to build a system that keeps individual patient data away from prying eyes that should not be able to see it, that logs everyone who accesses the data and adds to it or changes it, and at the same time brings it all together in one easy display to help any physician or other clinician work the case.

Imagine what the financial world would look like if its IT vendors had convinced each bank and brokerage to build software that would not talk to anybody else's. Interconnectivity is normal. The reason it's

---

180 Premier, Inc., "Accountable care organizations struggling with HIT interoperability, according to survey," September 24, 2014. Available at: https://www.premierinc.com/aco-interoperability-survey-9-24-14/

not normal in healthcare is that some or most of the vendors don't want it to be normal.

Here's one example, in a note from a clinician, of how incompatible EHRs slow clinicians down:

> One of my clinical sites recently changed EHRs. The theory was that someone would abstract the important information from each old EHR record when patients came in to the clinic for the first time after the new EHR was started. That works okay for some things, but I never know when I'm going to need to go back to the very first note to see which things were involved when a patient presented; or to want to count the cumulative number of milligrams of a particular drug a patient was previously given; or to verify whether a patient qualifies for a clinical study based on details such as how many other drugs have previously been tried (and being sure it was for an adequate dose and duration).
>
> The old records weren't imported wholesale into the new system directly, weren't printed out and scanned (and anyone who's ever had to review 300 pages of dense repetitive PDFs to find the needles in the haystack knows how that discourages you from attempting it at all), or printed and stored as hard copies. So now the tech support people have to maintain some degree of backward compatibility with the old EHR and forward compatibility with the new EHR. They are not happy, and nor are we who use those records. I keep one window open to the old EHR and one for the new EHR whenever I work in that clinic.[181]

Building good software on an enterprise scale for something as complex as healthcare is extremely hard. But this is not the hard part. If you are a software company working in healthcare, you can design the software to produce data to industry standards, with entry ports built in so that other systems can read it, just as my Mac produces .pdfs and .xml files

---

181 Diane Brown, MD, PhD, personal communication, November 22, 2014.

and .wav files that can be read by machines running Windows or Linux or Unix. You can build APIs (application program interfaces) into your software, sets of routines, protocols, and tools that allow other software suites and applications to interact with your software and access its data. Or you can make a different design decision, using proprietary coding that cannot be read by any other company's software.

Why would software companies make that decision and convince their clients to go along with it? Because they want the clients to stay in their walled garden, buying only their products. They do it for market share, that's all.

The idea that interoperability is difficult or impossible is a con. In a classic case of an industry driving government decisions, not the HiTech Act, nor the Affordable Care Act, nor the regulations implementing "meaningful use" have disallowed the con and demanded true interoperability.

We, as an industry, have largely fallen for the con. Some of the healthcare providers have been running their own con, trying to use a lack of interoperability to build their own "walled gardens" and gain market share. In a world of ACOs, population health management, and shifting partnerships and affiliations, that attitude is frustrating the doctors, hobbling new strategies, and killing patients.

Zane Burke, the president of the healthcare software company Cerner (which just bought Siemens, another major software firm), made a strong point about interoperability in an interview with *H&HN Daily*'s Matthew Weinstock:

> "We all owe it to the country … to really perform true interoperability and create openness…. You need platforms that don't just open up your APIs [application programming interfaces] but actually create ecosystems for other players … to perform well. We can't use the operating system at the EHR lever as a competitive advantage. It just can't be that way.
>
> "The industry community shouldn't compete on the platform layers. And we need our provider community to not compete based on connectivity of their organizations, even where they compete in their market. We need our provider community to

come together and say we need patient identifiers, interconnectivity, and interoperability to be ubiquitous across the U.S."[182]

It's Time

It's not like this is new. It's not like we didn't see this coming. I have been writing about and advocating for the digitization of healthcare for 30 years, as have many others. I have to tell you: We knew back then that interconnectivity through industry standards — and smart user interfaces that assist clinicians in their normal workflow rather than hinder them — were hard problems that needed solving.

It never occurred to me or anyone else who was writing about it at the time that the industry and its vendors would deliberately turn away from smart, clean, highly usable, highly interconnected design simply because of a fruitless quest for the lowest bid and a greed for market share. We did not imagine it because this deliberate turn-away would be so manifestly stupid, so wasteful of our money, of the time and talent of our clinicians, and of the lives and suffering of our patients.

It cost us millions to billions to get into this mess. It will cost as much, maybe more, to get out of it. It's time to quit digging the hole we are in, toss what does not work, start in again and do it right.

Where Are We Now?

Right now, at this writing, we are at some kind of hinge point. The HiTech Act of 2009 (part of anti-recession stimulus program) has driven the use of digital systems in healthcare from about 10 percent to about 70 percent. The first phase of the program demanded "meaningful use," meaning largely that healthcare providers couldn't just use the money to buy systems and then not use them. In order to not get penalized in Medicare reimbursements, they had to show in various ways that they actually used them.

---

182 Weinstock M, "Are Meaningful Use Numbers a Cause for Concern?" *H&HN Daily*, October 31, 2014. Available at: http://www.hhnmag.com/display/HHN-news-article. dhtml?dcrPath=/templatedata/HF_Common/NewsArticle/data/HHN/Daily/2014/Oct/ CIO-worry-meaningful-use-CHIME-blog-video-Weinstock

In the second phase (from 2012 on), though, the regulations were refined to specify exactly how the systems were to be used, right down to specific actions. For instance, it was no longer okay for the docs just to give handouts to their patients; they had to wait until the computer prompted them to. As one doctor and expert in practice redesign put it, meeting these new meaningful use (MU) requirements became "like [solving] some riddle or puzzle. Life is hard enough. Why are we making it so much harder?" As we approached the January deadline for qualifying for incentives under Stage Two of the MU program, 80 percent of the country's 333,454 eligible Medicare providers had qualified for Stage 1; less than one percent had qualified for Stage Two.[183] Even the Office of the National Coordinator for Health Information Technology (ONC) admitted that the regulations were overly "enthusiastic" and would have to be scaled back.[184] Whether they will or not is up in the air — especially since much of this regulatory regime has now been baked into other recent legislation.

But a true shift toward interoperability is showing up in various quarters.[185] The ONC has worked with 35 federal agencies to pull together a new *Federal Health IT Strategic Plan 2015-2020*[186] that includes a strong focus on interoperability and lays the groundwork for the early 2015 release of a Nationwide Interoperability Roadmap. This was backed up by language inserted into the "Cromnibus" federal appropriations bill passed in December 2014. Congress instructed the ONC to decertify any healthcare software that is not fully interoperable.[187] In March, 2015,

183 HIT Policy Committee, Centers for Medicare and Medicaid Services, "Medicare and Medicaid EHR Incentive Programs," November 4, 2014. Powerpoint presentation available at: http://www.healthit.gov/facas/sites/faca/files/HITPC_EHR_Incentive_Programs_2014-11-04_0.pptx

184 Wachter B, MD "RIP Meaningful Use Born 2009 – Died 2014?" *The Healthcare Blog*, November 26, 2014. Available at: http://thehealthcareblog.com/blog/2014/11/26/rip-meaningful-use-2009-2014/

185 For the current news on this front, go to http://www.healthcareitnews.com/directory/interoperability

186 Available at: http://www.healthit.gov/policy-researchers-implementers/health-it-strategic-planning

187 Slabodkin G, "EHRA Opposes Effort to Decertify EHRs Blocking Information Sharing," *Health Data Management*, December 18, 2014. Available at: http://www.healthdatamanagement.com/news/EHRA-Opposes-Congress-Effort-to-Decertify-EHRs-Blocking-Information-Sharing-49463-1.html

we saw the Senate holding hearings into the interoperability problem for the first time in nearly five years.[188] By May, a House committee was advancing the 21st Century Cures Act, which among other things would mandate steep penalties for using non-interoperable EHRs starting in January 2018.[189]

Meanwhile, in a private effort, the CommonWell Health Alliance, a group of healthcare IT companies, has been slowly expanding toward true interoperability between those clients that choose to opt in.[190] CommonWell has been criticized for high upfront fees, and uptake has been slow so far. On the other hand, Epic, the dominant company in healthcare IT, which has been criticized as the primary driver of this lack of interoperability, has developed and increasingly spread its CareEverywhere standard. This standard purports to allow permeability not only between Epic sites, but with outside sites if they follow industry standards. Because of the way Epic has built and customized its hundreds of sites across healthcare, though, the types of data that can be transferred even between Epic sites is limited, and even more limited with non-Epic sites. And one-way copying of data is a long way from true seamless interoperability.[191]

At the same time, a new and even larger effort has emerged that attempts to connect CommonWell systems, Epic systems, large private networks like Kaiser and Intermountain, payer networks, everybody across healthcare. Carequality, established by the not-for-profit Healtheway, is now in the pilot phase of connecting some 2,000 hospitals, 40,000 clinics, and 200,000 physicians through agreed national data standards.[192]

188 McCann E, "Interoperability (finally) takes center stage in Congress," *Healthcare IT News*, March 18, 2015. Available at: http://www.healthcareitnews.com/news/interoperability-finally-takes-center-stage-congress

189 Tahir D, "Stiff interoperability penalties in 21st Century Cures Act," *Modern Healthcare*, May 13, 2015. Available at: http://www.modernhealthcare.com/article/20150513/NEWS/150519953

190 "CommonWell Health Alliance and its Members Move Forward with Nationwide Expansion of Services," press release, November 19, 2014. Available at: http://www.commonwellalliance.org/news/commonwell-health-alliance-members-move-forward-nationwide-expansion-services-2/

191 Rand Corporation, "Redirecting Innovation in U.S. Health Care: Case studies," January 2015. Available at: http://www.rand.org/pubs/research_reports/RR308.html

192 Murphy K, "How Healthcare Interoperability, Data Exchange Move Forward," HealthIn-

Can Tech Drive Down Costs?

For decades, waves of technologies have washed through healthcare: robotic surgery, proton accelerators, digitization, ever faster and more detailed CTs and MRIs, on and on. Each new category, we are told, will Revolutionize Healthcare, making it orders of magnitude better — and even reduce costs by getting earlier, more accurate diagnoses and quicker, more thorough therapies. Yet the experience of the last three decades is that while some new technologies help doctors do better medicine, almost all new technologies add complexity and expense.

So what will it be? Will some of the new technologies now bursting into healthcare actually transform it this time, making it not only better but cheaper? Which ones? How can we know?

There is an answer, but it does not lie in the technologies. It lies in the economics. It lies in the reason we have so much waste in healthcare. As we have seen, we have so much waste because we get paid for it.

Yes, it's that simple. In an insurance-supported, fee-for-service system, we don't get paid to solve problems. We get paid to do stuff that might solve a problem. The more stuff we do, and the more complex the stuff we do, the more impressive the machines we use, the more we get paid.

A Tale of a Wasteful Technology

A few presidencies back, I was at a medical conference at a resort on a hilltop near San Diego. I was invited into a trailer to see a demo of a marvelous new technology — computer-aided mammography. I had never even taken a close look at a mammogram, so I was immediately impressed with how difficult it is to pick possible tumors out of the cloudy images. The computer could show you the possibilities, easy as pie, drawing little circles around each suspicious nodule.

But, I asked, will people trust a computer to do such an important job?

Oh, the computer is just helping, I was told. All the scans will be seen by a human radiologist. The computer just makes sure the radiologist does not miss any possibilities.

teroperability.com, April 14, 2015. Available at: http://healthitinteroperability.com/news/how-healthcare-interoperability-data-exchange-move-forward

I thought, Hmmm, if you have a radiologist looking at every scan anyway, why bother with the computer program? Are skilled radiologists in the habit of missing a lot of possible tumors? From the sound of it, I thought what we would get is a lot of false positives, unnecessary call-backs and biopsies, and a lot of unnecessarily worried women. After all, if the computer says something might be a tumor, now the radiologist is put in the position of proving that it isn't.

I didn't see any functional reason that this technology should catch on. I didn't see it because the reason was not in the technology, it was in the economics.

Years later, as we are trending toward standardizing on this technology across the industry, the results of various studies have shown exactly what I suspected they would: lots of false positives, call-backs and biopsies, and not one tumor that would not have been found without the computer. Not one. At an added cost trending toward half a billion dollars per year.[193]

It caught on because it sounds good, sounds real high-tech, gives you bragging rights ("Come to MagnaGargantua Memorial, the Hospital of the Jetsons!") — and because you can charge for the extra expense and complexity. There are codes for it. The unnecessary call-backs and biopsies are unfortunate, but they are also a revenue stream — which the customer is not paying for anyway. It's nothing personal, it's just business. Of course, by the time the results are in saying that any particular new technology does no good at all, you've got all this sunk cost you have to amortize over the increased payments you can get, plus the whole floor of the new wing that you've dedicated to it, and all those people you hired to service it and run it, and those physicians who make a good part of their living off of it. No way you're going to put all that fancy equipment in the dumpster and fire all those people just because the technology fails to do what you bought it for.

Is this normal? Or an aberration? Neither. It certainly does not stand for all technological advances in healthcare. Many advances are not only highly effective, they are highly cost effective. Laparoscopic surgery is

193 Fenton J *et al.*, "Influence of Computer-Aided Detection on Performance of Screening Mammography," *New England Journal of Medicine*, Vol. 356, 2007, pp. 1399–409. Available at: http://www.nejm.org/doi/full/10.1056/NEJMoa066099

a great example — smaller wounds, quicker surgeries, lower infection rates, less recovery time, what's not to like? But a shockingly large number of technological advances follow this pattern: unproven expensive technologies that seem like they might be helpful, or are helpful for special rare cases, adopted broadly across healthcare in a big-money trance dance with Death Star tech.

Tech Can Drive Down Costs

On the other hand, there are many ways in which new technologies can drive down costs, in the right context. Here are a couple of examples that use "big data." Remember the Alaska Native Healthcare Service? One feature of its rebuilt system is a "data mall" that shows each team in easy-to-use graphics just how they are doing with their panel of patients: hospital admissions, blood sugar scores, contacts — and cost. At the same time, it shows them how they compare with other teams. This frequently has a strong affect on the outliers, especially those who are doing worse than other teams, because they are all looking at the same data. Nobody wants to be displayed in front of their colleagues as the worst team in the place at getting people's eyes checked, or getting them in for prenatal exams.[194]

Or take Narayana Hrudayalaya,[195] a rapidly growing chain of hospitals and clinics in India, founded by a cardiac surgeon and centered on the world's largest heart hospital in Bangalore. Described by *Fast Company Magazine* as "Wal-Mart meets Mother Teresa," Narayana Hrudayalaya is a for-profit institution with a corporate mission of bringing more and better care to the poor, a mission that was indeed inspired by an encounter between its founder, famed cardiac surgeon Dr. Devi Shetty, and the sainted nun of Calcutta. It accomplishes its mission not

---

194 "A Formula For Cutting Health Costs," Editorial, *The New York Times*, July 21, 2012. Available at: http://www.nytimes.com/2012/07/22/opinion/sunday/a-formula-for-cutting-health-costs.html

195 The name means "God's compassionate home" in Sanskrit. Special note to aspiring public speakers: Imagine standing on a convention dais in front of a microphone with a PowerPoint clicker in your hand, speaking to a convention hall full of listeners. Glancing at your notes, you realize that in a few moments you are going to pronounce this name in public over the PA system, smoothly, without hesitation.

just by finding ways to give the poor access to expensive, high-quality treatment, but by making the treatments themselves far less expensive. An open heart operation at Narayana Hrudayalaya typically costs less than U.S. $2,000, a tiny fraction of what it would cost in the United States, and one-third of the average cost in India. It accomplishes this through a fanatical attention to process and detail, linked to a liberal use of high tech.

As one example, every morning every physician not only receives follow-up information on every patient, he or she receives a real-time profit and loss statement: Did you make us money yesterday or cost us money? Shetty and his colleagues want to grow the chain rapidly to provide more and better care for the poor, so it really matters that the physicians, who are salaried, know if they are helping the bottom line. The information allows and encourages them to constantly seek more efficiencies, as well as to fine-tune the adjustment of their patient load between the well-off patients willing to pay full freight with add-ons for special perks like private rooms and private nursing staff, and the less well-off getting discounted rates.

Narayana Hrudayalaya also uses tech to cheaply extend its reach. It owns or manages hospitals in 14 cities throughout India, but every physician uses Skype on his or her laptop to extend that care to 100 more facilities in India and 50 in Africa.[196]

While thinking about this, and imagining the layer on layer of other innovations this organization uses and the ferocity of intent with which those innovations are applied, remember that Narayana Hrudayalaya is for-profit. And profitable. And growing rapidly. It's not about your tax status. It's about your intent, your focus, and your business model: What are you trying to do? And how are you getting paid to do it?

Bars to Innovation

So hospitals and health systems follow fads as long as the fads come with reimbursements attached.

---

196 Salter C, "Narayana Hrudayalaya Hospitals: For Bringing Medical Care To The Masses," *Fast Company*, February 7, 2013. Available at: http://www.fastcompany.com/3017477/most-innovative-companies-2012/36narayana-hrudayalaya-hospitals

At the same time, though, institutions increasingly get in the way of innovation that might actually save money and make their operations more lean and efficient.

Think about this: A few years ago I was invited to speak by the Independent Medical Distributors Association. My host was the formidable and passionate Duke Johns, a medical entrepreneur and board member of the venerable Tuoro Infirmary of New Orleans. He welcomed me on the small exhibit floor. I asked him why there is an "independent" group of medical distributors.

He said, "The group is mostly small companies like mine, trying to discover and sell innovations that might actually make patient care cheaper. And we have a hard time penetrating hospitals and health systems."

"Why? Show me an example."

He steered me away from his own booth to someone who was showing off a simpler product: a walker, the kind recovering patients use to navigate the hospital hallway. "What do you think of that? Pretty cool, huh?"

"Yeah. But I can see how this guy would have trouble selling it."

"Why?"

"Because it must cost several times what the usual walkers do. They're usually flimsy, made of cheap aluminum tubing. This is powder-coated steel, with nice sturdy combination of feet and wheels. And I know that the hospital materials managers, who would be your buyer, often get bonuses based on getting the lowest unit cost."

"Ah. You're starting to see the problem. But just starting. What is the real cost of a walker? When you see a patient walking down the hospital corridor, what do you see with them? A flotilla of staff, holding the perfusion mast for the IV fluids, and maybe a cart with the electronic monitoring equipment, plus another person to help steady the patient. This walker eliminates the first two, because it has these racks for all that, and a sturdy enough design to carry it. So you only need one staff person to help them, or if they are a little more advanced, none at all."

"So you have a higher unit cost, but lower system costs — the cost of labor to accompany the person."

"Exactly."

"And the materials manager doesn't get paid to bring down system costs, only unit costs."

"Exactly."

It gets worse. You can't easily even get in the door to talk to the materials manager. If you design a new walker or some other gadget that cuts costs, you often have to pay an outside "vendor certification" firm a large fee just to be admitted to make your case to a hospital's materials manager. And every time you want to talk to another hospital, even one in the same chain, you have to get re-certified and pay another huge fee to the vendor certification firm. You certainly have no hope of talking to the hospital's chief financial officer, who would be able to see the systemic advantages of your innovation.

Cui Bono?

But that is in healthcare-as-it-has-been, not in healthcare-as-it-will be. How we think about the impact of new technologies is bound up with the changing economics of healthcare.

Under a code-driven fee-for-service system the questions about a new technology are:

- Is it plausible that it might be helpful? (Not proven, just plausible.)
- What are the startup costs in capital and in learning curve?
- Most importantly: Can we bill for it? Can we recoup the costs in added revenue?

In any payment regime that varies at all from strict code-driven fee-for-service (such as bundled payments, or any kind of risk situation), whether we can bill for it becomes irrelevant. The focus will be much more on efficiency and effectiveness:

- Does it really work?
- Does it solve a problem?
- Whose problem?

Many times, extra complexity and waste are added to the system for the convenience and profit of practitioners, not for the good of patients. For example, why do gastroenterologists like to have anesthesiologists assisting at colonoscopies, when the drugs used (usually a combination of propofol or midazolam [Versed] with fentanyl) do not provoke general anesthesia and can be administered by any doctor or nurse trained in their use? According to gastroenterologists I have interviewed the reason is simple: It turns a 30-minute procedure into a 20-minute procedure. Relieved of having to oversee the assistant's administration and monitoring of the drugs, the gastroenterologist can do three per hour instead of two per hour. In the volume-based healthcare economy, they make more money.[197] The use of the anesthesiologist adds an average of $400 per procedure to the cost without adding any benefit, lowering the value to the patient. Altogether this one practice adds an estimated $1.1 billion of waste to the healthcare economy every year.[198]

So in thinking about whether these new technologies will propagate across healthcare, we can ask how exactly they will fit into the ecology of healthcare, who will benefit from their use, and how that benefit will tie in to the micro economy of healthcare in that system, with those practitioners and those patients.

Six Ways

New technologies — especially new information technologies — can make healthcare better and cheaper in six ways:

1. **Big Data continual analysis of the organization** to find waste and quality problems, as well as to understand the very complex financials of operating in the hybrid-risk, fee-for-service, multipayer environment of the Next Healthcare.

---

197 Personal conversations with 12 gastroenterologists at medical conferences: May 1 and June 3, 2014.

198 RAND Corporation, "Eliminating Discretionary Use of Anesthesia Providers During Gastroenterology Procedures Could Generate $1.1 Billion in Savings per Year," March 2012. Available at: http://www.rand.org/pubs/research_briefs/RB9648.html

Liu *et al.*, "Utilization of Anesthesia Services During Outpatient Endoscopies and Colonoscopies and Associated Spending in 2003-2009," *Journal of the American Medical Association*, March 21, 2012, Vol. 307, No. 11. Available at: http://jama.jamanetwork.com/data/Journals/JAMA/22494/joc25018_1178_1184.pdf

2. **Big Data analysis of populations** to target high resource users and to hotspot problem areas.
3. **Doc-friendly and universal electronic health records (EHRs)** that give all physicians working with a patient immediate and intuitive grasp of the patient's situation and history.
4. **Artificial-intelligence-assisted clinical support:** We are looking at a future of more care, not less; care that is closer to the customer; care that happens in many places besides the exam room; care that happens earlier in the disease cycle — and with an increasing shortage of physicians. AI-assisted decision support will enable us to move a great deal of basic care "down license" to nurse practitioners, nurses, and physician assistants.
5. **Telehealth** programs that open as much of healthcare as possible to access via browsers and apps on computers and devices.
6. **mHealth,** the related world of apps, dongles, gadgets, and wearables that make up the world of mobile health — quick, inexpensive, easy-to-use ways to connect high-risk patients directly and constantly with the system.

That's the promise, that's the possibility. But the technology itself brings only a promise. The delivery on the promise depends crucially on how the technology is used, the details of its design and implementation, in the intelligent, even wise, knitting together of the technology with a fierce strategy for driving better healthcare at far lower cost.

So far, the actual record is not so good. So far, on average across healthcare, the expense, complexity, and difficulty of adopting new information technologies have not been overwhelmed by any measurable grand new efficiency.

Telehealth and mHealth

2014 seemed to be the year that we began to see hospitals and health systems get serious about telehealth, building programs for a variety of specific uses, such as:

- Virtual visits: Patients doing primary and urgent care visits from home or work
- eICU and virtual ED: Intensivists backing up onsite clinicians by monitoring patients remotely
- Virtual rounding: Both doctors visiting their patients through the use of audiovisual robots, and families coming along on rounds when they cannot visit in person
- Video-connected post-surgical and post-discharge follow-up: Checking on patients as they are recovering at home.
- Home monitoring of high-risk and frail elderly patients: Preventing unnecessary ED visits and admissions.

The payment systems are still catching up. At this point, some 22 states and the District of Columbia require insurers to reimburse virtual visits at the same rates as in-person visits, but Medicare still restricts telehealth to rural areas and not from the patient's home.

The deeper problem is the same as for many of the strategies we are talking about here: Successful use of telehealth reduces ED use and admissions and could prevent some serious acute episodes — which in a code-based fee-for-service system means lost revenues. On the other hand, when you flip the revenue streams to risk-based population health management or bundled services, the money saved is money earned.[199]

Change Is Systemic

After decades of bravely keeping them at bay, healthcare is beginning to be overwhelmed by inexpensive and easy-to-use new technologies, from BYOD ("bring your own device") tablets in the operating room, to apps and dongles that turn your smartphone into a Star Trek Tricorder, to 3-D printed skulls. (No, not a souvenir of the Grateful Dead, a Harley decoration, or a pastry for the Mexican Dia de Los Muertos, but an actual skullcap to repair someone's head. Take measurements from a scan, set to work in a cad-cam program, press Cmd-P and boom! There you have it: new ear-to-ear skull top, ready for implant.)

199 Aston G, "Telehealth Promises to Reshape Health Care," *Hospitals and Health Networks*, March 21, 2015. Available at: http://www.hhnmag.com/display/HHN-news-article.dhtml

A cardiologist in an examining room whips out his iPhone and snaps it into what looks like a special cover. He hands it to the patient, shows the patient where to place his fingers on the back of the cover, and in seconds the patient's EKG appears on the screen. Dr. Eric Topol, author of *The Creative Destruction of Medicine* (Basic Books, 2012), often performs a sonogram on himself on stage, while speaking, using a cheap hand-held device. These things are easy to imagine in isolation, as something a single doctor or nurse might do with an individual patient.

In reality, in most of healthcare, the things we need to do to incorporate such technologies are systemic. To be secure, reliable, HIPAA-compliant and connected to the EHR, they can't be used randomly by the clinicians who happen to like them. They must be tied into and supported by the IT infrastructure — and for the most part, they are not.[200]

Similarly, in moving from Volume to Value we are talking about changes that don't happen at the level of a single doctor or single patient. In most cases we cannot treat the patients for whom we are at risk differently from those we are treating on a fee-for-service basis.

When you are paid differently, you are producing a new product.

When you are producing a new product, you are a beginner.

The shift from Volume to Value demands and dictates broad systemic changes in revenue streams, which dictate changes in business models, compensation regimes, and governance structures. Getting good at these new businesses means changing practice patterns, collaboration models, and cultures.

Hospitals, integrated health systems, and medical groups face a stark choice: They can either abandon the growing part of the market that demands a Value business arrangement and stick to the shrinking island represented by old-fashioned Volume arrangements. Or they can transform their entire business.

The use and propagation of these new low-cost technologies are entirely wrapped up in that decision. In old-fashioned fee-for-service

---

200 "Epocrates Mobile Trends Report Reveals Mobile Behaviors Are Shifting Amid Historic Change in Healthcare; Nurse Practitioners, Physician Assistants, and Pharmacists Emerge as Top Engaged Users," athenahealth.com, June 17, 2014. Available at: http://news.athena-health.com/Press-Releases/2014-Epocrates-Mobile-Trends-Report-Reveals-Mobile-Behaviors-Are-Shifting-Amid-Historic-Change-in-He-1fb7.aspx

systems, they will be used only where their use can be billed for, or where they lower the internal costs of something that can be billed for. They will not be used to replace existing services that can be billed at higher rates.

"That's a Lot of Money"

Dr. Topol in his talks likes to make the point that there are over 20 million echocardiograms done in the United States every year at an average billing of $800. As he puts it, "Twenty million times $800 — that's a lot of money. And probably 70 percent to 80 percent of them will not need to be done, because they can be done as a regular part of the patient encounter."

Precisely: That is a lot of money. In fact, it's a big revenue stream. It's difficult to imagine that fee-for-service systems for which various types of imaging, scanning and tests represent large revenue streams are going to be early adopters of such technologies that diminish the revenue streams to revenue trickles.

When you are paid for waste, being inefficient is a business strategy.

In the Value ecology of the Next Healthcare, the questions are much more straightforward: Does it work? Does the technology make diagnosis and treatment faster, more effective, more efficient? Does it make it vastly cheaper?

In tech, looked at globally, "vastly cheaper" is the monster business opportunity space — one where other countries are threatening to steal the march on many U.S. firms. This become vivid when the South Korean government asked me to Seoul to keynote their "Chosun Biz" healthcare tech conference, and when the Israeli government and its private partners such as EY Israel invited me to keynote their "Start Up Nation" conference in Jerusalem.[201] They are intensely aware of the vast markets represented by the opportunity to bring low-cost high tech mobile medicine to the burgeoning markets of India, China, sub-Saharan Africa, the Central Asian states, and Latin America.

---

201 November 14, 2013 and September 11, 2014, respectively.

Imagine replacement bones (and matrices for regrowing bones) 3-D printed to order. Imagine replacement knee joints, now sold at an average price of €7,000 in Europe and $21,000 in the United States, 3-D printed to order. (Imagine how ferociously the legacy makers of implants will resist this change, and how disruptive it will be to that part of the industry.)

Imagine anesthesiologists replaced in many circumstances by a personal sedation machine (which is already in preliminary use at this writing).[202]

Imagine the relationship between the doctor, the nurse, and the patient with multiple chronic conditions, now a matter of a visit every now and then, turned into a continual conversation through mobile monitoring.

Imagine a patient at risk for heart attack receiving a special message accompanied by a special ring tone on his cell phone — a message initiated by nano sensors in his bloodstream — warning him of an impending heart attack, giving him time to get to medical care. This is no fantasy, but a system currently in testing by Dr. Topol and colleagues.

Imagine an inexpensive handheld device that can do tests for dozens of conditions from a single drop of blood. Again, not a fantasy, but already in human testing.[203]

Imagine an inexpensive handheld device which a patient can use at home to do a total physical working over the Internet with a doctor at the hospital or clinic. Not a fantasy, at this writing a crowd-funding project.[204]

Imagine all of this embedded in a system that is redesigned around multiple, distributed, inexpensive sensors, apps, and communication devices all supporting strong, trusted relationships between clinicians and patients.

---

202 Frankel T, "New machine could one day replace anesthesiologists," May 11, 2015. Available at: http://www.washingtonpost.com/business/economy/new-machine-could-one-day-replace-anesthesiologists/2015/05/11/92e8a42c-f424-11e4-b2f3-

203 "Robot doctor: Handheld device diagnoses 100s of conditions from single blood drop," *RT News*, November 16, 2014. Available at: http://rt.com/news/206039-rhealth-diagnostic-blood-nasa/

204 "MedWand - The 21st Century Digital House Call," available at: https://www.indiegogo.com/projects/medwand-the-21st-century-digital-house-call

Imagine all this technological change supported with vigor and ferocity because the medical organizations are no longer paid for the volume they manage to push through the doors, but for the extraordinary value they bring to the populations they serve.

That's the connect-the-dots picture of a radically changed, mobile, tech-enabled, seamless healthcare that is not only seriously better but far cheaper than what we have today.

Wise Use

Wise use of data tech goes way beyond the "meaningful use" mandated by the government. "Meaningful use" means having the hardware and software integrated into your workflow. But remember the rule of thumb: Anything can fail to help if you do it stupidly. Wise use means thinking deeply, continually, and actionably about what you are really trying to do, and what would help do it better. What we are trying to accomplish is not digitized healthcare. What we are trying to accomplish is better healthcare for far less money — for which computers, data, and communication tech can be a help or a hindrance, a powerful tool or an obstacle.

Convenience Is Clinical

"All these consumer medical apps and gadgets are just conveniences. They don't make a difference clinically." I hear the notion in many different disguises, but every one of them is wrong — and I suspect they are trotted out only by people who have never been a mother of young children or a caregiver to a frail elderly person.

You and I may think that health is so important that we can take it for granted that patients and caregivers would make it a top priority. But we would be wrong. A caregiver is very busy with all kinds of necessities of life — busy, distracted, and pretty darn tired a lot of the time. A sick person is pretty busy just being sick — busy, tired, and not a little mentally confused. They need help. They need convenience. If you want to actually help people be healthier, we not only have to make sure they are seen by a clinician, given prescriptions, and informed about how to manage their disease; we need to make everything about their health-care convenient. In a world in which I can deposit checks and pay bills using my smartphone, why should the most important thing — managing my body — be so much less convenient?

One Solution: Cook IT Yourself

Tom Sullivan, executive editor of HIMSS Media, makes the case for an emerging different method of assembling the IT that a healthcare institution needs: Partner with start-ups to build custom solutions that you can build into your IT.

> We all know the established way of acquiring IT products and services. Write a big check to a technology consultancy, pore through their research reports, and ultimately plunk down top dollar for one of three vendors qualifying as market share leaders.
>
> That's expensive. And it tends to be safe. But it can leave an organization with a solution that doesn't meet everyone's needs.
>
> By custom building applications, the IT staff can deliver software more likely to meet with widespread acceptance.[205]

In this approach, the in-house IT shops of healthcare providers such as the Bronx's Montefiore Medical Center and insurers such as Aetna research their needs, then find small or startup companies to work with to build them. There is some risk involved — you could get the needs wrong, the company may not be capable of producing what you need. But when it works you end up with software that does meet your needs exactly for often much less than the costs of the big system providers. It also may be a product you can market to other providers as Montefiore is doing with a population health analysis package developed with Streamline Healthcare Solutions.[206]

---

205 Sullivan T, "The bold art of build-your-own IT," Innovation Pulse, *Healthcare IT News*, February 20, 2015. Available at: http://www.healthcareitnews.com/news/innovation-pulse-bold-art-build-your-own-it

206 Streamline Healthcare Solutions: http://www.streamlinehealthcare.com

Entrepreneurs, Investors, Inventors: Build a Better EHR

The very aggressiveness of the largest medical record software companies have now made them vulnerable to serious competition. The market has rapidly expanded since the HiTech Act of 2009 and the Affordable Care Act laid out incentives for going digital and penalized any foot-draggers who did not achieve "meaningful use" right quick now. It is as if the government dictated that everyone retire their buggies, turn their horses out to pasture, and drive cars and trucks instead — in 1903, when cars were complicated and balky to run, few roads were paved, service stations didn't exist, and there were no stoplights.

Right now, the screaming of physicians and other clinicians is reaching a crescendo as more and more of them are being forced to use clunky, inadequate tools. Even the mad rush to bring your own tablet and smartphone has slowed and started to reverse, simply because most systems don't play nice with mobile devices. It doesn't matter that the physicians would much rather have the records and images in their hands wherever they are; most systems force them to sit down at a computer.

The complications of most medical records software slow down clinicians' work and actually affects patient care.

The market for EHRs will be hard to penetrate for new entrants. The monopolistic practices work, most of healthcare has now signed up with one or another large legacy player, and the investments in this sloppy, barely functional current technology is into the tens of millions even for a small suburban medical system.

Nonetheless, the clear failure of most of today's EHRs to solve physicians problems, let alone make healthcare easier to manage, means that the opportunity is there: Build a better EHR and they will come. Please, step forward and compete. Today's market leaders may well turn out to be the Reos, the Stanley Steamers, the Hupmobiles of the market.

Build in Seamless Importable Analytics

Analytics — discovering what works and what doesn't, building patient safety dashboards, monitoring high-risk patients and super-users, doing predictive analysis to ferret out patients most likely to experience sudden cardiac arrest or to be readmitted to the hospital — are key to making the Next Healthcare actually work in the hospital and health system environment. We are at the beginning of a massive effort all across healthcare to explore what actually works best in this data-rich new world to drive down cost and increase quality at the same time.

What could jump-start this effort? Sharing.

Building analytic software and algorithms from scratch or buying them custom-made can be expensive and slow for an individual institution. Apervita, a Chicago company, has established an analytics market in which major institutions such as Mayo can publish their algorithms for other institutions to build on, seamlessly incorporating them into their own analytic environment. Any health enterprise can publish its datasets of any type in a form that other enterprises can use, along with its medical algorithms and their associated results. The market becomes a community of learning whose participants have already created hundreds of algorithms covering such measures as readmission, mortality, morbidity, compliance, and prediction, along with disease-specific insights. Sophisticated analytics markets like Apervita's will be key to rebuilding medicine for the new environment.[207]

Knit in the Mobile and the Wearable

Mobile tech can be a powerful tool in the armamentarium of healthcare. But at the moment it is mostly isolated from the mainstream of healthcare information in the medical records and health information exchanges (HIEs).

Google Glass was the Wright Flyer of a whole new field: wearables. Before Sony popped the Walkman on us 35 years ago, no one would have imagined today's streets and subways filled with people with ear buds listening to their own world. Before Steve Jobs popped the iPhone on us, no one would have imagined rows of young people in parks, each intently thumb-typing away on a pocket-sized device. It is equally hard to imagine that we will be surrounded by people with invisible sensors,

207 Pennic F, "Mayo Clinic to Publish Its Algorithms to Improve Patient Outcomes," HIT-Consultant.net, February 27, 2015. Available at: http://hitconsultant.net/2015/02/27/mayo-clinic-publish-algorithms-patient-outcomes/
Apervita: Apervita.com

recorders, and computers woven into their clothes, belts, and jewelry, even embedded in their skin — or that we might be one of them. But it will happen, and it will happen especially for the most medically vulnerable, their vital signs being constantly and automatically monitored as they walk or garden or sit with friends, their medical records and physical state instantly available to the clinicians working with them. EHRs and HIEs must be re-built to accommodate these new streams of information.

The Internet of Things

Most of this is about how doctors communicate with patients, get lab results, and look at images, and how patients respond and look up things on the Internet. That's fine for traditional healthcare. But if the way you are paid changes, and you find yourself trying to monitor and manage the health of populations, you need tools that much more ubiquitous, analytical, subtle, and interwoven with daily life.

If you want to let the top of your head start to rotate and spin up like a quad copter, imagine billions of conversations going on between pill bottles, hospital bed sheets, blood glucose monitors, scales, even the toilet. The pill bottle can help track use, then trigger a prescription refill. The sensor sown into the hem of the bed sheet will signal when it was last washed, and at what temperature. The toilet can analyze our excreta for all kinds of things that might be medically useful. Implanted medical devices can report all manner of chemical checks via Bluetooth to a smartphone, and from there on to the cloud, where intelligent systems can analyze them, flag anomalies, and even alert human caregivers or practitioners if the patient needs a phone call, a visit, or an ambulance at his or her front door.[208]

The Internet of Things — the smart toaster, the programmable house, the car you can start from a distance (but won't let you in the driver's seat if you're drunk), the fork that is having issues with the lamb shank you're sticking it into — is the third stream of data that will have

208 Bresnick J, "What Does the 'Internet of Things' Mean for Healthcare?" *Health IT Analytics*, November 5, 2014. Available at: http://healthitanalytics.com/2014/11/05/internet-things-mean-healthcare/

useful things to add to your medical data if you ask it to, and if the EHRs and HIEs in the cloud can make use of them.

I predicted this when dinosaurs roamed the earth (in Internet years) in *Wired 2.01* in 1993.[209] Now over 20 years later we are seeing that prediction suddenly come true.

Right now most EHRs struggle to capture the information even from the medical system's own machines right on the premises. In the future, we can imagine a web of medical analysis going on automatically, autonomously, all the time, behind the scenes, for any of us who want or need it, through the Internet of Things.

---

209 Flower J, "The Other Revolution in Health Care," *Wired*, January 1993. Available at: http://archive.wired.com/wired/archive/2.01/healthcare_pr.html

Tech: The To-Do List

**Purchasers (Employers, Pension Plans, and
Other Purchasers of Healthcare):**

- **Shop for wise tech use:** In shopping for healthcare, find ways to give preference to medical organizations that display the greatest competence in the wise use of new communication and sensing technologies in all four ways mentioned above to drive down costs and keep quality up.
- **Shop for deep transparency:** Give preference to medical organizations whose records are deeply transparent not only across the organization and to the patient, but to other medical organizations.

Consumers:

- **Demand tech convenience:** Expect and demand convenience from the doctors and medical systems that provide you medical care — convenience, transparency, and easy contact at all times. You need it. If they are not going to provide it, they should get into some other business that's not so people-oriented. Maybe taxidermy. Or Comcast customer service.
- **Shop for convenience and transparency:** When you are shopping for healthcare, make convenience and transparency part of your

criteria. A doctor who does not do email? A system that does not allow you to make appointments, that gives you no access to your medical records? Take your business elsewhere.

- **Use tech to join the circle of trust:** Taking care of your health is not easy, especially if you are a young mother, or are getting older, or have chronic health conditions. There are a number of apps that not only tie you into the medical system, but into a circle of other patients (often your family or very closest friends) who help each other look after their health and stay fit. Look for these apps and use them.

Health Plans:

- **Target and segment:** Use your Big Data reach to find the small percentage of your customers who are using huge amounts of healthcare resources because they are being poorly cared for. Find ways to offer them better programs to keep them healthier and bring their costs down.
- **Share analytics:** Share the medical insights that can be gained from your massive collections of patient data in analytics markets such as Apervita's.
- **Shop for wise use of tech:** Use the better shopping techniques in the first chapter to help steer your customers to medical practitioners who make wise use of tech to drive their own costs down and to link more strongly to their customers.
- **Give your customers more info:** Supply your customers with information apps that will help them become better shoppers for healthcare.
- **Reimburse virtual:** In reforming any payment system, in any part that is still paying code-driven, fee-for-service, make sure that virtual visits, constant monitoring, and other interactions that are not face to face are reimbursed as well.
- **Redefine medical interactions:** Make sure that virtual interactions, autonomous monitoring, and other digital interactions are included in the medical interactions that your policies pay for.

Entrepreneurs, Inventors, and Investors

- **Get clear about the customer:** Don't confuse what you or I might think is cool with what the market will take up. We are outliers. The apps and gadgets that we might want to manage our own health represents a niche, not a mass phenomenon — because many people out there in the real world are not as educated, as interested in tech, and as sure of their own judgment as we are. What the market will take up is not things that we might like, but things that solve real problems for clinicians, for people running health-care institutions, and for everyday patients and their caregivers.
- **Go after the truly huge market:** Go for apps, dongles, and gadgets that are integrated into the medical experience, bringing patients into closer, more constant, more convenient contact with their clinicians and caregivers.
- **Work in the Internet of Things:** We have only begun to devise the devices, interfaces, and algorithms that we need to construct this vast intelligent web of helpers.
- **Compete for the core:** Build a better EHR that works for the clinician and is transparent across the organization and outside it, integrated into better enterprise software. There will be a vast market for it when the clinicians and healthcare organizations fully absorb the shortcomings of much of what is out there now.
- **Build in the analytics:** Hook enterprise healthcare software up with analytics markets like Apervita's to provide healthcare institutions with a wide base of algorithms and insights into their own operations.
- **Build artificial-intelligence-assisted clinical-support systems:** These can assist moving much basic care down-license to nurse practitioners, nurses, and physician assistants.

Hospitals, Physician Groups, and Healthcare Institutions

- **Start over:** Seriously. If your current tech environment is hard for clinicians to use, if it obfuscates important data, if it is not transparent in importing and exporting data from other systems or other parts of our system, it is getting in your way at a time when you need all the help you can get.

- **Envision the distributed system:** Imagine a medical system transformed to take full advantage of the possibilities of new communications, new devices, new big data techniques, new robotics, new wearables. Focus only on ways that these new technologies make your system more efficient and effective, not on what is the fad of the moment. In such a system, the interconnectivity of data, consultation, monitoring, and medical judgment is not a bolt-on, not an extra, but the central nervous system of the whole enterprise.

- **Invest in artificial intelligence-assisted decision support:** Imagine a medical system in which the EHR includes a strong decision-support system, providing the physician with information, decision pathways, choices, methods of differentiating diagnoses, in real time during the patient consultation, fed directly by the information the physicians is discovering in the patient history, narrative, and test results. Imagine automating this decision support so that we can move more basic care down-license to nurse practitioners, nurses, and physician assistants.

- **Build in analytics:** Make sure that your IT capabilities include deep analytics. Don't start from scratch or buy siloed customized analytics, but share in the medical insights and enterprise algorithms in analytics markets such as Apervita's.

- **Get the whole picture:** The environment is far more complex than the past. To guide our decisions and see their effects, we need enterprise software that combines patient medical data, finance and enterprise data, and population health data in one complex, moving, robust picture. For one example, take a look at Evolent's Identifi software suite.[210]

- **Design around the right needs:** Put the needs of your customers and doctors ahead of the convenience of the organization, and especially ahead of what vendors tell you is possible.

---

210 Evolent: http://www.evolenthealth.com

- **Build forward:** Set a strategic goal of building toward this vision stepwise.
- **Get the risk right:** Healthcare executives have hung back from bold use of tech, even though both their customers and most of their doctors seem eager for tech that actually works. They are afraid of making a big mistake and spending a lot of money in the wrong place or the wrong way, yet that is exactly what many of them have done. But disruptors from within the industry and outside it are itching to step up and take over. As Scott Lundstrom, group vice president of IDC Health Insights, warned skeptical healthcare leaders at a recent conference: "If you aren't willing to adapt to this role, to spend a little to save a lot, rest assured that your new owners will be."[211]

Federal, State, and Local Legislators and Policymakers

- **Mandate interoperability:** Proprietary systems that do not produce data that are legible to other systems are a public health hazard. If we can outlaw lead-based paint, certainly we can outlaw black-box software systems.
- **Reimburse virtual:** In reforming any payment system, in any part that is still paying code-based fee for service, make sure that virtual visits, constant monitoring, and other interactions that are not face to face are reimbursed as well.
- **Redefine medical interactions:** In all legislation and policy that defines or regulates medical interactions, make sure that virtual interactions, autonomous monitoring, and other digital interactions are included.

---

211 Eastwood B, "Why Healthcare IT Spending Needs to Shift Its Focus," *CIO*, July 8, 2014. Available at: http://www.cio.com/article/2450758/healthcare/why-healthcare-it-spending-needs-to-shift-its-focus.html

The Call

WHERE DID YOU come from? Who are your people? There is a grave in Calvary Cemetery in Los Angeles with my name on it, a tiny grave, the grave of an infant. Nearly my name: Joseph Edgar Flower. I am Joseph Edward. He was born to my mother in 1949 with, we are told, "a hole in his heart," lived 24 hours and died and broke my mother's heart. The condition today is fixable with delicate pre-natal cardiac surgery. In 1949, there was nothing one could do.

We are in this together. Compassion is not a hobby.

My dad was the son of a miner in the copper pits of Arizona — a violent man, a drunk. My father was determined not to be his father. While stationed at Pearl Harbor during World War II, he discovered peace in a garden kept by contemplative nuns in Honolulu, learned the Peace Prayer of St. Francis, was baptized and came home to marry a Catholic girl, daughter of Irish immigrants.

I was one of 10 children, not counting Joseph Edgar. I remember very few arguments between my parents, but one — loud, passionate — was when my brother lay dying. Jim was very sick. My mother would not call the ambulance because hospitals and doctors were expensive and we had little money, despite my father's job as a salaried oval badge at Lockheed. My father said, "We will pay the price. Call the hospital. He's my son." When they carried him out (half a century later the memory sticks), I wondered. I had never known that humans could be blue. He had, it turned out, spinal meningitis and pneumonia. He lived.

People die. People suffer.

My friend Tom's mother disappeared. She had, we were told, a "breakdown." We were not told what that meant, or if she would be back. One did not speak of those things.

Dad did things. As Los Angeles expanded he founded parishes, founded councils of the Knights of Columbus, gathered funds to build hospitals. In those segregated days he would regularly go to the other end of the San Fernando Valley to where the Mexicans lived to build houses and bring help to families who were down on their luck.

We are a society. We are who we are because of each other.

When my own first child was born in San Francisco, my wife nearly died when, in the handoffs between shifts, the nurses lost track of the fact that she had been in hard labor for over 24 hours and was fading in exhaustion. I was so exhausted just from tending her that I could barely speak, but I pointed out their mistake, and they rushed her into surgery. Lives matter. Yours, mine. Our children.

Dad died on the table in the surgical suite at 86 when a surgeon had convinced him that putting in a mitral valve at his age would be fine. It wasn't.

I am not special. Everyone has these stories. Where do you come from? Who are your people?

Life, liberty, and the pursuit of happiness. Is "life" some abstraction? Or does it mean, actually, your life, the lives of your children, your parents, your best friend? Actual lives? Does that mean that if we have here in our hands the magic elixir that will save you, the procedure, the real help, that we will give it to you, help you have it — or withhold it from you because you had not managed to put together the right combination of job and insurance this particular year?

There is nothing abstract about this. Healthcare, how we manage it, how we pay for it, is about life and death, your life and death, your children, your suffering, their very real suffering. It's about whether you have the power to do anything about it. I believe we do.

I think that's your phone ringing. I recognize that special ring tone. That's not your organization calling. That's not even healthcare calling. That's life calling.

You're a VP of development at a hospital system, you're a resident at a teaching hospital; you're an employer, a Fortune 500 CEO, or a partner in a brew pub with a dozen employees; you're an HR director; you're an entrepreneur, an investor looking for the next big thing; you're in the Senate or the House or a state legislature; you're a citizen, a patient, a parent, a child of aging parents. And you may never have thought that life would come calling, come knocking on your door, come saying this is the time, this is the moment that you were made for, this is why you are here. No, we don't know why, you and I, but it's here.

There will be times when the fight to revolutionize healthcare will not seem worth it. Some of the time it will seem like there is no movement, or like things are getting worse. That is the nature of struggle, that it seems impossible until the moment when it seems inevitable.

It may seem often that you have no allies. But you will find them. We are here, and we are in your organization, your community, your profession, your part of the market.

There are already victories to celebrate and congratulations to share and there will be more. The victories will often seem partial. But victories there will be. We will make this better.

We are engaged one way or another with a mighty industry that has us in its hands, all of us, our life and death and our suffering. We have our hand on this magic thing, this marvelous magic thing that can relieve the suffering, that can help us to an easy birth, a whole and powerful life, a good death. We have our hands on that, and we have a chance to bring it, we have a chance to make it work, we have this one chance. You have this one chance to do a great and mighty thing. What will you do?

Appendix 1: Resources

THESE ARE SOME resources that might help you in revolutionizing healthcare. This is by no means a comprehensive list. Feel free to contact me (joe@thechangeproject.com) with more resources that you find helpful.

Resources For Consumers:

- **Handbook for consumers:** We have gathered all this advice and these resources — and more — in a smaller handbook just for consumers at ImagineWhatIf.com/resources.
- **Getting covered**
  - Healthsherpa.com is a user-friendly interface for the ACA exchange websites. Think of it as TurboTax for Obamacare. Use this if you are sure that you are in the market only for an ACA exchange health plan, for instance if your income is low enough (e.g. under $95,000 per year for a family of four) that you qualify for subsidies.
  - Gravie.com establishes a full dashboard that brings all of your health insurance options into one place. Use this if you want a wide range of choices, both in the ACA exchanges and in the private market outside the exchanges.
- **Low-cost primary healthcare — the Federally Qualified Health Center:** There are over 1,200 FQHCs across the United States

that are specifically designed to help people who have difficulty finding help elsewhere because they are poor or have no insurance coverage. The ones I have visited have been well run and highly professional. If you aren't poor, don't worry; they will be happy to take your credit card or your insurance, for prices that are often far less than other primary or urgent care outlets near you. Because of whom they serve, they are particularly good at knowing what resources there are in the community to help you manage your health. The federal Health Resources and Services Administration describes their mission this way:

HRSA health centers care for you, even if you have no health insurance. You pay what you can afford, based on your income. Health centers provide

- checkups when you're well
- treatment when you're sick
- complete care when you're pregnant
- immunizations and checkups for your children
- dental care and prescription drugs for your family
- mental health and substance abuse care if you need it[212]

To find one, put terms like "federally qualified health clinic" or "community clinic" in your browser, along with the name of your town. Or go to: bit.ly/FindFQHC.

- **Tracking your health (and your family's health, and your posse's health):** Microsoft's HealthVault[213] is a comprehensive website/repository/set of apps that allow you to track everything about your health, link it with other apps and dongles for input, and share whatever information you want with your clinicians, your family and health posse, your health coach, or whomever you choose.

---

212 http://findahealthcenter.hrsa.gov/Search_HCC.aspx
213 https://www.healthvault.com

- **Apps and dongles:** The **HealthVault website**[214] lists 149 health apps and 233 consumer health devices.
- **Intervening earlier:**
  - **The Institute for Functional Medicine, or the California Center for Functional Medicine.**[215] Functional medicine provides a different way of looking at the body. Rather than waiting for a full disease process to set in, functional medicine starts earlier, bringing the body back into balance, using evidence-based treatments, often by means of supplements, diet, and exercise, and sometimes in combination with pharmaceuticals and surgery, depending on how advanced the condition already is.
  - **Mindfulness meditation**: A helpful way to begin centering and balancing the body and mind together. A good place to start is the Mindful Awareness Research Center[216] at UCLA's School of Medicine. Its website offers not only research but also tools, including guided meditations.
- **Choosing your treatment:** WiserTogether.com[217] leads you through a decision-making process that shows you the range of treatments, from lifestyle changes to drugs to surgery, for a particular condition, and helps you rank them, personalized to your situation, to find the solutions that are right for you.
- **Crowd-sourcing your information and support:** Online patient communities have grown to be a powerful resource for patients. Some deal with hundreds of conditions, some deal with specific conditions or rare ones. They are all a little bit different. Some involve physicians and other clinicians to guide the discussion and provide information. Some are set up entirely as patients asking the physicians; others are more explicitly peer-to-peer. Here are a few to look into:

---

214 http://bit.ly/HealthVaultDirectory
215 https://www.functionalmedicine.org
216 http://marc.ucla.edu
217 http://www.wisertogether.com

- **PatientsLikeMe**[218] is one of the oldest and largest. It was founded in 2004 to focus on ALS (amyotrophic lateral sclerosis, "Lou Gehrig's Disease"). Ten years in, it has 250,000 members covering over 2,000 conditions, and the largest community of ALS patients in the world.
- HealthBoards[219] is even older and larger, founded in 1998, with over 1 million members by 2014, 280 separate disease-specific forums, and 10 million monthly visits.
- **MedHelp**,[220] which dates back to 1994, features "Ask An Expert" forums along with community support forums.
- **MDJunction's**[221] 800 support forums ("People Helping People") bring some 16 million visits per year.
- Inspire[222] builds patient forums for national disease advocacy organizations, such as the Arthritis Foundation, the National Osteoporosis Foundation, and the American Liver Foundation.
- **HealingWell's**[223] forums focus specifically on chronic illness. Founded in 1996, today its 150,000 members take advantage of support communities, blogs, videos, articles, a newsletter, and other resources.
- **AskAPatient**[224] focuses specifically on Yelp-style patient reviews of medications.
- **HealtheTreatment's**[225] goal is "to create a user-generated database of conditions, symptoms, treatments and statistics to enable more proactive management of serious health conditions, and to improve the quality and speed of the patient-doctor dialog." It intends to become the "TripAdvisor or Yelp of chronic disease" by gathering and concisely presenting myriad patients' experiences with their conditions.

218 http://www.wisertogether.com
219 http://www.healthboards.com
220 http://www.medhelp.orghttp://www.medhelp.org
221 http://www.mdjunction.com
222 http://www.inspire.com
223 http://www.healingwell.com
224 http://www.askapatient.com
225 http://www.healthetreatment.com

- **HealthTap**[226] is not peer-to-peer, but doc-to-you. It is busy creating a "knowledgebase of doctor-created, -curated, and -edited health expertise," plus it puts a doctor in your smartphone. For a monthly fee, you have instant access to one of their 63,000 doctors who can actually see your records, listen to you, even take a look at the rash any time of day or night from anywhere in the world.
- **Price and quality information:**
  - **Paying Until It Hurts:**[227] Elizabeth Rosenthal's *New York Times* series, "Paying Until It Hurts" is a deep dive into all different aspects of the high cost of healthcare in the United States. Its tour of the trickery, waste, and overpricing of healthcare would be a good beginning to becoming a smart healthcare shopper.
  - **NewChoiceHealth.com**[228] crowdsources price information and solicits bids from providers in your area for the procedure or test that you need.
  - **INQUIREhealthcare** is an app that searches for nearby practitioners who meet national standards of quality. It's available on the web,[229] as well as for iOS on the iTunes store; and for Android devices at Google Play.
  - ClearHealthCosts.com[230] gives real prices for many procedures and tests, but as of this writing was still confined to New York City, San Francisco, Los Angeles, Dallas-Fort Worth, Houston, San Antonio, and Austin.
    - **HealthcareBlueBook.com**[231] mines databases for commercial pricing, and provides it for free to consumers and employers.

---

226 http://www.healthtap.com
227 http://bit.ly/PayingHurts
228 http://www.NewChoiceHealth.com
229 http://www.hci3.org/inquire_healthcare/
230 http://www.clearhealthcosts.com
231 http://www.healthcarebluebook.com

- Guroo: A product of the Healthcare Cost Institute, Guroo culls data from private insurers to give averages of costs for common procedures and tests locally and regionally.[232]
- A list of a number of cost-comparison sites is available at **Open Health News.**[233]
- **Castlight**[234] is a service provided by many insurance companies and employers that does the same thing, using insurance company data.
- An interactive map[235] from *The New York Times* (data are from 2011) can give you a sense of what different hospitals in your area charge for the same procedure.
- **How to negotiate doctor bills:** Kliff S., "The Secret to Negotiating a Lower Medical Bill," *Vox*, August 6, 2014.[236]
- **Medical claims advocates:**
  - Articles on claims advocates[237] and claims negotiators[238] at **Need Help Paying Bills?**
  - **"Hiring a Guide To the Medical Bill Maze"**[239]
  - **VersaClaim**[240]
  - **HealthAdvocate**[241]
  - **Alliance of Claims Assistance Professionals**[242]
  - **Medical Billing Advocates of America**[243]

Resources for Employers:
- **Price and quality information:**

---

232 http://www.healthcostinstitute.org/about-guroo
233 http://bit.ly/OpenSystems
234 http://www.CastlightHealth.com
235 http://bit.ly/HospitalsCharge
236 http://bit.ly/MedicalBill
237 http://bit.ly/BillAdvocates
238 http://bit.ly/BillNegotiators
239 http://bit.ly/MazeGuide
240 http://www.versaclaim.com
241 http://bit.ly/BillSaver
242 http://www.claims.org
243 http://billadvocates.com

- **Paying Until It Hurts:**[244] Elizabeth Rosenthal's *New York Times* series, "Paying Until It Hurts" is a deep dive into all different aspects of the high cost of healthcare in the United States. Its tour of the trickery, waste, and overpricing of healthcare would be a good beginning to becoming a smart healthcare shopper.
- **NewChoiceHealth.com**[245] crowdsources price information and solicits bids from providers in your area for the procedure or test that you need.
- ClearHealthCosts.com[246] gives real prices for many procedures and tests, but as of this writing was still confined to New York City, San Francisco, Los Angeles, Dallas-Fort Worth, Houston, San Antonio, and Austin.
- **ClearCostHealth.com**[247] provides transparency tools for employers, pension plans, and health plans. Yes, it is different from ClearHealthCosts.com.
- A list of a number of cost-comparison sites is available at Open Health News.[248]
- **HealthcareBlueBook.com**[249] builds custom websites for employers and health plans that pursue a transparency strategy. The seven-year-old company is a leader in bringing price transparency to consumers, self-insured employers, health plans, and third-party administrators.
- Guroo: A product of the Healthcare Cost Institute, Guroo culls data from private insurers to give averages of costs for common procedures and tests locally and regionally.[250]

---

244 http://bit.ly/PayingHurts
245 http://www.NewChoiceHealth.com
246 http://www.clearhealthcosts.com
247 http://www.clearcosthealth.com
248 http://bit.ly/OpenSystems
249 http://www.healthcarebluebook.com
250 http://www.healthcostinstitute.org/about-guroo

- Castlight[251] is a service provided by many insurance companies and employers that does the same thing, using insurance company data.
- An interactive map[252] from *The New York Times* (data are from 2011) can give you a sense of what different hospitals in your area charge for the same procedure.
- **The Leapfrog Group:** Leapfrog is a national, nonprofit business group dedicated to improving healthcare. Its flagship product is an annual hospital survey.[253] The survey is voluntary, with only about a quarter of American hospitals participating. But it can be very valuable. It also gives a Hospital Safety Score,[254] considered by some to be the gold standard of hospital safety ratings. This year, Leapfrog began working with Castlight to refine its ratings.
- **Help with the ACA exchanges:** If your work force is primarily low-wage, you and they may be better off if you provide them some cash and help them sign up on the ACA exchanges. Use Benefitter.com or Gravie.com to navigate the transition.
- **Medical claims advocates:**
  - VersaClaim[255]
  - HealthAdvocate[256]
  - Alliance of Claims Assistance Professionals[257]
  - Medical Billing Advocates of America[258]
- **Brokers and consultants:** Looking for more? Visit ImagineWhatIf.com/want-help to talk with me about I can help you think through framing this process to assist your customers.

---

251 http://www.CastlightHealth.com

252 http://bit.ly/HospitalsCharge

253 http://www.LeapfrogHospitalSurvey.org.

254 http://www.hospitalsafetyscore.org

255 http://www.versaclaim.com

256 http://bit.ly/BillSaver

257 http://www.claims.org

258 http://billadvocates.com

Resources for Health Plans:

- Apervita is a health analytics marketplace in which anyone with health data — healthcare providers, insurers, individual practitioners — can share their data, medical algorithms, and any other metrics, and take advantage of the knowledge other community members are sharing in order to drive better outcomes and lower costs.[259]
- **Castlight**[260] is a service provided by many insurance companies and employers that uses your claims data to provide your members with the information they need to make smart shopping choices.
- **HealthcareBlueBook.com**[261] builds custom websites for employers and health plans that pursue a transparency strategy. The seven-year-old company is a leader in bringing price transparency to consumers, self-insured employers, health plans, and third-party administrators.
- **HealthSparq**[262] offers decision support and transparency tools to 60 health plans that collectively provide coverage for more than 60 million lives. (http://www.healthsparq.com)
- **ClearCostHealth.com**[263] provides transparency tools for employers, pension plans, and health plans. Yes, it is different from ClearHealthCosts.com.

Resources for Entrepreneurs and Investors:

- Talk to me at ImagineWhatIf.com/want-help. We have resources on the site — and I may be able to help you personally to evaluate the products and services which will work best in the emerging economy of the Next Healthcare.

---

259 http://apervita.com
260 http://www.CastlightHealth.com
261 http://www.healthcarebluebook.com
262 http://www.healthsparq.com
263 http://www.clearcosthealth.com

- Health 2.0:[264] The best, most dynamic places to see the radical confluence of healthcare with new technologies and business models are the Health 2.0 conferences every fall in the San Francisco Bay Area, and at other intervals in Washington, D.C., Europe, India., or elsewhere. Its website puts it well: "Ready to revolutionize healthcare? Health 2.0 has introduced over 500 technology companies to the world stage, hosted more than 15,000 attendees at our conferences and code-a-thons, awarded over $6,494,000 through our developer challenge program and inspired the formation of 70 new chapters in cities around the globe."
- Healthcare's New Entrants[265] — **Who will be the industry's Amazon.com?** A market survey from PWC's Health Research Institute, April 2014.
- **Chilmark Research**[266] surveys the evolving field and issues reports[267] on the future market trends.
- **Exploring what's available:** Other places to see what products are becoming available in the field include:
  - **HealthVault website:**[268] Lists 149 health apps and 233 consumer health devices.
  - **Oxeon Partners:**[269] This innovative VC firm concentrates on making strategic investments and partnerships on the edge of healthcare change. They are specifically focused on fomenting deep change in healthcare. So their investment and partnership list is an interesting guide to what strategic directions some very smart, focused people are willing to put their money on.

---

264 http://www.health2con.com

265 http://bit.ly/NewEntrants

266 http://www.chilmarkresearch.com

267 http://www.chilmarkresearch.com/2015/03/11/inside-peak-to-forthcoming-phm-report/

268 http://bit.ly/HealthVaultDirectory

269 http://bit.ly/OxeonInvest

Resources for Hospitals, Physician Groups, and Healthcare Institutions:

- Talk to me at ImagineWhatIf.com/want-help. I can help you work through the implications for your organization in your market, with your capacities and the populations you serve.
- The Advisory Board Company[270] is the longest-established major consulting company in healthcare, but in recent years has also been leading the charge on change. It does studies and surveys, often sharing the results with non-members on its blog.[271] The tone of The Advisory Board is thoughtful and penetrating, not theoretical but practical, seriously engaged with the nuts and bolts of healthcare transformation.
- Evolent[272] is a two-year-old company based in Arlington, Virginia, and San Francisco. It grew out of the expertise of The Advisory Board and the experience of the UPMC Health Plan in implementing population-based, value-driven healthcare in western Pennsylvania. It is being built from the ground up specifically to spread the skills of building the Next Healthcare. Rather than coming in for a quick consulting job and then leaving, Evolent builds long-term partnerships with healthcare organizations, aligning its incentives with their success. It uses a technology platform called Identifi which fuses clinical, financial, billing, and population health data in a bid to allow executives to drive this complexity in real time.
- Apervita is a health analytics marketplace in which anyone with health data — healthcare providers, insurers, individual practitioners — can share their data, medical algorithms, and any other metrics, and take advantage of the knowledge other community members are sharing in order to drive better outcomes and lower costs.[273]

---

270 http://advisory.com
271 http://bit.ly/AtTheHelm
272 http://www.evolenthealth.com
273 http://apervita.com

- **Plan Design Build Community:** Architecture firms with large portfolios in the healthcare market are another emerging unusual resource for confronting the future. Adapting to a radically new future will almost inescapably mean new buildings, new uses for old buildings, indeed rethinking the entire physical structure of your institution.

- Committing yourself to bricks and mortar and steel and glass commits you to a particular vision of the future. Many architectural firms have recognized this and have committed major resources to helping their clients and potential clients think about the future in highly structured ways. For instance, Dr. Jennifer Flower and I have worked with **Perkins+Will** in mapping the future of healthcare systems large and small.

- The advantage of architecture firms in this kind of thinking is twofold: 1) By the nature of their work, they must think long-term and concretely. 2) By the nature of their work, they are intimately aware of the requirements and demands of the industry. But they stand outside healthcare, and so share fewer of the assumptions by which the industry has lived for decades.

- **Transformation Task Force:** In 2012 the California Hospital Association undertook Transform for Tomorrow, an ambitious project to help its members understand their options. The association assembled a task force of 50 CEOs from all different types of hospitals across the state. It hired the consulting company Deloitte to manage the process but, according to senior vice president Anne McLeod, "This was not a consultant-driven process." Perhaps what was most useful about the process was that it did not attempt to lay out a single future desirable for all. The task force identified five different strategic destinations available to different types of hospitals and systems in different markets, then laid out a variety of core strategies necessary to reach each of these different destinations. By the beginning of 2013 it had made a detailed, 104-page report available to its members. This report can be very helpful in guiding ways to think about the future possibilities for any hospital. The downside? It is proprietary to the members of the California Hospital Association. But maybe you can talk a friend into letting you see it.

- **HealthcareBlueBook.com**[274] builds custom websites for providers willing to advertise their wares and true, bundled prices in a transparency strategy.
- **Population Health:**
  - Association for Community Health Improvement:[275] This arm of the American Hospital Association is a powerhouse of data, case studies, and training for lowering healthcare costs by improving the health of the community. Once you have turned your business models around so that you do better by preventing disease, this kind of expertise is vital to the financial health of your organization.
  - The Healthy Communities Institute[276] helps "move the needle with your community and population health initiatives," as it puts it, with powerful databases of community resources embedded in geodata maps. (In spring 2015, HCI became a subsidiary of Midas+, a Xerox company.)
  - The Community Commons[277] brings powerful free, open source geodata to bear on the problems of population health and building healthier communities.
  - Small and Rural Hospitals' Population Health Report:[278] "The Role of Small and Rural Hospitals and Care Systems in Effective Population Health Partnerships," from the Health Research & Educational Trust and Hospitals in Pursuit of Excellence, both programs of the American Hospital Association.

---

274 http://www.healthcarebluebook.com
275 http://www.healthycommunities.org/
276 http://www.healthycommunitiesinstitute.com
277 http://www.communitycommons.org
278 http://bit.ly/SmallRuralPop

Appendix 2: The Acronymicon

(**N**OTE: THESE ARE not medical acronyms. That list would be vastly longer. These are healthcare system acronyms. A few actual medical procedures and devices are mentioned because they are prominent in the story of the healthcare system.)

ABC: The ABCs of healthcare are "assess, blame, and criticize."

ACA: The Affordable Care Act, aka the Patient Protection and Affordable Care Act, aka Obamacare. The healthcare reform law passed by Congress and signed by the President in 2010, found constitutional (except for one provision making Medicaid expansion mandatory in all states) by the Supreme Court in 2012, and fully implemented in January 2014.

ACO: Accountable care organization. A healthcare organization (or affiliation of healthcare organizations) defined by the ACA that can get some money back from the government ("shared savings") by meeting certain quality goals and saving the government some Medicare money. Also similar organizations that deal only with privately insured patients, for instance employees of a particular employer or beneficiaries of a particular pension plan.

ADA: Americans with Disabilities Act, which defines many requirements to give Americans with disabilities access to all the physical facilities and services open to the public.

AHA: American Hospital Association

AI: Artificial intelligence. Software that goes beyond computing to bringing in new contextually relevant information, asking appropriate questions, offering possible action plans, and generally supporting decision making. Expected to be widely deployed in clinical decision making.

AMA: American Medical Association

API: Application programming interface. Allows programs to interact with each other and share data.

AQC: Alternative quality contract. A payment system that in effect rewards primary care doctors for taking such good care of their patients that the patients require fewer visits to the emergency department, fewer hospitalizations, surgeries, and other expensive procedures.

BCBS: Blue Cross/Blue Shield.

BYOD: Bring your own device. The practices of clinicians using their own tablets or smartphones in a medical environment.

CBT: Cognitive behavioral therapy. A type of therapy that focuses on helping patients change their mental patterns and therefore their behaviors.

CHIP: Children's Health Insurance Program. Also called S-CHIP (State Children's Health Insurance Program). A Medicaid-like program that pays for basic medical care for poor children.

CDHP: Consumer-directed health plan. Also called CDHC (consumer-directed healthcare). Euphemism for plans that bundle a HDHP (high-deductible health plan) for catastrophic medical expenses with an HSA (health savings account) for routine medical expenses.

CEO: Chief executive officer.

CFO: Chief financial officer.

CMO: Chief medical officer.

CMS: The Centers for Medicare and Medicaid Services. The agencies within the federal Department of Health and Human Services that administers these two programs. Of enormous importance in shaping the healthcare marketplace.

CNM: Clinician network management. Software that distributes patient data and system information between clinicians in different healthcare organizations who are working together as a network. Cf: HIE.

CNO: Chief nursing officer.

CPOE: Computerized physician order entry, the software that allows a doctor to order tests and pharmaceuticals through a computer or other device.

CT: Computerized tomography. Same as CAT (for "computerized axial tomography"). A machine and technique for rapidly taking narrowly focused X-ray pictures of the body in order to build up a three-dimensional image.

CTO: Chief technology officer.

DRG: Diagnosis-related group. A system used to classify hospital cases for payment by Medicare and Medicaid.

EBITDA: Earnings before interest, taxes, depreciation, and amortization. A measure of profitability (though not of cash flow) and, generally, of an organization's ability to support debt. Leaves out several important items, such as the cash needed to fund working capital and to replace old equipment. Quoting EBITDA can be a way to make profit and loss statements look better while hiding some weaknesses in the overall financial picture. Since not-for-profits (NFP) pay no taxes on earnings, the NFP version is EBIDA.

ED: Emergency department. People often call this the "emergency room," but it's not a room, it's a department.

EHR: Electronic health record. Also called electronic medical record or EMR. Generated within and controlled by a medical provider. This contrasts with a PHR ("personal health record") controlled by the patient..

EKG: Electrocardiogram.

EMR: Electronic medical record. See EHR.

EMS: Emergency medical service. Ambulances, air ambulances, and other medical rescue services. The employer of EMTs.

EMT: Emergency medical technician. Ambulance crew member.

FDA: Food and Drug Administration. The federal agency responsible for regulating, among other things, medical drugs and devices.

FFS: Fee for service. The practice of paying for each separate service rendered in healthcare, as opposed to paying for, say, an entire operation, or all of one's diabetes care, or all of one's care.

FQHC: Federally Qualified Health Center. FQHCs are community-based clinics that provide comprehensive primary care and preventive care, including health, oral, and mental health/substance abuse services to persons of all ages, regardless of their ability to pay or health insurance status. A critical component of the healthcare safety net, their funding was greatly expanded under President George W. Bush, and again under

President Obama. They were given new funding and expanded roles under the ACA.

FSA: Flexible spending account. See HSA.

GDP: Gross domestic product. The sum total of the value of all goods and services produced in a nation's economy in any given period.

HCI3: The Health Care Incentives Improvements Institute, a think tank that focuses on the alignment of incentives in payment systems in healthcare.

HCO: Health care organization. Generic term for healthcare providers such as medical groups, clinics, hospitals, and various networks, affiliations, and systems that include all of the above.

HDHP: High-deductible health plan. Pays for catastrophic medical expenses.

HIE: Health information exchange, a system for securely sharing medical records between different providers, typically within a geographic region.

HIPAA: Health Insurance Portability and Accountability Act of 1996. Most current use, as in such declarations as "Of course, we've got to test this for HIPAA compliance," does not refer to the whole act but to its privacy provisions, which healthcare providers blame for all kinds of bizarre bureaucratic behavior, such as denying patients access to their own files and images, and building data systems that cannot transfer their data to any other system.

HIT: Health information technology. Cf.: IT.

HMO: Health maintenance organization. Pure HMOs are capitated; that is, their members pay them a set amount per month in return for all care. (Cf.: PPPM). Most actual HMOs these days combine the monthly payment with co-pays every time you see your doctor, have a procedure, or re-up a prescription. Kaiser is the largest and best known example of an HMO. Kaiser is a "staff model HMO," in which the doctors all work together in the same medical groups. Many other HMOs are purely insurance arrangements; the contracted doctors may not work in the same place or even know each other. In theory, an HMO is incentivized to maintain your health; that is, it will make more money and do better if it does whatever it can to help you stay healthy. In practice, HMOs can and often do interpret the incentive in a simpler way: They make more money by denying you care whenever possible. Just as fee-for-service healthcare is incentivized to do too much, an HMO can feel incentivized to do too little. How a particular HMO works in practice is worth digging into before you sign up with them. Kaiser, for instance, has done marvels with preventive care and population health management, but has not done well at all with mental health.

HRA: Health reimbursement account. See HSA.

HSA: Health savings account. Also HRA (health reimbursement account), FSA (flexible spending account), MSA (medical savings account). These are savings accounts, usually paired with an HDHP (high-deductible health plan), used to pay routine medical expenses. They are typically funded by the employer, or both employer and employee. The funding is considered a tax-deductible expense. The different kinds have somewhat different rules and are administered in somewhat different ways.

ICD: International Statistical Classification of Diseases. A detailed list of diseases, broken down by cause, signs, symptoms, complaints, and so forth. Maintained by the World Health Organization. Used in the United States as the basis for DRGs and similar codes of diseases and syndromes used as the basis for fee-for-service payment. The United States currently uses version nine (ICD-9). The World Health Organization promulgated the more complicated version 10 (ICD-10) in 1992. ICD-10 has many more codes than ICD-9, but much of multiplication of codes just pertains to positions on the body, i.e. a compound fracture of the left tibia has a different code than one on a right tibia. The United States finally adopted the new version in the fall of 2015.

ICU: Intensive care unit

IOT: Internet of Things, in which almost every object gets smart and connected: bed linens that can report out whether they have been washed and at what temperature; doors that record who goes through them; streets that get energy from the traffic passing over them and give back information on traffic jams, accidents, weather, and road surface wear.

IT: Information technology. Cf.: HIT.

MLR: The average percentage of the premium spent by a health plan on medical care. Under the Affordable Care Act, the MLR must be at least 80 percent or 85 percent, depending on the type of plan.

MRI: Magnetic resonance imaging. (Note: When it was first introduced it was called "nuclear magnetic resonance" or NMR, because the magnets excite the nucleus of the cell to create the image. The new technology had nothing to do with nuclear reactors or radiation, but the public thought it did because of the word "nuclear" and would run screaming for the hills when you announced you were going to install one. Some marketing genius got the hint, and the industry changed the name.)

MSA: See HSA.

MU: Meaningful use. A level of usage of digital technologies required by the federal government if hospitals and health networks are to avoid reductions in their Medicare and Medicaid reimbursements.

NFP: Not for profit. The legal classification under which most hospitals are not taxed, but also cannot raise capital on the equity markets.

NFP: Nurse-Family Partnerships. A program under which nurses seek out poor pregnant women to bring them prenatal care.

NICU: Neonatal intensive care unit. Like an ICU, but for newborns.

OECD: Organization for Economic Cooperation and Development. An international organization of the world's most-developed 34 countries, dedicated to facilitating economic development. Source of many of the international statistics on healthcare used in this book.

ONC: Office of the National Coordinator for Health Information Technology. The federal office charged with setting and promoting standards for the digitization of healthcare.

OPM: Other people's money. By far the preferred type of money to spend.

OWAs: Other weird arrangements. A highly useful term describing a wide variety of hinky deals. The Godfather makes you an offer you can't refuse; in healthcare financing and affiliation they'll make you an offer you can't understand. Note: This is not an illusion, nor an accident. It is true seeing. If you don't understand it, that means they explained it to you fully.

PAC: Potentially avoidable complications. One good measure that applies to all different types of patients, and serves as a general measure of quality (the lower the number the better).

PCI: Percutaneous coronary intervention. The practice of inserting catheters and instruments into the cardiac arteries for such purposes as installing coronary stents.

PCMH: Patient-centered medical home. A primary care practice that is paid a bit extra per patient per month to keep track of all of its patients in a database and make sure they are getting the attention they need for their chronic diseases.

PFP: Pay for performance. Bonuses paid to medical practitioners and organizations for meeting specific process goals, such as knowing the A1c scores of all their diabetes patients.

PHM: Population health management, as discussed in the chapter on prevention. Cf.: PPPM

PHR: Patient health record. An electronic medical record owned and controlled by the patient. Cf: EHR.

PoC: Point of care. The interaction between a clinician and a patient.

PPO: Preferred provider organization: A medical group that has signed up with a health insurer to provide medical services at a discounted rate. If you have a PPO-based health plan, doctors and hospitals who have signed up become "in network" for you.

PPP: Public-private partnership. A set of arrangements for financing particularly capital projects for public or not-for-profit organizations using private money combined with the not-for-profit's tax benefits. For instance, a healthcare organization might wish to build a new hospital or clinic, but lack the bond capacity or other source of capital that it needs. A developer might set up a for-profit corporation for the purpose, which buys the land and finances the construction, then leases the physical plant back to the healthcare organization.

PPPM: Per patient per month. An alternative way for healthcare organizations to get paid to provide healthcare for a population, instead of fee for service, especially for primary care. This is one version or element of a risk contract. By itself, this would encourage healthcare organizations to deny services as much as possible to each patient. This is what happened in many so-called "health maintenance organization" (HMO) setups in the 1990s fad for "managed care." Combined with proper quality markers and incentives, PPPM payment schemes encourage the healthcare organization to get into serious prevention and population health management.

RUC: Relative Value Scale Update Committee. An advisory committee to the Centers for Medicare and Medicaid which sets the relative values of the different medical specialties.

ROI: Return on investment. The percentage of an investment that is returned as profit within any given period of time.

SEC: Somebody else's credit. The preferred form of credit to use for capital expenditure when your own credit basis is insufficient, or it would not look good on the EBIDA statement. See OWA and OPM.

SGR: Sustainable growth rate. A formula built into the Balanced Budget Act of 1997 that limited how much physicians' Medicare rates could rise each year. Each year since then, physicians have lobbied to have the SGR fixed so that they can continue to receive higher reimbursements. Each year Congress has obliged, but only with a one-year fix. If you ever need a dictionary example of the cliché "kicking the can down the road," this would do just fine. In May 2015 Congress finally passed a permanent fix, which also pushed physician compensation more in the Volume to Value direction.

TDABC: Time-driven activity-based costing. A method of rigorously adding up everything that is necessary to produce a given outcome.

Appendix 3: Malpractice

A DOCTOR RECENTLY REACTED angrily to a brief précis of this book. He would not be coming to hear me speak, he said, since I had not even mentioned the single largest problem in healthcare today: malpractice suits.

He has likely skipped reading the book as well, and many who do read it will be wondering why the malpractice mess is relegated to a brief appendix.

Two reasons: First, this book is about how to change healthcare. Solving the malpractice mess, even if we could easily do it, would not be a major lever of change. Second: No, the malpractice mess is far from the single biggest problem in healthcare today.

The way we have traditionally dealt with malpractice claims is wrong, ineffective, and inefficient[279] in many ways, including:

- **Defensive medicine.** The threat of career-threatening malpractice claims, suits, and settlements drives physicians irresistibly to over-test and over-treat. If a computer program circles a cloudy mass in a mammogram as a possible tumor, the treating doctor cannot simply say, "Nah, not a tumor." Now he or she has to prove it's not a tumor by ordering a biopsy. Multiply this situation across all healthcare. In most situations, the physician cannot be

279 Studdart DM *et al.*, "Claims, Errors, and Compensation Payments in Medical MalpracticeLitigation," *New England Journal of Medicine*, Vol. 354, 2006, pp. 2024–33. Available at: http://www.atulgawande.com/documents/ClaimsErrorsandCompensationPaymentsinMedicalMalpracticeLitigation_000.pdf

hurt by ordering one more test or trying one more procedure, but could engender a massive claim if he or she missed something. By itself, fear of malpractice claims adds some unknown percentage to the cost of healthcare.

- **Timidity.** Fear of malpractice claims and huge malpractice insurance costs discourage doctors from entering the fields that are most open to such claims, such as anesthesiology, obstetrics, and high-risk perinatal care.

- **Fear of helping.** Someone collapses on an airplane and suddenly the purser goes on the PA and asks, "Is there a doctor aboard?" Many physicians feel afraid of stepping forward, even to save a life, because if the patient does not survive they could get blamed.

- **Physician burnout.** Fear of malpractice problems contributes to the stress of medical life and drives doctors out of practice, at a time when we need more doctors than ever.

- **Neglect of most real problems.** In the traditional way we deal with medical mistakes, the only way a patient or surviving family can get any recognition or redress at all is to mount a malpractice case. Since malpractice attorneys make their living from a percentage of the payouts, the clients have to have a pretty slam-dunk case with big, provable damages, ample evidence, and someone that it can be blamed on. That describes only a tiny percentage of actual medical mistakes. So most patients who are actually damaged by the medical system have no way to get help for the problem, or even to get the system to admit there is a problem.

- **No learning.** What we would really like to do with medical mistakes is use them as opportunities for learning how to fine-tune the system so that they cannot happen again. Physicians and institutions that follow the traditional legal advice to clam up, deny everything, and fight every claim lose any possibility of learning from the mistake.

Why No Solution Yet?

Many other countries do not have this problem. Direct costs of malpractice claims in Canada, for instance, run at about 10 percent of the U.S.

rate. For the most part, the reason other countries do not have this problem is that we treat it as an adversarial legal procedure, and they don't.[280]

The reason we have not fixed the problem is largely because our two great political parties have chosen to use it as one more battleground for political trench warfare. One claims to represent the needs of patients (and by the way the malpractice bar). The other claims to represent the needs of patients (and by the way the doctors). So the Democrats usually fight to keep the current system and the Republicans usually fight to keep the current system but limit payouts.[281] Neither of these strategies really solves the many problems we listed above.

Real Solutions?

The emerging solutions that really can make a difference in one way or another take the problem out of the adversarial court system.[282]

Apology and settlement. Some institutions have adopted a different way of dealing with malpractice claims. When a patient or family makes a claim, instead of clamming up, denying everything, and referring the whole thing to their lawyers, these institutions follow a four-step process:

1) Meet with the patient or family, acknowledge that the patient had a problem, and promise to investigate.

2) Actually look into the case to try to track down what went wrong.

---

280 Some examples in Library of Congress Reports (all dated September 23, 2011): United Kingdom (England and Wales): http://loc.gov/law/help/medical-malpractice-liability/uk.php;
Germany: http://loc.gov/law/help/medical-malpractice-liability/germany.php;
Canada: http://loc.gov/law/help/medical-malpractice-liability/canada.php.

281 Norman B, "Medical Malpractice Reform Efforts Stalled," *Politico.com*, November 8, 2011. Available at: http://www.politico.com/news/stories/1111/67780.html

282 Sage WM, "Medical Malpractice Insurance and the Emperor's Clothes," *DePaul Law Review*, Vol. 54, 2005, pp. 463–64. Available at: http://via.library.depaul.edu/cgi/viewcontent.cgi?article=1403&context=law-review
Studdert DM, Mello MM, and Brennan TA, "Medical Malpractice," *New England Journal of Medicine*, Vol. 350, 2004, p. 283. Available at: http://www.ncbi.nlm.nih.gov/pubmed/14724310
Boothman RC, *et al.*, "A Better Approach to Medical Malpractice Claims? University of Michigan Experience," *Journal of Health and Life Sciences Law*, Vol. 2, No. 2, 2009. Available at: http://www.med.umich.edu/news/newsroom/boothman%20et%20al.pdf

3) Meet with the patient or family again, show them the results of the investigation and, if the institution is at fault in one way or another, offer a settlement.

4) Use the incident as part of the institution's patient safety and quality program, changing procedures or education efforts so that it can't happen again.

There are now consultant legal groups that teach doctors and institutions this non-adversarial alternative strategy, including teaching doctors how to admit a mistake and apologize in ways that actually reduce the possibility of large malpractice claims. Institutions that have gone this route have generally discovered that the direct costs of malpractice claims drop considerably, even to half, at the same time that more patients and families get redress of some kind, physicians feel less under the gun, and quality improves.

Court changes. Some courts, particularly in New York State, have set up special pathways for medical malpractice cases. Judges volunteer to take classes on medical matters so they have a much greater ability to evaluate the claims made on both sides. They then move the cases through a rapid series of meetings in chambers, gathering information and giving both sides a clear sense of how strong the case is and how large a settlement is reasonable. They give the two sides a deadline to reach a settlement. If they don't meet the deadline, then the adversaries have to enter the massively expensive, years-long process of litigation.

This process, where tried, has been successful in moving more cases more quickly to resolution at far lower cost.[283]

Quality and standardization. A major way to reduce the malpractice claims problem is to actually reduce medical "adverse events" and "never events" (mistakes so catastrophic they really should never happen at all). Designing systems that consistently produce high-quality results and only rarely make mistakes has been a major study in industry over the past 30 years, and in this decade some healthcare institutions have finally gotten serious about it, with many adopting "lean manufacturing" programs and medical standards and guidelines. Any systems quality

---

283 Gallegos A, "Medical Liability: Cutting Costs from the Bench," amednews, October 31, 2011. Available at: http://www.ama-assn.org/amednews/2011/10/31/prsa1031.htm

control engineer can tell you that variation for no reason is a sign of a quality problem. Unnecessary handoffs, failures of communication, and unclear accountability make mistakes possible. So building standardized workflows and medical guidelines into healthcare, and using lean manufacturing principles to examine and refine every process will result in many fewer mistakes and problems.

At the same time, standardization and guidelines help physicians defend against malpractice suits. Without them, every decision is simply the physician's own judgment, and that judgment can be questioned and impugned by other for-hire experts. If the physician is working to guidelines, the decisions are supported by the collective judgment of his or her specialty.

Imagine plaintiff's counsel asking, "Why didn't you order the exploratory surgery that would likely have found the tumor?"

"In my judgment it was not needed."

"Obviously, your judgment was wrong, wasn't it, Doctor?"

A much more comfortable and defensible answer would be: "According to the guidelines of my profession for this situation, it was not needed. And every surgery carries its own risks. It would have been in violation of the guidelines of my specialty to have ordered an unnecessary surgery."

It is unlikely that we will come to a political solution to malpractice any time soon, since the two parties find it so useful for raising campaign funds from physicians and the malpractice bar. But as we move into the Next Healthcare, these three strategies may well reduce the cost, the fear, the waste and the cost in human lives that the current system represents.

Appendix 4: Regulation

HEALTHCARE IS OVER-REGULATED. More important, the regulations are a mess. They overlap, and every agency demands its compliance information in slightly different ways, using slightly different definitions of each measurement. Even worse, some regulations contradict other regulations, so that it is not possible to always be in compliance with all regulations.

One sign that this is not just the usual grumping about government interference: I hear it from all angles, from the customers and the providers. In Detroit recently I talked to Carl Camden, the CEO of worldwide Kelly Services, Inc., the temporary staffing agency with more than 8,000 employees of its own, and over half a million that it employs for clients in the course of a year. Carl would have a better than average view of the costs and difficulties of employing a worker. He has long supported the ACA for helping get especially low-wage employees healthcare coverage. His big complaint? Reporting requirements. "The law needs to be tweaked," he told me, "to help employers manage part-time workers and ease data reporting requirements, especially for small businesses."[284]

When I talked to John Strange, the CEO of the two-hospital, 14-clinic regional St. Luke's Healthcare System in Duluth, Minnesota, about what's growing and what's choking in the wake of the ACA, he jumped right to the regulations: "You should see my compliance group. I swear they're

---

284 Panel discussion chaired by the author, *Crain's Detroit Business* Health Care Leadership Summit, Thursday, November 6, 2014, Shriners Silver Garden Events Center, Southfield, Michigan.

breeding like rabbits down there. Pretty soon I'll have more compliance officers than doctors!"[285] A few months later, there I was in Los Angeles, at the other end of the size spectrum in healthcare, keynoting a meeting of the compliance departments of Kaiser — all regions (Northern and Southern California, Mid-Atlantic, Northwest, Georgia, Hawaii, Colorado). There were health plan compliance officers, medical compliance officers, medical group compliance officers, compliance officers from the pharmacies, from the national facilities services, from the IT departments, people working on compliance with the ACA exchanges, with IT "meaningful use" and the medical records shift to ICD-10, with RAC audits and MAC audits, access requirements, labor union requirements. The 500 attendees packed downtown L.A.'s vast Westin Bonaventure.

Regulatory compliance is the fastest-growing sector of healthcare these days, and that's not good news. The best estimate is that the documentation required of physicians, for instance, has doubled in just the last 10 years. According to a recent study by the federal Institute of Medicine, the average hospital or health system employs 50 to 100 people, at an average cost between $3.5 million and $12 million, just to answer regulatory compliance surveys.[286]

Hospitals and other healthcare institutions are regulated by (among other agencies):

- The Centers for Medicare and Medicaid Services (CMS)
- State health and insurance departments
- The Internal Revenue Service
- The National Committee for Quality Assurance (NCQA)
- The Joint Commission (formerly the Joint Commission on Accreditation of Healthcare Organizations or JCAHO)
- The federal Justice Department (for anti-trust issues)
- State "Certificate of Need" commissions

---

285 Personal conversation with author, St. Luke's board and staff retreat, April 27, 2013, Minnesuing Acres, Wisconsin.

286 Institute of Medicine, "Vital Signs: Core Metrics for Health and Health Care Progress," April 2015. Available at: http://www.iom.edu/~/media/Files/Report%20Files/2015/Vital_Signs/VitalSigns_RB.pdf

There are many more. When the Office of the National Coordinator for Health Information Technology (ONC) wanted to build a new strategic roadmap for healthcare IT, it had to consult with 35 different federal agencies. And that's just for health IT.

These regulations not only add an enormous burden to healthcare providers to prove their compliance, they also in many cases outlaw some of the very changes that would make healthcare cheaper and higher quality by baking currently favored industry practices into law and regulation. Many are protectionist, protecting one or another group in healthcare from innovation or outside competition. Examples are the "scope of practice" laws, the "corporate practice of medicine" laws and the "certificate of need" laws discussed in the "Shopping" chapter.

The Institute of Medicine has suggested scrapping almost all regulations at federal and state levels and replacing them with a standard set of 15 core measures.[287]

Unfortunately, this over-regulation will prove to be one of the hardest things to change in getting to the Next Healthcare. The problem is largely political: Those who run healthcare and those who buy it and pay for it complain about the burden of regulation, but much of that burden has arisen out of the efforts over decades of the powerful leaders of the legacy system to protect their interests. The movement to the Next Healthcare is not largely something that can be dictated by government; instead it is largely the result of existing economic forces interacting and competing more strongly toward normal economic goals: producing real value for the end user for a lower price than the competition. The winners in the legacy system will fight hard by lobbying legislators and regulators at the state and federal level to maintain their privileged positions and the bloated revenue streams that go with them, even as the regulations choke their ability to move forward.

---

287 *Ibid.*

Index